Praise for *SEAL Team Six*

P9-BBU-300

"A rare glimpse into the thinking, training, and tactics of the Special Forces at a time when their shadowy work is playing an increasingly crucial role in the war on terror."

—*San Diego Union-Tribune*

"*SEAL Team Six* is a masterful blend of one man's—*Waz-Man's*—journey from hard knocks to hard corps. Even better, Waz-Man and Templin can actually write as good as they can shoot. They capture your attention at every turn—not knowing if you're about to take a bullet to the head from a SEAL sniper or get hit in the gut with a punch line."

—Dalton Fury, former Delta Force Commander and *New York Times* bestselling author of *Kill Bin Laden*

"Great insights into the training and operations of one of America's premier counterterrorism units. Grabs you on page one and is hard to put down."

—General Henry H. Shelton, former commander in chief of the U.S. Special Operations Command and 14th chairman of the Joint Chiefs of Staff

"Wasdin is a true warrior and real hero. *SEAL Team Six* is a must-read." —Gunnery Sgt. Jack Coughlin, USMC, bestselling author of *Shooter*

"Working with Howard was not only encouraging, but fun. He demonstrated compassion to those less fortunate than himself yet vehemently confronted enemy opposition. He is, like many others, a true warrior in the order of King David."

—Randy (Kemo) Clendening, former SEAL, Team Two

SEAL TEAM SIX
MEMOIRS OF AN ELITE NAVY SEAL SNIPER

*Howard E. Wasdin
& Stephen Templin*

St. Martin's Paperbacks

SEAL TEAM SIX: MEMOIRS OF AN ELITE NAVY SEAL SNIPER

Copyright © 2011 by Howard E. Wasdin and Stephen Templin.

All rights reserved.

For information address St. Martin's Press, 175 Fifth Avenue, New York, NY 10010.

EAN: 978-1-250-05508-8

Printed in the United States of America

St. Martin's Press edition / May 2011
St. Martin's Griffin trade paperback edition / April 2012
St. Martin's Paperbacks edition / June 2014

St. Martin's Paperbacks are published by St. Martin's Press, 175 Fifth Avenue, New York, NY 10010.

10 9 8 7 6 5 4 3 2 1

CONTENTS

AUTHOR'S NOTE

Some names, places, times, and tactics have been changed or omitted to protect operators and their missions.

GLOSSARY

AC-130 Spectre: It superseded the Vietnam-era AC-47 gunship a.k.a. "Spooky" or "Puff the Magic Dragon." The spectre is an air force plane capable of spending long periods of time in the air, sometimes carrying two 20 mm M-61 Vulcan cannons, a 40 mm L/60 Bofors cannon, and a 105 mm M-102 howitzer. Sophisticated sensors and radar help it detect enemy on the ground.

AK-47: The name is a contraction of Russian: *Avtomat Kalashnikova obraztsa 1947 goda* (Kalashnikov's automatic rifle model of year 1947). This assault rifle fires a .308 (7.62 × 39 mm) round up to an effective range of 330 yards (300 meters) and holds 30 rounds. It was developed in the Soviet Union by Mikhail Kalashnikov in two versions: the fixed-stock AK-47 and the AKS-47 (S: *Skladnoy priklad*) variant equipped with an underfolding metal shoulder stock.

AT-4: An 84 mm, one-shot light antitank rocket.

Agency: Central Intelligence Agency (CIA). Also known as "Christians in Action."

Asset: Local personnel providing intelligence.

BDU: Battle Dress Uniform.

Blowout kit: Medical pouch.

Booger-eater: Generic term for "bad guy."

BS: Bull excrement. A synonym for "dishonesty."

BTR-60: *Brone-transporty* or "armored transporter," an Armored Personnel Carrier, the last one in the series was the 60PB, which had a boatlike hull and sloped armor.

BTR-60PB: Soviet eight-wheeled (8 × 8) armored personnel carrier armed with 14.5 mm KPVT heavy machine gun (500 rounds), and PKT coaxial 7.62 machine gun (3,000 rounds). It was replaced by the BTR-70.

BUD/S: Basic Underwater Demolition/SEAL Training.

CAR-15: Colt Automatic Rifle-15. One of the family of AR-15 (Arma-Lite Rifle) and M-16 rifle-based small arms. Later versions of the AR-15/M-16 assault rifles were short-barreled. Typically 11.5 inches for a Colt

Commando (Model 733), a 14.5 in. barrel for the M-4 Carbine, and a 20 in. barrel for an M-16. The CAR-15 is an earlier version of the M-4 assault rifle with a retractable telescopic buttstock, firing .223 (5.56 mm) rounds, and holding 30 rounds in the magazine. Colt wanted identification of the CAR-15 with its other products, but the CAR designation eventually wound up as a law-enforcement weapon and the M-16 as a military small arm.

CCT: Combat Control Team/combat controllers. Air force special operation pathfinders who can parachute into an area and provide reconnaissance, air traffic control, fire support, and command, control, and communications on the ground—particularly helpful in calling down death from above.

CO: Commanding officer.

CQC: close quarters combat.

CVIC: Aircraft Carrier Intelligence Center. The first *C* actually stands for "cruiser." The *V* comes from the French word *voler,* meaning "to fly." Used together, *CV* is the navy hull classification symbol for "aircraft carrier."

Cadre: Instructors. Sometimes means leaders.

Cammy, cammies: Camouflage.

Caving ladder: Portable wire ladders for climbing.

Chemlights: Glow sticks. Light sticks containing chemicals activated by bending.

Christians in Action: Nickname for Central Intelligence Agency.

Correct dope: Adjust the scope to adjust for windage and distance.

Cutvee: a cut down Humvee without a top, doors, or windows; a.k.a. M-998 cargo/troop carrier.

Dam Neck: Dam Neck, Virginia, home of SEAL Team Six.

Delta: Delta Force. The army's tier-one commando unit tasked with conducting counterterrorism and counter-insurgency.

Deuce-and-a-half: A truck that carries 2.5 tons.

Dope: knowledge, intelligence, poop (Navy Slang). *Also see* Correct Dope.

E&E: Escape and evasion. Getting out of Dodge.

Exfil: Exfiltrate.

External fixator: A device used in treating fractures. A surgeon drills holes into the uninjured part of the bone near the fracture, then screws pins into the bone.

Outside the limb, a metal rod attaches to the pins to hold them in place. The pins and rod make up the external fixator. A.k.a. "halo."

Fantail: A ship's stern overhang.

Fast-rope: Kick a thick rope out of the door. Then, wearing special gloves to prevent burning the hands, grab the rope with hands and feet while sliding down.

FFP: Final Firing Position; a sniper's hide, i.e., the camouflaged pit or tree blind from where a sniper fires.

Fireflies: Handheld infrared strobe lights.

Flashbang: Stun grenade using a nonlethal flash of bright light and loud blast to disorient enemies.

FOB: Forward operating base.

Full package: In Mogadishu, this was at least a hundred men, including a Humvee blocking force, Little Birds with Delta snipers, and Black Hawks with Rangers and Delta operators.

HAHO: High Altitude High Opening; a parachute jump by personnel at 25,000 to 35,000 feet wherein the parachute is opened quickly (while high in the air).

HALO: High Altitude Low Opening; a parachute drop made delivering supplies, equipment, or personnel by freefalling until the dropped objects are low enough to open the chute and safely land on target.

Helo: Helicopter.

HRT: Hostage Rescue Team.

HUMINT: Human intelligence. Intelligence gained and provided by human sources: agents, couriers, journalists, prisoners, diplomats, NGOs, refugees, etc.

IED: Improvised explosive device. A homemade explosive device used in unconventional (illegal) warfare.

JOC: Joint Operations Center.

JSOC: Joint Special Operations Command.

KIM: Keep In Mind; memorization games for scout-snipers.

Khat: A flowering plant native to Somalia, which contains a stimulant that causes excitement, loss of appetite, and euphoria (a.k.a. African "speed").

KN-250: Night-vision rifle scope. Night vision amplifies available light from sources like the moon and stars, converting images into green and light green instead of black and white. The result lacks depth and contrast but enables the sniper to see at night.

Knot: One knot equals roughly 1.15 miles per hour.

LAW: Light Antitank Weapon that fires one 66 mm unguided rocket. Replaced by the AT-4.

Little Bird: Special operations light helicopters. The MH-6 and AH-6 (attack variant) were both used in Mogadishu. Armament includes guns, rockets, and missiles.

LST: Lightweight Satellite Terminal; an encrypted radio that can send burst packets to a satellite for fast relay.

MRE: Meal, Ready-to-Eat. Field ration in lightweight packaging. Sometimes referred to as "Meal, Refusing-to-Exit" because the low dietary fiber content can cause constipation.

Macawi: A colorful Somali kiltlike garment.

NOD: Night Optical Device.

NVA: North Vietnamese Army—the regular Communist military that fought the South Vietnamese and Americans during the Vietnam War.

OP: Observation post.

Op: Operation.

Ouija board: Flat surface on which miniature airplanes or other objects are moved around to indicate position and status of aircraft on the deck of a carrier.

P-3 Orion: Navy spy plane.

PJ: Air force pararescue special operations unit focused on rescuing pilots downed in enemy territory and providing emergency medical treatment.

PLO: Palestine Liberation Organization. A political, paramilitary, and terrorist organization recognized by a hundred states as representative of the Palestinians.

PT: Physical training.

PTs: Gym shorts and T-shirt worn during PT.

Pasha: Code name for our safe house in Mogadishu.

QRF: Quick Reaction Force made up of the army's 10th Mountain Division, 101st Aviation Regiment, and 25th Aviation Regiment.

Rangers: A rapid light infantry unit that can fight against conventional and special operations targets. The Army Rangers in Mogadishu came from Bravo Company, 3rd Ranger Battalion.

RPG: Rocket-propelled grenade.

SAS: Special Air Service, Britain's tier-one special operations commando unit. Australia and New Zealand derived their SAS from this British unit.

SATCOM: Cryptographic (scrambled) portable satellite communication radio used by SEALs.

SEALs: The U.S. Navy's elite SEa, Air, and Land commandos.

SERE: Survival, Evasion, Resistance, and Escape.

JSOC: Joint Special Operations Command, located at Pope Air Force Base and Fort Bragg in North Carolina. JSOC commands Special Mission Units that include SEAL Team Six, Delta, and the air force's 24th Special Tactics Squadron.

SIG SAUER P-226 Navy 9 mm: Schweizerische Industrie Gesellschaft—German for "Swiss Industrial Company." Pistol with phosphate corrosion-resistant finish on the internal parts, contrast sights, and an anchor engraved on the slide. Holds fifteen rounds in the magazine. Designed especially for the SEALs.

SIGINT: Signals Intelligence. Intelligence gathered intercepting signals between people (communications intelligence) and electronic signals (electronic intelligence) not directly involved in communication such as radar. Also the people responsible for gathering such intelligence.

Staph infection: "*Staph*" is short for "*staphylococcal*," a strain of bacteria that produces toxins similar to those in food poisoning, which can kill.

Task Force 160: Nicknamed the "Night Stalkers," this army helicopter unit usually operates at night, flying fast and low, to avoid radar detection.

Thermite grenade: Grenade containing thermite, a chemical that burns at approximately 4,000°F/2,200°C.

UDT: Underwater Demolition Team. The frogmen, ancestors of SEALs.

UNOSOM: United Nations Operation in Somalia.

Unit: U.S. Army Delta Force.

VC: Vietcong. Guerrilla and regular Communist units that fought the South Vietnamese and America during the Vietnam War.

Whiskey Tango Foxtrot: Like other military units, SEALs often use the military phonetic alphabet "*Whiskey Tango Foxtrot*"—WTF to mean "What the f***?"

Win Mag: Winchester Magnum. The .300 Win Mag holds four rounds of .300 ammunition. Usually used with a Leupold 10-power scope. For evening, a KN-

250 night-vision scope slides over the top of the Leupold.

XO: Executive officer. Number two man in charge of a command. The number one man is the commanding officer (CO).

PART ONE

I like shooting, and I love hunting. But I never did enjoy killing anybody. It's my job. If I don't get those bastards, then they're gonna kill a lot of these kids dressed up like Marines.

—Gunnery Sergeant Carlos Hathcock,
MARINE CORPS SNIPER

1.
REACH OUT AND TOUCH SOMEONE

When the U.S. Navy sends their elite, they send the SEALs. When the SEALs send their elite, they send SEAL Team Six, the navy's equivalent to the army's Delta Force—tasked with counterterrorism and counterinsurgency, occasionally working with the CIA. This is the first time a SEAL Team Six sniper's story has been exposed. My story.

Snipers avoid exposure. Although we prefer to act rather than be acted upon, some forces are beyond our control. We rely on our strengths to exploit the enemy's vulnerabilities; however, during the war in the Persian Gulf I became vulnerable as the lone person on the fantail of an enemy ship filled with a crew working for Saddam Hussein. On yet another occasion, despite being a master of cover and concealment, I lay naked on an aircraft runway in a Third World country with bullet holes in both legs, the right leg nearly blown off by an AK-47 bullet. Sometimes we must face what we try to avoid.

* * *

In the morning darkness of September 18, 1993, in Mogadishu, Somalia, Casanova and I crept over the ledge of a retaining wall and climbed to the top of a six-story tower. Even at this early hour there were already people moving around. Men, women, and children relieved themselves in the streets. I smelled the morning fires being lit, fueled by dried animal dung and whatever else people could find to burn. The fires heated any food the Somalis had managed to obtain. Warlord Aidid knew fully the power of controlling the food supply. Every time I saw a starving child, I blamed Aidid for his evil power play that facilitated this devastation of life.

The tower we were on was located in the middle of the Pakistani compound. The Pakistanis were professional and treated us with great respect. When it was teatime, the boy in charge of serving always brought us a cup. I had even developed a taste for the fresh goat milk they used in the tea. The sounds and scents of the goatherd in the compound reached my senses as Casanova and I crawled onto the outer lip at the top of the tower. There we lay prone, watching a large garage, a vehicle body shop that had no roof. Surrounding the garage was a city of despair. Somalis trudged along with their heads and shoulders lowered. Helplessness dimmed their faces, and starvation pulled the skin tight across their bones. Because this was a "better" part of town, multilevel buildings stood in fairly good repair. There were concrete block houses instead of the tin and wooden lean-to sheds that dominated most of the city and countryside. Nevertheless, the smell of human waste and death—mixed with hopelessness—filled the air. Yes, hopelessness has a smell. People use the term "developing countries," but that is bullcrap. What developed in Somalia were things such as hunger and fighting. I think "developing countries" is just a term used to make the people who coined it feel better. No matter what you call them, starvation and war are two of the worst events imaginable.

I calculated the exact distances to certain buildings. There are two primary considerations when making a sniper shot, windage and elevation. Because there was no significant wind that could throw my shot left or right, I didn't have to compensate for it. Elevation is the variable considered for range/distance to the target. Since most of my potential targets were between 200 yards (garage) and 650 yards (intersection beyond the target garage), I dialed my scope in at 500 yards. This way I could just hold my rifle higher or lower depending on range. When the shooting began, there would be no time to dial in range corrections on my scope between shots.

We started our surveillance at 0600. While we waited for our agent to give us the signal, I played different scenarios over in my mind: one enemy popping out at one location, then another popping up at another location, and so on. I would acquire, aim, and even do a simulated trigger pull, going through my rehearsed breathing and follow-through routine while picturing the actual engagement. Then I simulated reloading and getting back into my Leupold 10-power scope, continuing to scan for more booger-eaters. I had done this dry firing and actual firing thousands of times—wet, dry, muddy, snowbound, from a dug-in hole in the ground, from an urban sniper hide through a partially open window, and nearly every which way imaginable. The words they had drilled into our heads since we began SEAL training were true, "The more you sweat in peacetime, the less you bleed in war." This particular day, I was charged with making sure none of my Delta Force buddies sprang a leak as I covered their insertion into the garage. My buddies' not bleeding in war was every bit as important as my not bleeding.

Our target for this mission was Osman Ali Atto—Warlord Aidid's main financier. Although Casanova and I would've been able to recognize the target from our previous surveillance, we were required to have confirmation of his identity from the CIA asset before we gave the launch command.

The irony wasn't lost on me that we were capturing Atto instead of killing him—despite the fact that he and his boss had killed hundreds of thousands of Somalis. I felt that if we could kill Atto and Aidid, we could stop the fighting, get the food to the people quickly, and go home in one piece.

It wasn't until around 0815 that our asset finally gave the predetermined signal. He was doing this because the CIA paid him well. I had learned firsthand while working with the CIA how payoffs could sway loyalty.

When we saw the signal, Casanova and I launched the "full package." Little Bird and Black Hawk helicopters filled the sky. During this time, the Delta operators literally had their butts hanging out—the urban environment provided too much cover, too much concealment, and too many escape routes for the enemy. All a hostile had to do was shoot a few rounds at a helo or Humvee, jump back inside a building, and put his weapon down. Even if he reappeared, he was not considered hostile without a weapon. Things happened fast, and the environment was unforgiving.

Delta Force operators fast-roped down inside the garage, Rangers fast-roped around the garage, and Little Birds flew overhead with Delta snipers giving the assault force protection. Atto's people scattered like rats. Soon, enemy militia appeared in the neighborhood shooting up at the helicopters.

Normally, snipers operate in a spotter-sniper relationship. The spotter identifies, ranges the targets, and relays them to the sniper for execution. There would be no time for that on this op—we were engaged in urban warfare. In this environment, an enemy could appear from anywhere. Even worse, the enemy dressed the same as a civilian. We had to wait and see his intention. Even if he appeared with a gun, there was a chance he was part of a clan on our side. We had to wait until the person pointed the weapon in the direction of our guys. Then we would ensure the enemy ceased to exist. There would be no time for makeup or second shots. Both Casanova and I wielded .300 Win Mag sniper rifles.

Through my Leupold 10-power scope, I saw a militiaman 500 yards away firing through an open window at the helos. I made a mental note to keep my heart rate down and centered the crosshairs on him as my muscle memory took over—stock firmly into the shoulder, cheek positioned behind the scope, eye focused on the center of the crosshairs rather than the enemy, and steady trigger squeezing (even though it was only a light,

2-pound pull). I felt the gratifying recoil of my rifle. The round hit him in the side of the chest, entering his left and exiting his right. He convulsed and buckled, falling backward into the building—permanently. I quickly got back into my scope and scanned. *Game on now.* All other thoughts departed my mind. I was at one with my Win Mag, scanning my sector. Casanova scanned his sector, too.

Another militiaman carrying an AK-47 came out a fire escape door on the side of a building 300 yards away from me and aimed his rifle at the Delta operators assaulting the garage. From his position, I'm sure he thought he was safe from the assaulters, and he probably was. He was not safe from me—300 yards wasn't even a challenge. I shot him through his left side, and the round exited his right. He slumped down onto the fire escape landing, never knowing what hit him. His AK-47 lay silent next to him. Someone tried to reach out and retrieve the weapon—one round from my Win Mag put a stop to that. Each time I made a shot, I immediately forgot about that target and scanned for another.

Chaos erupted inside and outside of the garage. People ran everywhere. Little Birds and Black Hawks filled the skies with deafening rotor blasts. I was in my own little world, though. Nothing existed outside my scope and my mission. Let the Unit guys handle their business in the garage. My business was reaching out and touching the enemy.

This wasn't the first time I'd killed for my country. It wouldn't be the last.

A few minutes passed as I continued scanning. More

than 800 yards away, a guy popped up with an RPG launcher on his shoulder, preparing to fire at the helicopters. If I took him out, it would be the longest killing shot of my career. If I failed . . .

2.

ONE SHOT, ONE SILL?

A year earlier I'd been stationed at SEAL Team Six in Virginia Beach, Virginia. While on standby, I wore my hair longer than standard navy regulations, so I could travel anywhere in the world at a moment's notice without being marked as military. Usually I stayed clean-shaven. When I deployed with SEAL Team Two to Norway, I wore a beard, but normally I didn't like wearing facial hair.

Waiting for a callout, I practiced my skills in a building called the "kill house," used for urban counterterrorist training, and on the shooting range.

After standby would come three months in individual training phase, when we could go off to school: Bill Rogers's shooting academy, driving school, free climbing, or whatever we put in for. The great thing about being at SEAL Team Six was that I got to go to almost any of the best schools anywhere I wanted. Training phase was also a good opportunity to take leave, maybe a vacation with the family, especially for those returning from an overseas deployment. Then came three months of getting together for Team training: diving, parachuting, and shooting school—each part of training followed by a simulated operation using the skill recently trained in.

One night I was sitting in a pizza place called the Ready Room (the same place Charlie Sheen and Michael Biehn stood outside of arguing in the movie *Navy SEALs*) talking about golf with my seven-year-old son, Blake, and a playful grizzly bear of a guy nicknamed Smudge. In the background, a Def Leppard tune was playing on the jukebox. We inhaled a pepperoni, sausage, and onion pizza—my favorite. When on standby, I wasn't allowed to drink more than two beers. In SEAL Team Six, we took the limit seriously.

Our drink was Coors Light. Whenever traveling in groups, my Teammates and I used the cover story that we were members of the Coors Light skydiving team—our explanation for why thirty buff guys, most of us good-looking, would walk into a bar wearing Teva flip-flops, shorts, tank tops, and a Spyderco CLIPIT knife in our front pocket. Every time we walked into a bar, the men started changing their drinks to Coors Light. Then the women would begin drinking Coors Light. Coors should've sponsored us. The cover worked well because if people asked us about skydiving, we could answer any question. Besides, our story was too preposterous not to be real.

At around 1930 hours, before I finished my pizza and Coors Light, my pager went off: *T-R-I-D-E-N-T-0-1-0-1.*

A code could mean "Go to the SEAL Team Six compound." Or a code might tell me which base gate to use. This time, I had to go straight to the plane.

My bags would meet me on the bird. Each bag was taped up and color-coded for its specific mission. If I didn't have everything packed up correctly, I just wouldn't have it. On one op, a guy forgot the ground liner to put on the outside of his sleeping bag to keep the water from getting in. His good night's sleep wasn't very good.

During standby, we were on a one-hour leash. No matter where the heck I was, I had one hour to get my tail on the plane and sit down ready for the brief. Now, time was already ticking. Blake and I hopped into the car, a silver Pontiac Grand Am, and I drove home, just down the road from the Ready Room. Inside the house, my wife, Laura, asked, "Where you going?"

I shrugged my shoulders. "Don't know."

"Is this the real thing?"

"Don't know—and if I did, I couldn't tell you. See ya later."

That was another nail in the coffin for our marriage: leaving at any time and not knowing when I'd be back. Who can blame her? I was married to the Team way more than I was married to her.

Smudge picked me up at home and dropped me off at Oceana Naval Air Station's airfield. My eyes scanned the special blacked-out C-130. Some have jet-assisted takeoff (JATO) bottles on them for taking off on short runways and getting in the air a lot quicker, a good thing to have when people are shooting at you. If I'd seen JATO bottles, I would've known our destination wasn't going to be good, but there were no JATO bottles this time.

I boarded the plane well before my 2030 drop-dead time. The inside was darked out. Under a red light, I made sure my bags were there, made sure they were the right ones, and made a mental note of where they were so I knew where to return when I needed to start gearing up.

Three SEAL snipers joined me: Casanova, Little Big Man, and Sourpuss. In the Teams, many of the guys went by nicknames. Some guys called me Waz-man. Others had tried to call me Howie, but that didn't stick because I wouldn't answer to it. Sometimes a guy gets his nickname for doing something really stupid—there's a reason a guy gets named "Drippy." Other times a difficult name like Bryzinski becomes "Alphabet." A Team Two friend of mine was called "Tripod."

Casanova was my shooting buddy. We'd been together since sniper school in Quantico, Virginia. He was the ladies' man. More panties were thrown at him than onto a bedroom carpet. Little Big Man had a bad case of the small man complex, which is probably why he always carried that big-ass Randall knife on his hip. Everybody teased him, "Little man, big knife." Sourpuss, the senior man, had zero personality—the one guy in the group who wasn't a cutup, fun-loving type of guy. He was too interested in getting back home to "Honey," his wife, and didn't seem to care about the op or what any of us had going on. He whined a lot, too. None of us really liked him.

We sat down in front of a flip chart near the cockpit. *Just the four of us. Probably a real-world op.* The guy giving the brief was someone I'd never seen before—someone from Joint Special Operations Command (JSOC). He was all business. Sometimes in the Teams there's a little chuckling during a brief. The SEAL briefer might crack a joke about the guy with the weak bladder: "OK, we're going to patrol in here about two clicks. This is where Jimbo will pee the first time. Then, over here, this is where Jimbo will pee the second time." Now, there were no jokes. We kept our mouths shut.

After the 1980 failed attempt to rescue fifty-three American hostages at the American Embassy in Iran, it became clear that the army, navy, air force, and marines couldn't work together effectively on special operations missions. In 1987, the Department of Defense grafted all the military branches' special operations onto one tree—including tier-one units like SEAL Team Six and Delta. SEALs and Green Berets are truly special, but only the best of those operators make it to the top tier: Team Six and Delta. JSOC was our boss.

Mr. JSOC flipped the chart to an aerial photo. "OK, gentlemen, this is a TCS op." Major General William F. Garrison, JSOC commander, had called us out on a Task Conditions and Standards (TCS) operation. General Garrison had thrown the BS flag. *Could we do what we advertised—anything, anytime, under any conditions—including an 800-yard killing shot on a human?*

Mr. JSOC continued, "You're going to do a night HALO onto a known target." HALO meant High Altitude Low Opening: We would jump from the airplane and free-fall until we neared the ground and opened our parachutes. It also meant that anyone on land might have a chance of seeing or hearing the plane flying so close to the area. On a High Altitude *High* Opening (HAHO), we might jump at 28,000 feet, fall five seconds, open our chutes, and glide maybe 40 miles to the landing zone—which allowed us to avoid detection more easily. On a training jump over Arizona, both Phoenix and Tucson, over a hundred miles apart, we looked barely separated. The bad thing about a HAHO is how bitterly cold it is at 28,000 feet—and it stays cold. After landing, I would have to stick my hands under my armpits to thaw them out. Because this jump was a HALO, the cold would be less of a factor.

Mr. JSOC showed us the plane route, the drop point, and, more importantly, the landing point—where we needed to park our parachutes. He told us where to stow our chutes after we touched ground. In hostile territory, we would dig holes and bury them. This was a training mission, though, and we weren't going to bury parachutes worth a couple of thousand dollars each.

"This is the route you're going to patrol in." He gave us the time for a ten-minute window of opportunity to take out our target. If we were late and missed our window of opportunity or missed the shot, there would be no second chances. One shot, one kill.

We stripped off our civilian clothes. Like every other SEAL I know, I went commando in my civvies—no underwear. For sniper work, I put on North Face blue polypropylene (polypro) undershorts, also used in winter warfare, to wick moisture away from the body. We put on woodland cammies, camouflage tops and bottoms. I wore wool socks. After going through winter warfare training with SEAL Team Two, I learned the value of good socks and spent money on the best civilian pair I could find. Over the socks I wore jungle boots. In one pocket I carried a camouflage boonie hat for the patrol in and patrol out. The boonie hat has a wide brim and loops sewn around the crown for holding vegetation as camouflage. In a knife case on my belt, I carried a Swiss Army knife, my only knife on sniper ops. I used a cammy kit, like a pocket-sized makeup kit, to paint my face dark and light green. I painted my hands, too, just in case I took off the Nomex aviator gloves that kept my hands warm. I had already cut out the thumb and index finger at the first knuckle on the right glove. This helped when I had to use fine finger movement for things like adjusting my scope, loading ammo, and getting a better feel for the trigger.

My sidearm was the SIG SAUER P-226 Navy 9 mm. It has a phosphate corrosion-resistant finish on the internal parts, contrast sights, an anchor engraved on the slide, and a magazine that holds fifteen rounds. Designed especially for the SEALs, it was the best handgun I'd ever fired, and I had tried nearly every top handgun there was. I kept one magazine in the pistol and two on my belt. My gear included a map, a compass, and a small red-lens flashlight. In a real op, we could use GPS, but this time General Garrison wouldn't let our map and compass skills go untested. We also carried a medical pouch, called a blowout kit.

We didn't wear body armor when doing a field sniper op like this over land, relying instead on being invisible. If we were doing an urban op, we'd wear body armor and helmets.

Each of us carried water in a CamelBak, a bladder

worn on the back with a tube that runs over a shoulder and can be sucked on (hands free) to hydrate.

Our long guns were the .300 Winchester Magnum rifle. Wind has less effect on its rounds, the trajectory is lower, the range is greater, and it has a hell of a lot more knockdown power than other rifles. For hitting a hard target, such as the engine block in a vehicle, I'd choose a .50 caliber rifle, but for a human target, the .300 Win Mag is the best. I already had four rounds loaded in my rifle. I would put a fifth round in the chamber when I got on target. On my body I carried twenty more rounds.

My sniper scope was a Leupold 10-power. Power is the number of times the target appears closer. So with a 10-power, the target appears ten times closer. The marks called mil dots on the scope would help me judge distance. We had laser range finders that were incredibly accurate, but we wouldn't be allowed to use them on this op. Over the Leupold scope I slid a KN-250 night-vision scope.

Although SEAL Team Six snipers sometimes use armor-piercing and armor-piercing incendiary ammunition, for this op we used match rounds—projectiles specially ground to be symmetrical all the way around. They cost nearly four times more than regular bullets and came in a brown generic box that read MATCH on the outside. These rounds shot nearly the same as the Win Mag rounds made by Winchester.

For other missions, we'd carry an encrypted satellite communication radio, the LST-5, but tonight was a one-night op, and we didn't have to report back. *Go in, do the hit, and exfiltrate.* We carried the MX-300 radio. The *X* didn't stand for "excellent"; it stood for "experimental." Our radios could get wet and cold and they still worked. From our sniper positions, we could quietly speak into the mike and pick each other up crystal clear. SEAL Team Six was always trying the latest and greatest stuff.

As the jumpmaster, I had to check everyone's parachute—the MT-1X. Again, the *X* didn't stand for excellent.

"Thirty minutes!" the loadmaster called.

If I had to urinate, now was the time to do it, in the piss tube mounted on the wall. I didn't have to, so I went back to sleep.

"Ten minutes!"

Awake.

"Five minutes!" The ramp on the back of the C-130 lowered. I gave a final look over each sniper's parachute. We walked to the ramp but not on it.

With the ramp down, it was too noisy to hear anymore. Everything was hand signals now. At three minutes, I got on my belly on the ramp. Remembering the aerial photo from the brief, I looked down to make sure the plane was over the area where it was supposed to be.

"One minute!" Everything on the ground looked familiar. I could've just trusted the pilots, but I'd done a lot of walking in the past, so I wanted to confirm the drop point.

"Thirty seconds!" The plane was a little off course. My left hand steadied me on the ramp as I used my right hand to signal. Looking into the plane, I flashed five fingers and jerked my thumb right, signaling the loadmaster in front of me. The loadmaster told the pilot to adjust the nose of the aircraft 5 degrees starboard. If I flashed two sets of five fingers, he would adjust 10 degrees. I never had to adjust more than 10 degrees. Some jumps I didn't have to adjust at all. It was nice to have great pilots.

The light on the ramp changed from red to green. Now it was my decision whether to jump or not. *It's going to take about five seconds to get everyone out of the plane.*

I signaled the guys. Little Big Man took the first step off the plane—12,000 feet above ground. We usually jumped in order of lightest to heaviest, so the heaviest jumper wouldn't land away from everybody. Next jumped Sourpuss, then Casanova. I jumped last because as the jumpmaster I had to make sure everyone exited the plane, help cut away anyone who got hung up, etc. In the air, our rucksacks hung from a line attached to our chests. There was a time when I'd think, *I sure hope this crap works.* Probably for the first hundred jumps I pleaded, *God, please. Please let it open.* Now I had hundreds of free falls under my belt, and I packed my own chute. Some guys experienced malfunctions with their primary parachute and had to go to their secondary, but not me. My chute always opened. I never so much as sprained a toe—even after 752 jumps.

I positioned my body so I could fly closer to the landing zone. After free-falling for a little under a minute, I pulled at 3,000 feet. At 2,500 feet I was under canopy. I looked up to make sure the chute was OK and loosened the straps attached to my rucksack, so the straps weren't cutting off my circulation. My feet helped support the weight of my rucksack. I flipped on my night optical device (NOD). An infrared chemlight glowed on the back of each of our helmets. These are known as glow sticks in the civilian world; just bend the plastic stick until the fragile glass container inside breaks, mixing two chemicals together that glow. Invisible to the naked eye, the infrared lights shone in our NODs. We stacked our canopies on top of each other. Behind and above Little Big Man descended Sourpuss. Behind and above Sourpuss came Casanova. I descended behind and above Casanova. Our parachutes looked like stairs as we flew into the target.

Nearing the ground, I flared my parachute, slowing my descent. I eased my rucksack down, so it wouldn't trip me up on my landing. Little Big Man landed first. Without the rush of wind, his 10′–12′ canopy immediately collapsed in the dirt. He quickly got out of his parachute and readied his weapon as Sourpuss came down next. Likewise Sourpuss released his chute and prepared his weapon. Casanova and I came down on top of Little Big Man's and Sourpuss's parachutes. The four of us had landed together in an area the size of a living room. Little Big Man and Sourpuss guarded the perimeter, each covering 180 degrees, while Casanova and I took off our chutes. After we concealed our chutes, I took the point, leading us out. JSOC's lane graders were out looking to see if they could find us taking shortcuts. It was tempting to cheat—all four of us could put our chutes away at the same time without having two on security and maybe shave five minutes off our time—but it wasn't worth the risk of getting caught by the lane graders. We knew we'd better be playing the game like it was hostile territory. The more you sweat in peacetime, the less you bleed in war.

The wind blew rain at us. Perfect weather to forgive tactical sins—a noise here, a sudden movement there. We patrolled a little over half a mile, then stopped at a rally point. Little Big Man and Sourpuss held security while Casanova and I reached in our rucksacks and pulled out our ghillie suits, camouflage clothing that looks like heavy foliage, made from loose burlap strips. Each of us hand-made our suits and owned two, one for green foliage and one for desert. This time we used the green type. I replaced my camouflage boonie hat with my ghillie suit boonie hat. For clothing, it's important to blend into the environment. In urban environments, colors become darker close to the ground, so two-tone clothes work effectively: the darker jungle camouflage trousers and lighter desert camouflage top.

Casanova and I checked out each other's war paint: hands, neck, ears, and face. When painting the skin, it's important to appear the opposite of how a human being looks: Make the dark become light and the light become dark. That means making sure the parts of the face that form shadows (where the eyes sink in, etc.) become light green and the features that shine (forehead, cheeks, nose, brow, and chin) become dark green. If the sniper's face is seen, it shouldn't resemble a face. Disappear and remain invisible.

We separated into two teams and took two different routes to the target. Even if one team got compromised, the other pair could still complete the mission. Casanova and I stalked through the night to our objective.

Each of us slowly lifted one foot and moved it forward, clearing obstacles with the toes straight to the front, feeling for twigs or anything we were about to step on. Taking short steps, I walked on the outside edges of my feet, slowly rolling between the balls of my feet and the heels, gradually shifting my weight forward.

At what we determined to be 900 yards to the target, we arrived at a partially open area. Casanova and I lay flat on the ground. Maintaining separation so we wouldn't look like some moving blob, we low-crawled. We had to move slowly enough not to be seen but fast enough to arrive in time to take our shot. I was careful not to stick my rifle muzzle in the dirt, which would degrade its accuracy, and careful not to stick it in the air, which would expose our position. Remaining flat, I slowly pulled the ground with my arms and pushed with my feet, face so close to the ground that it pushed mud. Six inches at a time. I became one with Mother Earth and cleared my mind of other thoughts. During stalks, I often told myself, *I am one with the ground. I am a part of this dirt.*

If I saw the target or a roving patrol, I wouldn't look directly at or think about it. A buck deer will snort and stomp the ground because he can smell you but can't locate you. He's snorting and stomping the ground trying to get you to move so he can locate you. Humans don't have a buck deer's sense of smell, but they do have a sixth sense—they know when they're being watched. Some are more attuned to it than others. When you think you're being watched and you turn around to find that someone is looking at you, you're using that sense. The sniper tries not to arouse this sense and avoids looking directly at the target. When it comes time to take the shot, of course, I look at the target in my crosshairs; even then, the concentration is on the crosshairs.

I paused for a moment. Then moved again.

Finally, at what we estimated to be 500 yards to the target, we arrived at our final firing position (FFP). Time: 0220. I pulled my green veil over my scope to break up the outline created by my head and night-vision scope. If you've never lain down in a puddle wearing a soggy ghillie suit with the rain pounding down and the wind howling, and all the while trying to stay on your scope and do your job, you're missing out on one of the best parts of life.

Ahead of us was an old house. Somewhere inside was our target. Casanova and I discussed range, visibility, etc. We used color codes for each side: white, front; black, rear; green, the building's own right; and red, the building's left. The color coding for the sides originated with ships, which use green lights for the right (starboard) side and red for the left (port). The phonetic alphabet designated each floor: Alpha, Bravo, Charlie, Delta . . . Windows were numbered from left to right: one, two, three . . . If someone moved in the front left window on the second floor, I'd report the window: White, Bravo, One. Thus we cut down on needless chatter, making communication concise and streamlined. It was also universal among Team Six snipers, allowing us to quickly understand others we may not have worked with before.

We also kept a log, which included the enemy's size, activity, location, unit, time, and equipment (summarized as SALUTE). Patrol information is important for an assault team. For example, the assault team might want to go in immediately after the enemy patrol reentered the house. If the patrol is only two people, the assault team might decide to abduct them during their patrol. Or three snipers might simultaneously shoot the two patrol members outside and the target inside. If this were a hostage situation, we would note where the hostages were, where the terrorists were, the leadership, eating times, sleeping times, etc. We were soaking wet, cold, and miserable, but we didn't have to like it; we just had to do it.

I mil-dotted the window. Knowing that a typical window is one yard tall, I multiplied that by one thousand. Then I divided by the mil dots on my scope to figure out the range.

A lane grader appeared. "What's the range to the target?"

"Six hundred yards," was my updated response.

A figure wearing a balaclava on his head and a big army trench coat appeared in the window—the target, which was a mannequin. Usually only one sniper in a pair takes the shot, and the other logs information, spots the target, and guards the perimeter. This time, all four of us would fire. General Garrison wanted to know if each, or any, of us could do what we claimed. I heard a shot from the other pair. Each would only get one try—cold bore. This first shot is the worst because the round has to travel through the cold bore of the rifle. After that round warms up the barrel, the next one fires more accurately—but General Garrison wouldn't give us second shots. Neither would the enemy.

A lane grader checked the target but didn't tell us

the results. Then the second shot went off. Again, my team didn't know the results.

It was our turn now. Casanova lay to my right close enough so I could hear him whisper, if needed. Close enough so we could look at a map together. His position also helped him spot the vapor trail of the bullet downrange, helping him see the bullet splash into the target so he could give me correction for a second shot—but today was all or nothing. It had only been about six hours ago when I was having hot pizza with my son in the warmth of the Ready Room. Now I was in the cold, damp woods in the middle of nowhere taking a cold-bore shot at my target. Most people have no idea of the degree of training and commitment required for sniper work.

The butt of the rifle rested tightly in my right shoulder pocket. My shooting hand held the small of the stock firmly but not stiffly, and my trigger finger calmly touched the trigger. My rear elbow gave me balance. Cheek firmly contacting my thumb on the small of the stock, I inhaled. After a partial exhale, I held my breath, a skill that frogmen excel at, keeping my lungs still so they wouldn't throw the shot. I had to stop breathing long enough to align my crosshairs over the target, but not so long as to cause blurred vision and muscular tension. My finger squeezed the trigger—*bang*.

I still didn't know if I'd hit the target or not. It's not like the movies, where the shot disintegrates the target. In reality the bullet goes through the body so fast that sometimes people don't even realize they've been shot, as I would later witness in Somalia repeatedly with the .223 rounds.

After Casanova took his shot, we crawled out of the

area using a different route from the one we'd taken to come in. Anyone who found our tracks and waited for us to return on the same path would be waiting a long time. We patrolled near the designated landing zone and waited there until dawn.

In the morning, we headed out for the helicopter pickup. A lane grader gave the code that the op was officially over: "Tuna, tuna, tuna." We could relax: stand up straight, stretch, crack our knuckles, relieve ourselves, and joke around.

A Black Hawk helicopter picked us up in an open field and shuttled us to a nearby airfield, where we boarded a plane.

After returning to SEAL Team Six, the four of us wouldn't get to go home yet. We had to debrief, then downstage our gear by cleaning it, inspecting it for damage, and repairing it if necessary. Then we had to upstage our gear, preparing for the next callout, whether practice or real world. After three hours, our gear would be ready for when the balloon went up again.

The four of us walked into the briefing room for the debrief at 1100 feeling like hammered turds. General Garrison, along with our SEAL Team Six skipper, our Red Team leader and Red Team chief, and eight or ten other key brass in their entourage, sat in front of us. William F. Garrison didn't choose the military; the military chose him. Drafted during Vietnam, he served two tours as an officer, earning a Bronze Star for valor and a Purple Heart for combat wounds. He had operated in the Phoenix Program to dismantle the Vietcong's leadership infrastructure. Later, he worked in the U.S. Army Intelligence Support Activity and Delta from 1985 to 1989. A tall, slender man with gray hair in a tight crew cut, he chewed half an unlit cigar hanging out the side of his mouth. He was the youngest general in the army—ever.

Our skipper didn't always attend training op debriefings, but with Papa Garrison at the dinner table, the skipper wanted to make sure that his bastard navy children looked good—and, more importantly, got their slice of the pie.

Our Red Team chief was Denny Chalker, nicknamed Snake, a former Army 82nd Airborne paratrooper who became a SEAL in Team One's counterterrorist unit, Echo Platoon, before becoming one of the original members of SEAL Team Six—a plankowner.

We reported: the briefing on the plane, the parachute jump, the whole op. The lane graders had been secretly watching our designated landing zone. They saw two of us hold security while the other two secured their parachutes. Fortunately, we practiced like we operated.

General Garrison said, "The good news is that your sniper craft skills were remarkable—stalking, navigating, blending with the environment, getting into position, observation—and you got off your shots. But it doesn't mean crap when all four of you miss the target! You told the lane grader that the target was at a distance of six hundred yards, but it was at a distance of seven hundred and forty-two yards. One of you shot so far off target that you hit the windowsill. Your only hope was that the enemy might die of a heart attack from being shot at."

We snipers looked at each other. Our faces sagged like we'd been kicked in the gut.

Our skipper's face looked about to split.

General Garrison kept two secrets from us, though. The first was that the Gold Team snipers had also botched their mission. Their jumpmaster failed to put them in the landing zone. Gold Team's snipers had to hump eight miles through the woods. By the time they made it to the target, they were too late: Their ten-minute window of opportunity had closed. They didn't even get off a shot.

The second secret: The general's own Delta Force had failed, too.

An even larger problem existed: SEAL Team Six and Delta Force had been run as two separate entities. Why should SEAL Team Six take down an aircraft on a runway when Delta does it better? Why should Delta take down a ship under way when SEAL Team Six does it better?

The most glaring example of this larger problem arose when Delta had one of several mishaps with explosives. A Delta operator put an explosive charge on a locked door to blow it open. He was using an Australian mouse—one slap initiates the five-second timer, which, after five seconds, detonates the blasting cap. The blasting cap makes a small explosion that detonates the larger explosion of the door charge. Unfortunately, the small explosion blew straight through the timer and immediately detonated the larger charge, blowing off the Delta operator's fingers.

Even though *nobody* does explosives better than SEAL Team Six—the most high-tech, state-of-the-art, you-only-thought-you-knew-about-explosives type of team there is (we even have our own special Explosive

Ordnance Disposal unit that does only explosives)—
SEAL Team Six trained and operated separately from
Delta.

General Garrison also understood that SEAL Team
Six and Delta were going to have to get realistic about
our capabilities. He spoke with a Texas drawl. "I don't
care what you can do some of the time. I want to know
what you can do every time anywhere in the world under any conditions." That's what you had to love about
Garrison.

SEAL Team Six and Delta would need to learn to
play together and face a reality check. Especially if we
were going to survive one of the bloodiest battles since
Vietnam—and that battle lay just around the corner.

3.
HELL IS FOR CHILDREN

As a child, I learned to endure forces beyond my control. My mother had me when she was sixteen years old—a child having a child—on November 8, 1961, in Weems Free Clinic, Boynton Beach, Florida. She couldn't afford a regular hospital. Born two months prematurely, with hazel eyes and black hair, I only weighed 3 pounds 2 ounces. The clinic was so poor that it didn't have the incubator a little one like me needed. I was so small, and a baby carrier would've been so big, that my mother literally carried me home in a shoe box. The bassinet at home was too large, so they pulled out a drawer from one of the dressers, put blankets in it, and that's where I slept.

My mother, Millie Kirkman, came from Scottish ancestry and was hardheaded as bricks in a wall. She didn't show emotion and didn't show flexibility toward life, working hard every day in a sewing factory to help support my sisters and me. I probably inherited my hardheaded, refusing-to-quit-if-you-think-you're-right attitude from her—to a fault.

When I was nine years old, she would tell me that

Ben Wilbanks, my biological father, had run off and abandoned us. I hated him for that.

The earliest memory I have of my childhood is in West Palm Beach, Florida, when I was four years old— awakened in the middle of the night by a huge man reeking of liquor. His name was Leon, and my mother was dating him. She first met Leon while working as a waitress at a truck stop.

They had just come back from a date. Leon snatched me out of the top bunk, questioning me about why I'd done something wrong that day. Then he slapped me around, hitting me in the face, to the point where I could taste my own blood. That was Leon's way of helping my mother keep her male child on the straight and narrow.

This was only the beginning. It didn't always happen at night. Whenever Leon came to the house, he took it upon himself to discipline me. I was terrified, dreading Mom's next date—literally shaking. My heart felt as though it would beat out of my chest. *How bad is it going to be this time?* A beating could happen when Leon arrived at the house while my mother got ready or when they came home. Leon wasn't picky about when he let me have it.

One day after kindergarten, I ran away. On purpose, I got on the wrong school bus. *This guy isn't going to beat me anymore. I'm outta here.* The bus took me out in the country somewhere. I had no idea where I was. There were only a few kids left on the bus. It stopped. A kid stood up. I followed him off the bus. The kid walked down the dirt road to his house. I didn't know what to do at that point—at five years old, I hadn't put a lot of thought into it. I walked down the dirt road until I got to the house at the end. Then I hung around outside not knowing what to do except stay away from the main road.

After a couple of hours, a man and a woman came home to find me sitting on the back porch, staying out of sight from the main road. The woman asked, "What's your name?"

"Howard."

"You must be hungry." They took me in and fed me.

Later, the woman said, "You know, we got to get hold of your parents. Get you back home."

"No, no," I said. "Please, please don't call my mom. Is there any way I could just live here with y'all?"

They laughed.

I didn't know what was so funny, but I didn't tell them the situation. "No, don't call my mom. Can I just live here with y'all?"

"No, honey. You don't understand. Your mama's probably worried sick. What's your phone number?"

I honestly didn't know.

"Where do you live?"

I tried to tell them how to get to my house in Lake Worth, Florida, but the bus had taken so many winding roads and turns that I couldn't remember. Finally, they took me back to my school. There they found my aunt looking for me.

My escape plan had failed. I lied to my mom, telling her I got on the wrong bus by accident.

Within a year or two, my mom married Leon.

Soon afterward, we moved to Screven, Georgia, and we went to see the judge there. In the car, my mother said, "When we see the judge, he's going to ask you if you want Mr. Leon to be your daddy. You're supposed to tell him yes." Leon was the last thing in the world I wanted in my life, but I knew damn well I better say yes, because if I didn't, I'd probably be killed when we got home. So I did my duty.

The next day, before I went to school, my parents told me, "You tell them at school you're not a Wilbanks anymore—you're a Wasdin." So I did.

Now I was the adopted child and had to see Leon every day. When a lion acquires a lioness with cubs, he kills them. Leon didn't kill me, but anything that was not done exactly right, I paid for. Sometimes even when things were done right, I paid.

We had pecan trees in the yard. It was my job to pick up the pecans. Leon was a truck driver, and when he came home, if he heard any pecans pop under his wheels, that was my ass. Didn't matter if any had fallen since I had picked them all up. It was my fault for not showing due diligence. When I got home from school, I'd have to go straight to the bedroom and lie down on the bed, and Leon would mercilessly beat me with a belt.

The next day at school, whenever I used the toilet, I would have to peel my underwear away from the blood and scabs on my butt to sit down. I never got mad at God, but sometimes I asked Him for help: "God, please kill Leon."

After so much, it got to the point that when the 250-pound man's belt cut across my lower back, butt, and legs, I wasn't afraid anymore. *Calm down. Stop shaking. It isn't going to make it any better or any worse. Just take it.* I could literally lie there on the bed, close

down, and block out the pain. That zombielike state
only pissed Leon off more.

My first sniper op came after Christmas when I was
seven years old. A ten-year-old boy named Gary, who
was the school bully, was big for his age and had beaten
up one of my friends. That afternoon, I gathered four
of my buddies together. We knew Gary was too big for
us to fight using conventional means, but most of us got
BB guns for Christmas. "Tomorrow morning, bring
your guns to school," I said. "We'll wait in the tree at
the edge of the playground and get him when he walks
to school." Gary would have to walk down a narrow
pathway that served as a natural choke point. The next
day, we waited. We had the tactical advantage in numbers, firepower, and high ground. When Gary entered
the kill zone, we let him have it. You'd think he'd start
running after the first shot—but he didn't. He just stood
there screaming like he'd been attacked by a swarm of
bees, grabbing his shoulders, back, and head. We kept
shooting. Ms. Waters, one of the teachers, ran toward
us screaming bloody murder. Another teacher shouted
for us to get down from the tree. Gary had curled up on
the ground and hyperventilated as he cried. I felt bad
for him because blood was streaming down his head,
where most of the BBs had hit him, but I also felt he
deserved it for beating up my buddy the previous day.
Gary's shirt was stuck to his back. A teacher took out
his handkerchief and wiped Gary's face.

We had to go to the principal's office. Our local law
enforcement officer sat in, trying not to laugh. I ex-

plained, "This kid's bigger than all of us, and he beat up Chris yesterday." In my mind, I didn't understand what we'd done wrong. They confiscated our guns and called our parents. Of course, my dad let me have it big-time when I got home.

Years later, prior to becoming a SEAL, I came home on leave from the navy and sat in a truck with Gary as he drove for my dad. Gary asked me, "You remember shooting me with the BB gun?"

I felt embarrassed. "Yeah, I remember. You know, we were kids."

"No, no, it's OK." He pointed to his left shoulder. "Feel right here."

I touched his left shoulder—and felt a BB beneath his skin.

"Every once in a while, one of those will work its way out," he said matter-of-factly. "Sometimes they come out of my scalp. Sometimes they come out of my shoulder."

"Oh, man. I'm so sorry."

Later we had a couple of beers and laughed about it.

When I was eight years old, I returned to Florida with Leon and some others to do some peddling, riding around selling produce out of the back of a pickup truck. I handled the sales from the back of the truck while an alcoholic redneck named Ralph Miller drove us around. He would often stop at a liquor store. "I'm stopping here to get some tomato juice. Don't you like tomato juice?"

"I guess I like tomato juice."

He would buy a can of tomato juice for me. Later, he

started buying a light, zesty tomato juice mixed with onions, celery, spices, and a dash of clam juice: Mott's Clamato. Ralph drank the same himself.

One time, from the back of the pickup truck, I snuck a peek into the cab. Ralph unzipped his pants and pulled out a bottle of vodka, mixing it in his own Clamato drink. *What's the fun in that? He's just messing up some good Clamato.*

We drove through some of the most dangerous parts of town, selling watermelons and cantaloupes. Once when we stopped in a town called Dania, two guys came up to the back of the truck asking for the price of our produce. One took a watermelon, put it in his car, and then walked to the cab as if to pay Ralph.

Pow!

I turned around and saw the man pointing a .38 revolver at Ralph. Ralph's leg was bleeding. Shaking, Ralph handed the man his wallet.

The man with the gun asked Ralph, "You didn't think I'd shoot you, did you?"

I moved to get off the truck.

The gunman's accomplice told me, "Just stay there."

Then the gunman pointed his pistol at me.

I jumped off the passenger side of the truck tailgate and hauled butt, expecting to get hit by a bullet any second. I ran so fast that my favorite red straw cowboy hat, which I got from Grandma Beulah's dime store, flew off my head. For a split second I thought about running back to get my hat, but I decided, *That man is going to shoot me if I go back.*

I circled around a couple of blocks and found Ralph pulled up to the phone booth in front of a convenience store. I was so happy that he was still alive. Ralph called an ambulance.

The police arrived shortly before the ambulance. As I listened to the cops question Ralph, I found out that he had offered to give the two thugs his money, but not his wallet. That's when Ralph got shot.

While Ralph went into surgery in the hospital, the police took me to the Dania police station. The detectives questioned me, took me back to the scene, and had me talk through the incident. They had a suspect but realized I was too young and too shocked by what happened to be a credible witness.

It was the first time I had been around such professional men. They took time with me, told me what it was like to be a police officer, and told me what they had to do to become police officers. I was amazed. A narcotics detective showed me all the different kinds of drugs they had taken off the street. They gave me a tour of the police station, and the paramedics next door gave me a tour of their facility. *Man, this is so cool.* The paramedics even let me slide down the pole. I would never forget them.

That night, they still couldn't find my dad, so a detective drove me to his home to spend the night. His wife asked, "Have you had anything to eat yet?"

I hadn't eaten since breakfast. "No, ma'am."

"Are you hungry?"

"A little bit."

"OK, let me fix you something to eat."

The detective said, "We brought him to the station this afternoon, but none of us thought about feeding him."

"Don't you know he's a growing boy?" She gave me a plate of food.

I ate ravenously. *Maybe I could just live with these people forever . . .* After my meal, I fell asleep. I was awakened at five o'clock the next morning. The detective took me to the police station, where Dad and his brother, my uncle Carroll, were waiting for me.

The two of them owned a watermelon field where I started working after school and during the summer. Those two were all about work. When they weren't working their farm, they were driving trucks. As I started contributing to the family, my relationship with Dad, who had stopped drinking, improved.

In South Georgia, where the heat exceeded 100 degrees and the humidity neared 100 percent, I would walk through the field cutting 30-pound watermelons off the vine, place them in a line to throw them over to the road, and then toss them up onto the pickup truck. One of the older guys would back the truck up to the trailer of an 18-wheeler, where I helped pack the watermelons onto the rig. After loading thousands of watermelons, I'd ride on the truck up to Columbia, South Carolina, in the early hours of the next morning to unload and sell the watermelons. I'd get about two hours of sleep before riding back.

When there was an hour or two to spare, my family would sometimes go for a picnic. On one of these picnics, I taught myself how to swim in the slow-moving waters of the Little Satilla River. I had no swimming technique whatsoever, but I felt at home in the water. We went there on a number of weekends: swimming and fishing for largemouth bass, crappie, redbreast, and bluegill.

Occasionally, after working in the watermelon patch, the crew and I went blackwater swimming in Lake Grace. Because of all the tannic acid from the pine trees and other vegetation, both the Little Satilla River and Lake Grace are so black on a good day that you can't see your feet in the water. In the summer, dragonflies hunt down mosquitoes. From the surrounding woods, squirrels chirp, ducks quack, and wild turkeys squawk. Those dark waters hold a mysterious beauty.

By the time I was thirteen or fourteen, I was running the field crew. I'd leave the side of town where the whites lived and cross the tracks to the Quarters, where the blacks lived. I'd pick up the fifteen to twenty people who were going to work in the field that day and drive them out to the field, organize them, and then work beside them, even though they were almost twice my size.

After work one day, my watermelon crew and I had a contest to see who could swim the farthest from the pier underwater at Lake Grace. The occasional family picnic had offered me the time to improve my swimming. As I swam beneath the surface of the dark brown water, I swallowed with my mouth closed and let a little air out. When I came up, someone said, "You had to be farting. There's no way you had that much air in your lungs." Times like this were very rare for me. They were the few times I could truly relax and enjoy myself. Occasionally, we built campfires and talked at night.

Dad didn't mind if we spent a few hours swimming or fishing, but we never went hunting. My dad let me shoot his gun once in a while, but hunting was an all-day event. That would take too much time away from work. Work was his focus. If I made a mistake or didn't work hard enough, he beat me.

In junior high school, I hurt my leg playing football in gym class. One of the coaches said, "Let me check your hip out." He pulled my pants down so he could examine my right hip. He saw the hell that covered me from my lower back down to my upper legs where my dad had recently beaten me. The coach gasped. "Oh, my . . ." After checking my hip, he pulled my pants up and never said another word. In those days, whatever happened in the home stayed in the home. I remember feeling so embarrassed that someone had discovered my secret.

Despite everything, I loved my parents. It wasn't entirely their fault they were uneducated and didn't know how to nurture children. It was all they could do to put food on the table and keep four kids clothed. In Maslow's hierarchy of needs, we never got up to self-actualization because we were still on the bottom of the pyramid—trying to feed and clothe ourselves. For the most part, my parents never used bad language. They were God-fearing people. Mom took my sisters and me to church every Sunday. They saw nothing wrong with their child-rearing skills.

Because I was the older brother, Dad expected me to take care of my sisters, Rebecca, Tammy, and Sue Anne. Tammy was always the bigmouthed, crap-stirring troublemaker. From the time she started elementary school,

I lost track of how many times she ran her mouth and I had to stick up for her. When I was in the fifth grade, she mouthed off to a guy in the eighth grade. The eighth grader cleaned my clock, giving me two black eyes, a broken nose, and a chipped tooth. When I got home, my dad was the proudest man there was. Never mind that Tammy had done something senseless and provoked a fight. I looked like road kill. No matter how badly that kid beat me, though, if I hadn't stood up to him, my dad would've beaten me worse.

At the age of seventeen, the summer of my junior year in high school, I returned home one afternoon from working all day in the watermelon field, took a shower, and sat in the living room wearing nothing but a pair of shorts. A little while later, Tammy came in the door crying.

My hair was still wet from the shower. "What is it?"

"My head hurts."

"What do you mean your head hurts, baby?"

"Feel right here."

I felt her head. She had a knot on top of it.

"We were playing volleyball at the church. When I spiked the volleyball, Timmy picked it up and threw it at me. So I threw it back. He grabbed me and put me in a headlock. Then he punched me on top of the head."

I went through the roof. Now I was a bull seeing red. Possessed. I ran out of the house, off the porch, vaulted the chain link, and ran down the road one block to the First Baptist Church. Kids and parents were coming out of church from summer Bible school. Deacons stood out front. I spotted Timmy, a boy my age—the boy who'd hurt my little sister.

He turned around just in time to see me coming. "Howard, we need to talk."

"Oh, no we don't, you son of a bitch." I nailed him right in the face, plowing him. I got on top of the boy, straddled his upper body, and pummeled him half to death, cussing up a storm. All I could see in my mind was my baby sister crying with a knot on her head.

A deacon tried to pull me off, but I was seventeen years old and had worked like a dog every day of my life. It took several more deacons to separate me from the boy.

Brother Ron appeared. "Howard, stop." I believed in Brother Ron and looked up to him. He was like the town celebrity.

I stopped. Brother Ron had exorcised the demon.

Unfortunately, the incident started a feud. The guy's dad was kind of a psycho, and my dad was a hothead who wouldn't back down from anybody.

Psycho drove to my house.

Dad met him outside.

"If I see that bastard son of yours somewhere, he may not be making it back home," Psycho said.

Dad walked into the house and grabbed a shotgun. As he exited the front door, my grandfather met him outside. With my grandfather stood Brother Ron. Dad was about to put a load of double-aught buck in Psycho's ass. Grandfather and Brother Ron calmed Dad down.

The next weeks were tense for me, looking over my shoulder for a grown man everywhere I went. Timmy had two brothers, too. I rounded up my posse to protect me and didn't go anywhere alone.

Brother Ron got Dad and Psycho together and had a peaceful "Come to Jesus" meeting. It turned out that things didn't happen quite the way my smart-mouthed sister had said. Tammy had done something to Timmy. After that, he'd only given her a playful noogie—rubbing his knuckles on her head. I had imagined a bigger bump on her head than there actually was. Our fathers agreed to put everything aside.

Now, I knew I was going to be in big trouble.

Instead, Dad said, "You know, I'd have done the same exact thing, though I might not have cussed as much as you did in the churchyard."

I wore that like a badge of honor. In spite of my dad's faults, protecting his family was important to him, and I respected his desire to protect me.

Brother Ron was the glue that held the community together, and the community helped shape who I was.

Besides Brother Ron, another man who influenced me was Uncle Carroll, Dad's older brother. Uncle Carroll didn't have a hot temper. He may not have been well educated, but he was intelligent—especially in his dealings with people. Uncle Carroll had friends everywhere. He taught me how to drive a truck because Leon didn't have the patience. Leon would be angry at the first mistake I made picking watermelons, driving, or anything—it didn't matter. Uncle Carroll took the time to explain things. When I was learning how to drive an 18-wheeler, Uncle Carroll said, "Well, Howard, no, you shouldn't have flipped the split axle right then. You should get your RPMs up a little bit more. Now gear back down and go back up . . ." Being around Uncle Carroll, I learned people skills. Leon and I would be in a truck driving from West Palm Beach, Florida, to Screven, Georgia—eight hours—and hardly speak. We didn't have conversations. He might say something like, "Do you need to go to the bathroom?" Unless it concerned bodily functions or getting something to eat, we didn't talk. Both Mom and Dad told us, "Children are supposed to be seen, not heard." They weren't BSing, either. If we were ever out in public and said something without someone asking us a question, when we got home, we knew what we were in for. Uncle Carroll was the only one who ever showed me any affection. On occasion, he'd put his arm around my shoulders if he knew Leon had been on my tail unrelentingly the way he usually was. He gave moral support, even a kind word on occasion. Through everything, Uncle Carroll's support was priceless. If he and I were in the truck, we would stop, go into a restaurant, and eat: breakfast and lunch. With Leon, we would go into a grocery store and get some salami and cheese and make a sandwich in the truck while driving—Leon couldn't be slowed down. The best thing was that Uncle Carroll gave me words of encouragement. His influence was as critical as Brother Ron's, maybe even more. Without them, I would've harbored some dark thoughts. Probably suicide.

I spent my high school years as an Air Force Junior Reserve Officer Training Corps (JROTC) geek. I loved JROTC, with its discipline, structure, and nice uniform. I was always the outstanding cadet: ranking officer, color guard commander—it gave me something to do and excel at. The light came on, and I learned that I could lead pretty easily.

When it came to girls, though, I was a late bloomer. In October, a month away from being eighteen years old, I asked a buddy, "How does this whole French kissing thing work? What do you do?"

"Howard, you just reach over, put your mouth on hers, stick your tongue in, and go to town."

I needed a date for the JROTC military ball. My JROTC buddy had a sister named Dianne; everyone called her Dee Dee. I hadn't really thought about her, but now I figured maybe she would go with me to the ball. Scared and embarrassed, I asked her, "Will you go to the military ball with me?"

"Yes," she said.

After the dance, Dee Dee said, "Let's go to the Ghost Light." I took her to the old make-out spot—where legend said that the ghost of an old decapitated railroad worker walked the railroad tracks searching with his lantern.

When we parked the car, I was petrified. *When do I put my lips on hers? What the hell does "stick your tongue in and go to town" mean? Do I go around in circles? What am I supposed to do?* So I pretty much talked myself out of it. I turned to tell Dee Dee, *You know, we better get back home.* She had already moved in for the kill. Her face was right on mine. She gave me my first French kiss. Needless to say, I figured out, *This is not quantum physics, and this is OK.* We dated the rest of the school year until spring.

The prom was coming, but someone had already

asked Dee Dee to it. During home economics class, I asked her friend Laura to the prom—our first date. Laura had a nice body and big breasts. After the prom, in the car, we kissed for the first time. Well, she kissed me and I didn't resist. Because I grew up in a family that didn't show affection, her interest in me meant a lot.

Thinking back on my teenage years, I can remember my first surveillance op. There's not a lot to do in Screven, Georgia, so sometimes we had to create our own fun. One Friday night, Greg, Phil, Dan, and I drove down to the river. We found an old suitcase that had fallen off somebody's car. We opened it. Inside were some clothes. We threw it in the back of Greg's truck and thought nothing else about it. As we camped near the river, sitting around a campfire drinking beer and roasting wieners, a malnourished, mangy cat approached us. It looked too wild to come near us, but it must've been desperate for food. We threw it a piece of wiener, and the cat gulped it down. One of us tried to pick up the feline, and it went berserk—claws and teeth everywhere. That cat was bad. We used the suitcase to set a trap for it, propping the lid open and putting a wiener inside. When the cat went inside to eat, we dropped the top and zipped up the suitcase. We laughed. Hearing the cat go crazy in the suitcase made us laugh harder. The cat kept going until it was exhausted.

I got an idea. "You know how we wanted to open the suitcase? If we put this on the road, someone will stop and open it." So we took the suitcase to the road and stood it up on the shoulder near a bridge. Then we concealed ourselves nearby, lying flat on a slope that descended from the street. We waited awhile before the first car drove by. It wasn't a well-traveled road.

Another car came by, and the brake lights flashed. Then it proceeded forward, did a U-turn, and came back. It passed us and did another U-turn, finally stopping next to the suitcase. An overweight black woman stepped out of the car and picked up the suitcase. After she returned to the car and closed the door, we heard excited talk, as if they had dug up a treasure chest. The car moved forward. Suddenly, the brake lights came back on and the car screeched to a halt. Three of the four doors popped open, and three people ran out of the car cussing at the top of their lungs.

We tried not to laugh.

One of the passengers threw the suitcase down the hill.

"Get it out from under the seat!" another yelled.

A third person grabbed a stick and started poking inside the car to get the cat out from under the seat. The cat finally escaped.

We hadn't expected them to open the suitcase in the car while it was moving, and we hadn't intended to harm anyone. Fortunately no one was hurt. The incident gave us a story to keep the laughter roaring at night. I'll bet those people never picked up anything from the side of the road again. It also became my first covert observation operation.

When I graduated from high school, I stood 5'11" tall, and I'd saved up money for a car and Cumberland

College in Williamsburg, Kentucky—a Christian school. All the work saving up for a car had been to no avail, because Tammy totaled my blue 1970 Ford LTD before I even left home, so I had to take the bus instead. Before I stepped on the bus, my mother told Dad, "Hug Howard." Then she told me, "Go hug your daddy." Leon put his arms out. We did an awkward hug. It was the first time we had ever hugged each other. Then I had a rare hug with my mother. I got on the bus glad to get the hell out of there.

4.
RUSSIAN SUB AND GREEN HERO

At the age of twenty, after a year and a half of college, I used up the last of my hard-earned money and couldn't afford to go back to school. There wasn't a lot of financial aid available at the time, and I was tired of washing with leftover soap and was weary of searching for lost change on Thursdays so I could enjoy three-hot-dogs-for-a-dollar night at the nearby convenience store. I decided to visit the military recruiters at the shopping mall in Brunswick, Georgia, hoping to join, save enough money, and return to college. A poster of a Search and Rescue (SAR) swimmer in a wetsuit hung outside the navy recruiter's office. Later, I signed up to do Search and Rescue for the navy.

Before shipping out, I decided to marry Laura.

My mom had one request. "Talk to Brother Ron first."

I knew our preacher didn't like Laura. I knew he didn't agree with her Mormon religion. "No, Mom, I won't do that. I'm not going to talk to Brother Ron. I love her, and I'm marrying her."

Leon came into my room and with both hands pushed both of my shoulders, knocking me back a few steps.

That was his big way of asserting dominance. If I looked at him or stepped forward, he would interpret that as a sign of aggression. I had learned to lower my head and stay back. "If you can't listen to your mom about this one thing, you pack up and get the hell out of my house!"

I couldn't believe my ears.

"Yeah, I saw you just look at me," Dad said. "You want to try me? Go ahead and try me. I'll go through you like a dose of salts." Epsom salts were used for constipation, and that was the South Georgia way of saying, "I'll go through you like crap through a goose." He had just threatened me for the last time.

I packed everything I could fit into a small suitcase, walked out the door, and headed down the street to a pay phone. After I called Laura's house, her parents sent her to pick me up.

Laura's family acted much different from my family. The kids and the parents *talked*. They had conversations. The parents were nice to the kids. Her father even told them good morning. That blew me away. They were loving and affectionate. I loved what their family had as much as I loved Laura.

Her parents let me live with them until I could get a temporary construction job and a small apartment. Months after I left my home, Laura and I married in her church on April 16, 1983. My parents grudgingly attended the small wedding. We lived in a town where it would've reflected poorly on them if they hadn't come. After Laura and I exchanged vows, my dad gave me a hundred-dollar bill and shook my hand without saying anything—no "Congratulations" or "Go to hell." Needless to say, my parents didn't stay for cake.

French kissing and lovemaking came naturally for me. Doing things like telling her I loved her and holding her hand were difficult. I was switched on or off—there was no in-between. I lacked a role model for being a husband and father. Dad never put his arm around my mother or held her hand. Maybe he did when I wasn't around, but I never saw it. Most of their conversation had only been about work or us kids.

On November 6, 1983, I arrived at navy boot camp in Orlando, Florida. Two days later, we all had fresh buzz cuts and smelled like denim. At lights-out, I told the guy in the bunk below me, "Hey, today was my birthday."

"Yeah, man. Happy birthday." He didn't give a crap. No one did. It was a bit of a reality check.

The lack of discipline and respect among the recruits amazed me. So many got in trouble for forgetting to say "Yes, sir" or "No, sir." I was raised to never forget my manners and never forget attention to detail. The guys doing extra duty—push-ups, stripping and waxing the floor—looked like morons. *Making your bed and folding your underwear isn't rocket science.* I was raised to make my bed and fold my underwear.

The company commander and I developed a bond— he'd had the same Search and Rescue job as an air crewman that I wanted. He put me in charge of half the barracks. After finishing almost four weeks of boot camp, a quarter of the recruits were still having problems. I couldn't understand it.

Anyone who got in serious trouble had to go to Intensive Training (IT). I told my company commander, "I want to go to IT to get in shape for my Search and Rescue physical screening test, sir." I don't remember what the exact SAR requirements were then, but today's candidates must swim 500 yards in 13 minutes, run 1.5 miles in 12.5 minutes, do 35 push-ups in 2 minutes, perform 50 sit-ups in 2 minutes, and do 2 pull-ups. If I failed the test, I would miss my big reason for joining the navy—Search and Rescue.

My company commander looked at me like I had a mushroom growing out of my head. "Wasdin, do you know what they do at IT?"

"The guys that got in trouble told me they do a lot of exercise."

He laughed.

After evening chow, I arrived at IT and found out why he was laughing. IT busted my rump. We did push-ups, sit-ups, drills holding rifles over our heads, and much more. I looked to the left and to the right—the men on either side of me were crying. *This is tough, but why are you crying?* I'd experienced much worse. Sweat and tears covered the gym floor. I sweat, but I didn't cry. The people who ran IT didn't know I had volunteered for it. After showing up there for an hour nearly every evening seven, eight, nine times, they wanted to break me of my evil ways. I never told them any different. When I left boot camp, they must've thought, *Wasdin was the biggest screwup who ever came through here.*

I took the Search and Rescue screening test. At the pool, I saw a guy with an unfamiliar insignia on his chest. At the time, I didn't know he was a Navy SEAL, and I didn't know what a SEAL was. Most people didn't. The IT may have helped me prepare for the Search and

Rescue test—if not physically, mentally. I passed. Even so, I was only 70 percent confident that I would be accepted to aircrew school. *My fate lies in the hands of the navy. What job will they make me do if I don't pass this?*

Toward the end of the three-month navy boot camp, my air crewman company commander gave me a smile and orders to attend aircrew school. "I'll see you in the fleet," he said. I'd passed. That was the best day of my life. Laura came out to Florida to see me at boot camp graduation, staying the weekend. I had to remain in uniform even when we were off base. While we were eating dinner in a restaurant, a couple gave us tickets to Disney World—and picked up my check on the way out. The next day, we explored the Magic Kingdom.

There would be no married housing where Laura could stay with me while I attended aircrew school in Pensacola, Florida. At aircrew school, I got to wear flight suits, learned how to deploy the rescue raft out of an aircraft, ran the obstacle course, and boxed in the navy "smoker" matches. Toward the end of the six-week-long school, I attended a week of survival training. The instructors simulated our aircraft being shot down, and we had to survive: tie knots, cross a river, and build a tent out of a parachute, with only minimal food like broth and apples. During the last three days of the survival training, we only ate what we could find and were willing to put in our mouths. I wasn't ready to eat grub worms yet.

My first boxing match was the night after returning from survival training. I told the coach, "I've been out in the woods three days without eating. You think I'll be OK?"

"Hell, yeah. This jarhead has been cleaning our clocks. We need you to go in there and fight him."

Thanks a lot, pal.

My friends Todd Mock and Bobby Powell came to watch and provide moral support.

Todd stood in my corner. I told him, "Wish I had more time to get ready for this fight."

"Just hit him more than he hits you."

Great advice.

The smokers were three three-minute rounds. Not a lot of pacing, just dumping everything you've got into every round. In the first round, I felt the marine and I fought about evenly. In the second round, I didn't react quickly enough and got caught a couple of times. *He's outclassing me.* My arms felt weak. The 16-ounce gloves felt like 40 pounds.

In the third round I went to touch gloves with him, a silent courtesy that boxers show each other at the beginning of the last round. I put my right hand out, and he sucker-punched me. It hurt. Oh, did it hurt. Knocked me down on my knee. I stood up but had to take an eight-count.

I wasn't Rocky—I was scared of getting hit again. After the eight-count, I came out whaling on the marine with everything I had, scared to death he was going to hurt me again. In the end, I won the fight. The navy fans went wild. I sat on the stool in my corner, exhausted. Looking at Todd, I said, "You and Bobby are going to have to help me get out."

They literally carried me to the parking lot and put

me in a car. After helping take off my gloves, they changed me into some sweats and drove me to a Wendy's, where we ate. Later, they took me to the barracks and tucked me into bed.

The next morning, I thought something was wrong with me. My face had puffed up, and one eye had swollen shut. The other eye had partially closed. *What happened?* I was sick for three or four days. Fortunately, it was near the end of aircrew school, and I graduated on time.

In spite of the separation, Laura and I wrote each other letters, and I called her. She came out to visit me for the weekend following graduation. Our relationship seemed fine.

After aircrew school, Todd, Bobby, and I moved down the street and started twelve weeks of Search and Rescue school. The place was intimidating: names on the wall, gigantic indoor pool, mock door of an H-3 helicopter, and SAR instructors in their shorts and blue T-shirts.

Man, these guys are gods.

SAR school challenged me. We got comfortable being in the water, jumped in with all our gear on, swam to the rescue hoist, hooked our pilot to it, did hand signals, lit the Mark-13 flare, and simulated rescues.

At the end of the school, for my final test, I had to complete a rescue scenario. One pilot sat in his raft. The other lay facedown in the water. In the huge indoor pool, I jumped out of the mock helicopter door and into the pool, then took care of the facedown man. The pilot in the raft screamed at me. "Hey, man. Get me the hell out of here! He's dead. Don't worry about him."

When I reached out to touch the facedown pilot, he sprang to life and grabbed me. I swam underwater, where drowning men don't like to go. After maneuvering around him, I started a spinal highway on him: checking to see no parachute cord was wrapped around his body. He seemed OK, so I started swimming, but he wouldn't budge. I checked him again and found parachute cord around both his legs. After clearing the cord, I swam him over to the other guy's raft. The pilot in the raft started yelling at the pilot in the water, "It's your fault. You screwed up."

I can't put this pilot in the same raft as the trouble-maker pilot. After inflating his flotation device, I left him in the water tied to the raft. Entering the raft, I checked on the troublemaker. I hooked him up to the helicopter hoist and sent him up first. He fought me, so I had to wrestle him before sending him up. Then I hooked myself up with the pilot in the water and went up with him.

Back in the locker room, some of my classmates hadn't returned. It hadn't dawned on me that they might've failed—I was still recovering from my rescue. Five or six instructors stood around me. "Wasdin, what did you do wrong?"

Holy crap. I just failed Search and Rescue school, and I have no idea why.

They took a J-hook, used for cutting parachute cord, and cut off my white T-shirt.

I tried to figure out what I'd missed.

"Congratulations, Wasdin. You just made it through SAR school." They gave me my blue shirt and threw me in the pool with my buddies, who were treading water.

All of them laughed their asses off at my traumatized face—they'd all been through the same.

SAR graduation was more special than boot camp or aircrew graduation because SAR training seriously challenged me physically and mentally.

After SAR school, I got even more schooling: antisubmarine warfare at Millington, Tennessee. Even though there was still no married housing, Laura and I rented a small apartment off base. When she became pregnant, she returned to live with her parents until the baby was born.

Then the navy assigned me to a training squadron in Jacksonville, Florida, to put together everything I'd learned in aircrew, SAR, and antisubmarine warfare. Still in Jacksonville, I reported to my first real duty station at HS-7 Squadron—the "Dusty Dogs"—assigned to the aircraft carrier USS *John F. Kennedy* (CV-67). Although the *Kennedy* was stationed in Norfolk, Virginia, my squadron would stay in Jacksonville except for when the *Kennedy* deployed out to sea.

On the morning of February 27, 1985, Bobby Powell came into my room in the barracks and told me, "Your wife is having a baby."

"Holy crap," I said. It would be a two-hour drive from Jacksonville to the military hospital in Fort Stewart, Georgia. I called Laura's family.

Her father answered the phone. "She's had a boy," he said.

Still wearing my flight suit, I drove as fast as I could. Everything was OK until I got within twenty minutes of the hospital. Police lights flashed at me from the rear—Georgia State Highway Patrol. I pulled over and stopped.

The officer parked behind me, stepped out of his vehicle, and strolled over to my door. "Where you off to so fast, son?"

Nervous and upset, I explained, "My wife had a baby, and I've got to get to the hospital, sir."

"Driver's license."

I handed it over.

He looked at it. "I'll tell you what. I'll escort you to the hospital. If we get there and your wife really has had a baby, I'll give you your license back." He put my license in his shirt pocket. "If she hasn't, you're going to take a ride with me."

He escorted me to the hospital parking lot, then walked with me into Laura's room. Among the visitors stood my mother—still mad at me for leaving home to marry Laura but excited about her grandson. The patrol officer spoke with her.

I held my beautiful baby boy, Blake, for the first time. I was so proud to be a father, and an elite SAR swimmer. Life was good. After a while, I noticed the officer had disappeared. "Where's the state patrol officer? I need my driver's license back."

My mom handed it to me. "The officer said to tell you congratulations."

After Blake grew old enough, he and Laura moved down to Jacksonville to join me.

* * *

On October 6, 1986, a Russian Yankee-class nuclear submarine (K-219) sailing off the coast of Bermuda experienced a failed seal on the missile hatch. Seawater leaked in and reacted with the missile liquid fuel residue, causing an explosion that killed three of its sailors. The sub limped toward Cuba. The *John F. Kennedy*'s task force sent my helicopter out to track the Russian vessel. Usually, we were supposed to fly within approximately 30 miles of our carrier group, but we had special permission to fly out farther.

I wore my booties, a short-sleeve wetsuit top called a shorty, and my white cotton briefs—tighty-whiteys. Most guys wore wetsuit bottoms, but I took my chances that I might have to rescue someone in my tighty-whiteys. For outerwear, I wore my flight suit. We picked up the Russian sub on active sonar. Following close, we kept popping its butt with sonar pings.

Suddenly, our pilot said, "Look at the temperature gauge on our main rotor transmission."

Oh, my . . . The gears burned hot enough to shear off.

The pilot tried to take us to a hover just before we fell out of the sky. We didn't hit the water as hard as I expected, but we hit hard enough. "Mayday, mayday . . ."

As the first swimmer, I rushed to the copilot to help him attach the sea anchor and put it out the window. Next, I made sure the pilot and copilot exited the aircraft through the front escape window. Then I hurried to the rear of the cockpit, where I made sure the first crewman had exited the side door. I took off my flight suit and put my swim fins, mask, and snorkel on. Finally, I kicked the raft out, inflated it, and helped the two pilots in. The other rescue swimmer was an older guy, in his forties. Instead of inflating his life vest and swimming to the raft, he hung on to a cooler for dear life, drifting out to sea. So I had to swim him down, bring him back to the raft, and get him inside. A disturbing thought occurred to me: *What am I going to do if that Russian sub rises up underneath us?*

An antisubmarine jet, an S-3 Viking, flew over. Its low-pitched hum sounded like a vacuum cleaner. The plane came back to us at a 90-degree angle, probably noting our position. Thirty minutes later, a helicopter arrived. I took the green sea dye marker, which looked like a bar of soap, and swished it in the water around the raft. We became a huge fluorescent green target for the rescue helicopter to see.

The helicopter came in low, and I signaled for them not to jump their swimmer. I put the pilots' helmet visors down to protect them from the stinging sea spray the helicopter blades blasted. Then I swam everyone over to the rescue hoist, riding up myself with the last guy. After the adrenaline dump of the crash, swimming the other swimmer down, and getting everyone to the hoist, I was wasted. In the helicopter, my buddy Dan Rucker, also a Search and Rescue swimmer, gave me a thumbs-up.

Our rescue helicopter landed on the aircraft carrier. We stepped out onto the flight deck, and everyone cheered, slapping me on the back, congratulating me for the rescue. Walking across the flight deck, I carried my swim fins, looking like the hero, except for my tighty-whiteys. Now my cotton briefs were tighty-fluorescent-greeneys. My whole body glowed from the fluorescent green dye marker. It was embarrassing as hell. I would've given a million dollars for my wetsuit bottom. Later, to my horror, others and I watched the scene all over again on the ship's video.

A couple of weeks before my active duty contract with the navy expired, I noticed five guys from a unit I'd never heard of: SEALs. In retrospect, they weren't even a standard seven- or eight-man SEAL squad. They seemed like a laser op team: two laser target designators, two spotters, and the lieutenant in charge—probably also running communications. They were in our Search and Rescue berthing space, so I started following them around asking questions about the SEALs.

During World War II, the first navy frogmen were trained to recon beaches for amphibious landings. Soon they learned underwater demolitions in order to clear obstacles and became known as Underwater Demolition Teams (UDTs). In the Korean War, UDTs evolved and went farther inland, blowing up bridges and tunnels.

Years later, after observing Communist insurgency in Southeast Asia, President John F. Kennedy—who had served in the navy during World War II—and others in the military understood the need for unconventional warriors. The navy created a unit that could operate from sea, air, and land—SEALs—drawing heavily from

UDTs. On January 1, 1962, SEAL Team One (Coronado, California) and SEAL Team Two (Little Creek, Virginia) were born.

One of the first SEALs was Rudy Boesch, a New Yorker and chief from UDT-21. Wearing his hair in a perfect crew cut, he led the newly formed SEALs at Team Two in physical training (PT). On his dog tag in the space for RELIGION was written PT. To stay in shape, Rudy and his Teammates played soccer for hours— thirty-two men on each team. Broken legs were common. The SEALs used a variety of tactics to get out of Rudy's fitness runs—making excuses, going to the restroom and not returning, and ducking into the bushes during the runs.

Rudy also served as chief of 10th Platoon, which relieved 7th Platoon in My Tho, Vietnam, on April 8, 1968. After a week of learning what 7th Platoon had been doing and going out on ops with 7th Platoon SEALs, 10th Platoon set out to do their thing. Rudy carried an imported version of the German Heckler & Koch 33. The assault rifle used the same .223 ammo as the standard-issue M-16 but was much easier to maintain in the jungle—and it had magazines that could hold forty rounds! He carried the large magazines in the pouches of a Chinese AK-47 chest pouch, two straps tied around his lower back and two straps across his chest, with the three largest pouches suspended over his stomach. Rudy stored his inflatable UDT life vest in one of his trouser pockets.

The SEALs' meat and potatoes were snatch-and-grabs. At night, Rudy and his Teammates crept into a thatched hut and grabbed one of the Vietcong (VC) out of his hammock. They wrapped the VC up and disappeared with him. Most VC had enough sense not to struggle against the green-faced men who came at night. The SEALs turned him over to the CIA for interrogation (the SEALs also used the South Vietnamese police to conduct interrogations). Then Rudy and his Teammates would act on that intelligence the next evening and snatch a VC who was higher up in the food chain. One of the prisoners switched sides to join the SEALs. The defector offered to take the green-faced men to their next target. The SEALs kept the turned VC in the front as their guide, letting him know that if he led them into an ambush, he would likely be the first killed—and if the enemy didn't kill the guide in an ambush, a SEAL would. After the guide worked hard enough to earn the trust of Rudy and the other SEALs, they made him a scout and gave him an AK-47.

With their Vietnamese scout, Rudy and six other SEALs rode through the night on a Landing Craft, Mechanized nicknamed the "Mike boat" that was loaded with weapons—M-60 and .50 caliber machine guns, a 7.62 minigun, and an M-29 mortar. It dropped them off on the shore, and they patrolled a mile until they came to a paddy dike. Rudy brought up the tail as rear security. Then they crawled in 8-inch-deep water until they reached a trail. The SEALs set up three claymore mines facing the trail, preparing to ambush an eight-man squad of VC. Twenty minutes later, Rudy and the others were fighting off sleep when at least eight VC showed up on the trail. The SEALs were waiting for all of the enemy to enter the kill zone when the VC's point man noticed some tracks, stopped, and called back to the others in Vietnamese, "Someone is here." The SEALs' Vietnamese scout shot the point man, and the green-faced men launched their ambush. Twenty-one hundred steel balls exploded from the claymores in 60-degree arcs. SEALs fired. The ambush literally tore the enemy apart. When the smoke cleared, the commandos hurried in, gathered weapons, and searched the scattered body parts for intelligence. While they were searching, AK-47 rounds came at them from the darkness—visitors. Soon muzzle flashes appeared. The VC were closing in. Rudy and his teammates decided it was time to bug out and reversed back to the river. The point man became rear security, while Rudy led them sloshing through the rice paddy. The volume of fire from behind increased. They had stirred up a hornets' nest. Rudy had never led a run of SEALs at Little Creek who were so motivated. The radioman called the Mike boat and said, "Drop mortar," requesting prearranged mortar fire. The Mike boat lobbed an 81 mm mortar shell over the SEALs' heads that missed the enemy. The radioman talked the next mortar round closer to the SEALs' rear, giving the enemy a loud surprise. When the SEALs neared the Mike boat, it opened up with all its guns on the pursuing enemy. The incredible firepower shredded trees and VC, silencing them. The SEALs climbed aboard the Mike boat and motored up the black river.

By the end of the war, SEAL Teams One and Two had been decorated with 3 Medals of Honor, 2 Navy Crosses, 42 Silver Stars, 402 Bronze Stars (one of them Rudy's), and numerous other awards. For every SEAL killed, they killed two hundred. In the late seventies,

Rudy helped in the formation of Mobility Six (MOB Six), SEAL Team Two's counterterrorist unit.

The SEALs on the *John F. Kennedy* probably got tired of me, but they shared some of the horror stories of Basic Underwater Demolition/SEAL (BUD/S) Training. They told me about skydiving, scuba diving, shooting, and blowing things up—and catching shrimp in the Delta. They worked hard and played hard. Lots of camaraderie. One told me that he got his orders to BUD/S as a reenlistment incentive. I wanted what they had.

During a six-month deployment, the *John F. Kennedy* stopped in Toulon, France, home of France's aircraft carrier *Charles de Gaulle*. I had a serious talk with the SEAL lieutenant about what it took to become a SEAL. To reenlist or not to reenlist—it was too big a bargaining chip with the navy to waste. Talk about divine intervention—meeting the right people at the right time. I went to my commanding officer's stateroom and knocked.

He cracked his door open.

"Commander Christiansen, if you can give me orders to BUD/S before my contract expires, I'll reenlist, sir."

"Get your ass in here." He opened the door.

I walked in and stood before him. It hadn't occurred to me that I might have hurt his feelings. I thought I'd joined an elite unit before, but now I knew about a unit that was more elite. There would be no satisfaction staying where I was.

"You don't know what you're asking. BUD/S is not what you really want to do. Take your money, go back home, and finish your education. You have no idea what it takes to become a SEAL." He spent the better part of an hour telling me what a crazy thing I was asking.

"Thank you, sir."

Still in France, three days before I returned to civilian life, my commanding officer's right-hand man, the executive officer (XO), called me in. "You've been a great crewman, and we'd like to keep you around. What do we have to do to keep you in the navy?"

"I already told Commander Christiansen, sir. If you can give me orders to BUD/S, I'll reenlist."

I went to my hotel, preparing to fly back to the States and become a civilian again. The day before I got on my Air France flight, my buddy Tim showed up at my door. "We just got a teletype in this morning with your orders for BUD/S."

"Bull."

"Seriously, the skipper told me to bring you back to the boat, so he can talk to you."

They're screwing with me. This is going to be some kind of farewell surprise.

I went back to the ship and entered the ready room, packed with pilots, crew members, and others. Squadron officers sat in airliner-type armchair seats. A coffee machine and magazines rested on a table. On the "Ouija board," little airplanes showed the position of each aircraft on the flight deck. A black-and-white monitor displayed landings on the flight deck. The commanding officer called me to the front. He handed me my orders to BUD/S. Everyone clapped and gave me a send-off.

The orders were contingent on me passing the physical screening test for BUD/S in Jacksonville. I flew back home to Georgia, and Laura drove me down to

Florida. During the nearly six months I'd spent on a deployed aircraft carrier, I didn't have much time to swim—except for rescuing the crew of my crashed helicopter. Before that, I mostly swam with fins on. The test was without fins. I hadn't practiced the sidestroke and breaststroke required for SEAL training, either. Although I don't remember the exact physical screening test requirements when the SEALs tested me, they were similar to today's: a 500-yard swim within 12.5 minutes, rest 10 minutes, 42 push-ups in 2 minutes, rest 2 minutes, 50 sit-ups in 2 minutes, rest 2 minutes, 6 pull-ups before dropping off the bar, rest 10 minutes, run 1.5 miles wearing boots and trousers within 11.5 minutes.

Twelve of us showed our IDs and paperwork. Then we stripped down to our swim shorts. I was nervous. At the sound of the whistle, we swam. As I neared the end of the 500-yard swim, the SEAL called out the time remaining, "Thirty seconds." Fighting to swim against each second, I finally reached the end with only fifteen seconds to spare. One applicant was not as fortunate.

Eleven of us got dressed in T-shirts, long pants, and boots. We did our push-ups and sit-ups. Again, I passed. Two more applicants failed.

After the two-minute rest, I jumped up on the pull-up bar. The stress of failure can sometimes cause people to implode. I passed, and two others failed.

Only seven of us remained. Each activity by itself wasn't so difficult, but doing one after the other *was*. We stepped onto the running track. The SEAL wished us good luck. I passed. One guy failed. Out of the twelve of us who started, only six of us were left.

The cuts didn't stop there. Some applicants didn't score high enough on the Armed Services Vocational Aptitude Battery (ASVAB), the intelligence test all potential recruits take before entering the military. During dental, medical, and hyperbaric chamber tests, more guys failed. Some guys failed for poor vision or being color-blind. Others failed the psychology testing. One psychology questionnaire asked the same questions over and over. I wasn't sure if they were checking the reliability of the test or my patience. One question asked, "Do you want to be a fashion designer?" I didn't know if fashion designers were crazy or if I was crazy for not wanting to be one. It also asked, "Do you have thoughts about suicide?" *Not before this test.* "Do you like *Alice in Wonderland*?" *How should I know? I never read it.* The prophet Moses would've failed the psychology test: "Have you had visions?" "Do you have special abilities?" After the paper test, I met with the psychiatrist and told her what she wanted to hear. I passed.

For the hyperbaric pressure testing, the chamber was a large torpedo-looking thing. I heard that some guys freaked out during the testing—the claustrophobia, air pressure, or both got to them. I stepped inside, sat down, and relaxed: slow breathing, slow heartbeat. The dive officer sealed my door shut. I went down 10 feet, 20 feet. I could feel the air pressure increasing. At 30 feet, I was already yawning and swallowing in order to relieve some of the pressure on my ears. The pressure inside the chamber simulated going down 60 feet underwater and staying there. No problem. After ten minutes at 60 feet under, the dive officer slowly relieved the pressure inside my chamber until it had returned to normal.

"Good job," the dive officer said.

Out of a hundred applicants, I was the only one who passed all the tests. I was beyond excited.

Laura and I returned home in time for Thanksgiving, and I didn't have to report to BUD/S until early January. It felt good to be home with her and Blake for the holidays, smiling and laughing, eating warm turkey with hot mashed potatoes and steaming gravy. *The only easy day was yesterday.*

5.

THE ONLY EASY DAY WAS YESTERDAY

When I showed up at the Naval Special Warfare Center in Coronado, California, I walked over the sand berm and saw the Pacific Ocean for the first time. Huge waves crashed in. *Holy crap.* I jumped into the balmy California water. It wasn't balmy—especially in comparison to the Florida gulf waters I'd trained in. *That's freezing.* I popped out quicker than I'd jumped in. *Wonder how much time we're going to have to spend in that.*

During the days leading up to training, SEAL Master Chief Rick Knepper helped prepare us with early-morning swims in the pool and late-afternoon calisthenics on the beach. Master Chief looked like an ordinary guy in his forties, calmly exercising as we grunted and groaned. He didn't seem to break a sweat.

Master Chief didn't tell us about his experiences in Vietnam. We would have to find out about them from others. Master Chief had served with SEAL Team One, Delta Platoon, 2nd Squad. His squad thought they knew about Hon Tai, a large island in Nha Trang Bay. From a distance, the island looked like a big rock sitting in the ocean for birds to take a crap on. Then two Vietcong, tired of fighting and being away from family, defected from the island and told U.S. intelligence about the camp full of VC they left behind.

Under the cover of darkness, Master Chief Knepper's squad of seven SEALs arrived by boat. Not even the moon shone. His squad free-climbed a 350-foot cliff. After reaching the top, they lowered themselves into the VC camp. The seven-man squad split into two fire teams, taking off their boots and going barefoot to search for a VIP to snatch. Going barefoot didn't leave behind telltale American boot prints in the dirt. It also made it easier to detect booby traps, and bare feet were easier to pull out of mud than boots. In the camp, though, the VC surprised the SEALs. A grenade landed at Lieutenant (j.g.) Bob Kerrey's feet. It exploded, slamming him into the rocks and destroying the lower half of his leg. Lieutenant Kerrey managed to radio the other fire team. When the team arrived, they caught the VC in a deadly crossfire. Four VC tried to escape, but the SEALs mowed them down. Three VC stayed to fight, and the SEALs cut them down, too.

A hospital corpsman SEAL lost his eye. One of the SEALs put a tourniquet on Kerrey's leg.

The SEAL squad snatched several VIPs, along with three large bags of documents (including a list of VC in the city), weapons, and other equipment. Lieutenant Kerrey continued to lead Master Chief Knepper and the others in their squad until they were evacuated. The intel received from the documents and VIPs gave critical information to the allied forces in

Vietnam. Lieutenant Kerrey received the Medal of Honor and would go on to become Nebraska's governor and senator.

Our mentors were among the best in the business.

On the first morning of indoctrination into BUD/S, we had to do the physical screening test again. After a cold shower and some push-ups, we began the test. Afraid of failing the swim, I kicked and stroked for all I was worth. Somehow, I completed it in time. Then we did the push-ups, sit-ups, chin-ups, and run. One guy failed; he hung his head as the instructors sent him packing.

That evening, the SEAL instructors stood before us and introduced themselves. At the end, Lieutenant Moore told us we could quit if we wanted to by walking outside and ringing the bell three times.

"I'll wait," Lieutenant Moore said.

I thought the lieutenant was bluffing, but some of my classmates began ringing the bell.

A number of my remaining classmates were impressive: an Iron Man triathlete, a college football player, and others. One evening in the barracks, I looked at myself in the mirror. *These guys are like racehorses. What the hell am I doing here?*

The next day, Iron Man rang the bell. I couldn't understand why.

One of our first training evolutions included the obstacle course (O-course). One night a SEAL might have to exit a submerged submarine, hang on for dear life as his Zodiac jumps over waves, scale a cliff, hump through enemy territory to his objective, scale a three-story building, do his deed, and get the hell out. The O-course helps prepare a man for that kind of work. It has also broken more than one trainee's neck or back—climbing over the top of the 60-foot cargo net is a bad time to lose arm strength. Much of our training was dangerous, and injuries were common.

We lined up in alphabetical order by our last names. I stood near the end, watching everyone take off before me. When my turn came, I took off like a cruise missile. I couldn't understand why I was passing so many people.

Partway through, I ran to the bottom of a three-story tower. I jumped up and grabbed the ledge to the second floor, then swung my legs up. I jumped up and grabbed the ledge to the third floor, then swung my legs up. Then I came back down. As I moved on to more obstacles, I noticed someone stuck behind on the three-story tower. There stood Mike W., who had played football at the University of Alabama, tears of frustration streaming down his face because he couldn't make it to the third floor.

With a hint of Georgia in his accent, Instructor Stoneclam yelled, "You can run up and down a college football field, but you can't get up to the top of one obstacle. You sissy!"

I wondered what the hell was wrong with Mike W. He was in way better shape than I was. *Wasn't he?* (Mike would severely injure his back, but Captain Bailey kept him around doing therapy for almost a year. Later, he became an outstanding SEAL officer.)

A number of the racehorses were the biggest crybabies. They'd probably been number one much of their lives, and now when they had their first taste of adversity—BUD/S style—they couldn't handle it.

What the hell is wrong with these prima donnas?

Although running and swimming came hard for me, the obstacle course turned out to be one of my favorite events. Bobby H. and I were always pushing each other out of the number one ranking. Instructor Stoneclam advised a student, "Look how Wasdin attacks the obstacles."

I'd rather be doing this than picking watermelons.

Danger had become a constant companion. Danger or no danger, one of our instructors always spoke in the same monotone. In a classroom at the Naval Special Warfare Center, Instructor Blah's jungle boot stepped on a 13-foot-long black rubber boat resting on the floor in front of my class. "Today, I'm going to brief you on surf passage. This is the IBS. Some people call it the Itty-Bitty Ship, and you'll probably have your own pet names to give it, but the navy calls it the Inflatable Boat, Small. You will man it with six to eight men who are about the same height. These men will be your boat crew."

He drew a primitive picture on the board of the beach, ocean, and stick men scattered around the IBS. He pointed to the stick men scattered in the ocean. "This is you guys after a wave has just wiped you out."

He drew a stick man on the beach. "This is one of you after the ocean spit you out. And guess what? The next thing the ocean is going to spit out is the boat."

Instructor Blah used his eraser like a boat. "Now the hundred-and-seventy-pound IBS is full of water and weighs about as much as a small car, and it's coming right at you here on the beach. What are you going to do? If you're standing in the road, and a small car comes speeding at you, what are you going to do? Try to out-run it? Of course not. You're going to get out of the road. Same thing when the boat comes speeding at you. You're going to get out of the path it's traveling. Run parallel to the beach.

"Some of you look sleepy. All of you drop and push 'em out!"

After push-ups and more instruction, we went out-side, where the sunshine had dimmed. Soon we stood by our boats facing the ocean. Bulky orange kapok life jackets covered our battle dress uniforms (BDUs). We tied our hats to the top buttonholes on our shirts with orange cord. Each of us held our paddle like a rifle at the order-arms position, waiting for our boat leaders to come back from where the instructors were briefing them.

Before long they returned and gave us orders. With boat handle in one hand and paddle in the other, all the crews raced into the water. Losers would pay with their flesh—*it pays to be a winner.*

"Ones in!" our boat leader, Mike H., called.

Our two front men jumped into the boat and started paddling.

I ran in water almost up to my knees.

"Twos in!"

Two more jumped in and started paddling.

"Threes in!"

I jumped in with the man across from me, and we

paddled. Mike jumped in last, using his oar at the stern to steer. "Stroke, stroke!" he called.

In front of us, a seven-foot wave formed. I dug my paddle in deep and pulled back as hard as I could.

"Dig, dig, dig!" Mike called.

Our boat climbed up the face of the wave. I saw one of the other boats clear the tip. We weren't so lucky. The wave picked us up and slammed us down, sandwiching us between our boat and the water. As the ocean swallowed us, I swallowed boots, paddles, and cold seawater. I realized, *This could kill me.*

Eventually, the ocean spit us out onto the beach along with most of the other boat crews. The instructors greeted us by dropping us. With our boots on the boats, hands in the sand, and gravity against us, we did push-ups.

Then we gathered ourselves together and went at it again—with more motivation and better teamwork. This time, we cleared the breakers.

Back on shore, a boyish-faced trainee from another boat crew picked his paddle up off the beach. As he turned around to face the ocean, a passengerless boat filled with seawater raced at him sideways.

Instructor Blah shouted into the megaphone, *"Get out of there!"*

Boy-Face ran away from the boat, just like the instructors told us not to. Fear has a way of turning Einsteins into amoebas.

"Run parallel to the beach! Run parallel to the beach!"

Boy-Face continued to try to outrun the speeding boat. The boat came out of the water and slid sideways like a hovercraft over the hard wet sand. When it ran out of hard wet sand, its momentum carried it over the soft dry sand until it hacked Boy-Face down. Instructor Blah, other instructors, and the ambulance rushed to the wounded man.

Doc, one of the SEAL instructors, started first aid. No one heard Boy-Face call out in pain. The boat broke his leg at the thigh bone.

As training progressed, dangers increased. Later in training, instead of landing our boats on the sand under the sun, we would land our boats on boulders at night in front of the Hotel del Coronado while ocean currents cut at us from two directions. Legend has it that those boulders used to be one rock before BUD/S trainees cracked it with their heads.

The sun lay buried in the horizon as we marched double-time through the Naval Amphibious Base across the street. Wearing the same green uniforms, we sang out in cadence, looking confident, but the tension in the air was thick. *If anybody is going to die, this is going to be the time.*

We arrived at the pool located at Building 164 and stripped down to our UDT swim shorts. An instructor said, "You are going to love this. Drown-proofing is one of my favorites. Sink or swim, sweet peas."

I tied my feet together, and my swim partner tied my hands behind my back.

"When I give the command, the bound men will hop into the deep end of the pool," Instructor Stoneclam said. "You must bob up and down twenty times, float for five minutes, swim to the shallow end of the pool, turn around without touching the bottom, swim back to the deep end, do a forward and backward somersault underwater, and retrieve a face mask from the bottom of the pool with your teeth."

The hardest part for me was swimming the length of the pool and back with my feet tied together and hands tied behind my back. I had to flip around like a dolphin. *Even so, I'd rather be doing this than being awakened from a dead sleep and slapped around.*

Although I did my duty, others didn't. We lost a muscular black guy because his body was so dense that he just sank like a rock to the bottom of the pool. A skinny redheaded hospital corpsman jumped in the water, but instead of swimming straight, he swam in a horseshoe. An instructor told him, "Swim in a straight line. What the hell is wrong with you?" The instructors found out later that Redhead was almost blind. He had forged his medical records to get to BUD/S.

For every guy who would do anything to get in, there were guys who wanted to get out. Stoneclam wouldn't let them.

"You can't quit now!" Instructor Stoneclam screamed. "This is only Indoc. Training hasn't even started yet!" We were still only in the indoctrination phase.

After three weeks of Indoc, we began First Phase, Basic Conditioning. Our class continued to shrink due to performance failures, injuries, and quitting. I wondered how much longer I could continue without being dropped because of a performance failure or an injury.

Of course, most evolutions were a kick in the crotch, designed to punish us. Woe to the trainee who let the pain show in his face. An instructor would say, "You didn't like that? Well, do some more." Likewise to the trainee who showed no pain. "You liked that? Here's another kick in the crotch." The torment continued throughout each day—push-ups, runs, push-ups, calisthenics, push-ups, swims, push-ups, O-course—day after day, week after week. We ran a mile one-way just to eat a meal. Round-trip multiplied by three meals made for 6 miles a day just to eat! We never seemed to have enough time to recover before the next evolution hit us. On top of everything, the instructors poured on the stress with verbal harassment. Most of them didn't need to raise their voices to tell us, "Grandma was slow, but she was old."

Each one of us seemed to have an Achilles' heel—and the instructors excelled at finding it. The hardest evolutions for me were the 4-mile timed runs on the beach wearing long pants and jungle boots. I dreaded them. Soft sand sucked the energy out of my legs, and waves attacked me when I tried to run on the hard pack. Some guys ran out in front, some stayed in the middle, and others like me brought up the rear. Almost every time, at the 2-mile marker at the North Island fence, an instructor would say, "Wasdin, you're getting behind. You're going to have to kick it on the way back." With each run, the time demands became tougher.

I failed one 4-mile timed run by seconds. While everyone else went back to the barracks, the four or five others who also failed joined me to form a goon squad. After having spent nearly everything I had on the run,

I knew this was going to suck. We ran sprints up and down the sand berm, jumped into the cold water, then rolled up and down the sand berm until our wet bodies looked like sugar cookies. The sand found its way into my eyes, nose, ears, and mouth. We did squat thrusts, eight-count bodybuilders, and all manner of acrobatic tortures until the sand rubbed our wet skin raw and nearly every muscle in our bodies broke down. It was my first goon squad—and the only one I ever needed. *I may die on the next timed run, but I ain't doin' this crap again.* There was one guy who swam like a fish but ended up in goon squad time and time again for not keeping up on the runs. I wondered how he ever survived all the goon squads.

In First Phase, one thing sucked more than the four-mile timed runs: Hell Week—the ultimate in *train the best, discard the rest.* It began late Sunday night with what is called breakout. M-60 machine guns blasted the air. We crawled out of the barracks as an instructor screamed, "Move, move, move!"

Outside on the grinder, an asphalt-covered area the size of a small parking lot, artillery simulators exploded—an incoming shriek followed by a boom. M-60s continued to rattle. A machine pumped a blanket of fog over the area. Green chemlights, glow sticks, decorated the outer perimeter. Water hoses sprayed us. The smell of cordite hung in the air. Over the loudspeakers blasted AC/DC's "Highway to Hell."

Terror covered the faces of many guys. Their eyes looked like two fried eggs. Only minutes into it, the bell started ringing—people quit. *You can't be serious. What the hell's wrong? Yeah, instructors are running around shooting off machine guns and everything, but no one has smacked me in the face or beat me with a belt yet.* I couldn't comprehend why people were quitting already. Of course, my tough childhood had prepared me for this moment. More than physically, I knew that mentally I had mastered pain and hard work, and I knew I could master more. My father's expectations for high performance from me produced my own expectations for high performance. In my mind, I strongly believed I wouldn't quit. I didn't need to express my belief in words—talk is cheap. My belief was real. Without such a strong belief, a tadpole has already guaranteed his failure.

One legendary Hell Week event occurs on a steel pier where the navy docks its small boats. We took off our boots and stuffed our socks and belts in them. My fingers were so numb and shaky that I had a tough time taking off my boots.

Wearing our olive drab green uniforms, we jumped into the bay with no life jackets, shoes, or socks. I immediately laid out in a dead man's float while I undid the fly on my trousers. Still in a dead man's float, when I needed air I'd bring my face out of the freezing water and take a quick bite of oxygen, then resume my position facedown in the water. When I started to sink too much, I kicked a couple of strokes. Meanwhile, I pulled off my trousers. Then I zipped the fly shut.

With my trousers off, I tied the ends of the legs

together with a square knot. Then, using both hands, I grabbed hold of the waist and kicked until my body straightened up from its float. I lifted my pants high in the air, then slammed them forward and down on the water, trapping air in the trouser legs.

As my upper body hung over the valley in the V of my homemade trouser flotation device, I felt relief. I had been so concerned about drowning that I had forgotten how frigid the water felt. Now that I wasn't drowning, I started to remember the cold.

Some of our guys swam back to the pier. We tried to call them back, but they'd had enough. *Ring, ring, ring.*

Instructor Stoneclam said, "If one more of you rings the bell, the rest of you can come out of the water, too. Inside the ambulance we have warm blankets and a thermos of hot coffee."

After one more ring of the bell, Stoneclam said, "Everybody out of the water!"

"Hooyah!"

We crawled out of the water and onto the floating steel pier.

Instructor Stoneclam said, "Now strip down to your undershorts and lie down on the pier. If you don't have shorts, your birthday suit is even better."

I stripped down to my birthday suit and lay down. The instructors had prepared the pier by spraying it down with water. Mother Nature had prepared the pier by blowing cool wind across it. I felt like I was lying down on a block of ice. Then the instructors sprayed us with cold water. Our muscles contracted wildly. The spasms were uncontrollable. We flapped around on the steel deck like fish out of water.

The instructors took us to the early stages of hypothermia. I would've done almost anything to get warm. Mike said, "Sorry, man, I gotta pee."

"It's OK, man. Pee here."

He urinated on my hands.

"Oh, thanks, buddy." The warmth felt so good.

Most people think it's just gross—they've obviously never been *really* cold.

Wednesday night—halfway through Hell Week—was the one time I thought about quitting. The instructors wasted no time beginning Lyon's Lope, named after a Vietnam SEAL. We paddled our black inflatable boat about 250 yards out to pylons in San Diego Bay, turned the boat upside down, then right side up (called "dump boat"), paddled back to shore, ran half a mile on land carrying only our paddles, tossed our paddles into the back of a truck, sat in the bay to form a human centipede, hand-paddled 400 yards, ran 600 yards, grabbed our paddles and used them to centipede-paddle 400 yards, grabbed our boats, and boat-paddled out to the pylons, then back to shore. We all had Stage Two hypothermia. Stage One is mild to strong shivering with numbness in the hands—most people have experienced this level of hypothermia. Stage Two is violent shivering with mild confusion and stumbling. In Stage Three, the core body temperature drops below 90 degrees, shivering stops, and a person becomes a babbling, bumbling idiot. There is no Stage Four—only death. The instructors calculated air and water temperatures along with how long we stayed in the water in order to make us as cold as possible without causing permanent damage or killing us.

It was standing room only at the bell. My classmates rang it like Coronado was on fire. The instructors had backed up ambulances and opened the doors. Inside sat my former classmates wrapped up in wool blankets drinking hot chocolate. Instructor Stoneclam said, "Come here, Wasdin. You're married, aren't you?"

"Yes, Instructor Stoneclam." My muscles felt too exhausted to move, but they shivered violently anyway.

"You don't need this. Come here." He walked me to the backs of the ambulances, so I could feel their warm air hit me in the face. "Have a cup of this hot chocolate."

I held it in my hand. It was warm.

"If we'd wanted you to have a wife, we would've issued you one," he explained. "Go over there and ring that damn bell. Get this over. I'll let you drink that hot chocolate. Put you in this warm ambulance. Wrap you up in a thick blanket. And you don't have to put up with this anymore."

I looked over at the bell. *It would be that easy. All I have to do is pull that mother three times.* I thought about the heated ambulances with blankets and hot chocolate. Then I caught myself. *Wait a minute. I'm not thinking clearly. That's quitting.* "Hooyah, Instructor Stoneclam." I gave him back his hot chocolate.

"Get back with your class."

Handing him back that cup of hot chocolate was the hardest thing I'd ever done. *Let me go back and freeze while I get my nuts kicked some more.*

Mike H. and I had a six-man boat crew before the

other four quit. Now it was only the two of us strug-
gling to drag our boat, weighing nearly 200 pounds,
back to the BUD/S compound—instructors yelling at
us for being too slow. We cussed at the quitters. "You
sorry pieces of crap." When Mike and I arrived at the
compound, we were still angry.

Mike and I had gone from being their comrades to
cussing them out for abandoning us. It's why the training is so brutal. To find out who has your back when all
hell breaks loose. After Wednesday night, I don't remember anyone else quitting.

Early Thursday morning, I sat in the chow hall.
*They're going to have to kill me. After everything I've
been through, they're going to have to cut me up in little
pieces and mail me back to Wayne County, Georgia,
because I'm not quitting now.* Inside me, something
clicked. It no longer mattered what we did next. I didn't
care. *This has got to end sometime.*

Deprived of support in our environment and the support of our own bodies, the only thing propping us up
was our belief in accomplishing the mission—complete
Hell Week. In psychology this belief is called self-
efficacy. Even when the mission seems impossible, it is
the strength of our belief that makes success possible.
The absence of this belief guarantees failure. A strong
belief in the mission fuels our ability to focus, put forth
effort, and persist. Believing allows us to see the goal
(complete Hell Week) and break the goal down into
more manageable objectives (one evolution at a time).
If the evolution is a boat race, it can be broken down
into even smaller objectives such as paddling. Believing allows us to seek out strategies to accomplish the

objectives, such as using the larger shoulder muscles to paddle rather than the smaller forearm muscles. Then, when the race is done, move on to the next evolution. Thinking too much about what happened and what is about to happen will wear you down. Live in the moment and take it one step at a time.

Thursday night, we'd only had three to four hours total sleep since Sunday evening. The dream world started to mix with the real world, and we hallucinated. In the chow hall, while guys' heads were bobbing in and out of their food and their eyes were rolling back in their heads from sleep deprivation, an instructor said, "You know, Wasdin, I want you to take this butter knife, go over there, and kill that deer in the corner."

Slowly rising from my oatmeal daze, I looked over and, sure as hell, there was a buck standing in the chow hall. It didn't dawn on me why the deer was in the chow hall or how it got there. *Now I'm on a mission.* I stalked up on it with my Rambo knife and got ready to make my death leap.

Instructor Stoneclam yelled, "Wasdin, what are you doing?"

"Getting ready to kill this buck, Instructor Stoneclam."

"Look, that's a tray table. It's what they haul trays in and out of the kitchen with."

What the . . . ? How did it turn into a tray table?

"Just sit your dumb ass down and finish eating," Instructor Stoneclam said.

The instructors had a big laugh about it.

* * *

Later, Mike H., Bobby H., and the rest of our crew paddled from the Naval Special Warfare Center south to Silver Strand State Park. It felt like we were paddling to Mexico, but the trip was only 6 miles. Paddle, fall asleep, paddle, fall asleep . . . Suddenly, Bobby banged the bottom of the boat, yelling, "Aaagh!"

"What the hell?" I asked.

"Big snake!" Bobby yelled.

We helped him kill the snake. "Snake!"

One guy stopped. "That's the bowline." We were beating the rope that's used to secure the front of the boat.

We all looked at the rope and returned to our senses.

Five minutes later, Mike yelled, "Aaagh!"

"Is the snake back?" I asked.

Lights from the city glowed in the sky. "I just saw my dad's face in the clouds," Mike said.

I looked up. Sure enough, I saw his dad's face in the clouds. I'd never met his dad and didn't know what his dad looked like, but I saw Mike's dad's face in the clouds.

Another guy in our class, Randy Clendening, was bald. Everywhere: head, eyebrows, eyelashes, armpits, nut sac—like a snake. As a child, he ate some red berries and had a fever so high that it killed all his hair follicles. (When he made it to SEAL Team Two, someone called him Kemo—short for chemotherapy. The nickname stuck.) During Hell Week, Randy wheezed and sputtered.

"You OK, Randy?" I asked.

"The instructors just told me I had a dirty carburetor."

"Wow, that must suck to have a dirty carburetor." It hadn't occurred to me that Randy had fluid in his lungs. The instructors discussed rolling him back to another class so he could recover, but that would mean doing Hell Week again—and we were so close to finishing.

On Friday, the instructors took us out into the surf zone. We sat in the frigid ocean facing the sea with our arms linked, trying to stay together. Instructor Stoneclam stood on the beach talking to our backs. "This is the sorriest class we've ever seen. You couldn't even keep the officers in your class." Officers and enlisted men undergo the same training together. "You didn't support them. You didn't back them up. It's your fault you don't have any officers left. This last evolution, you had the slowest time in history. We have just received permission from Captain Bailey to extend Hell Week one more day."

I looked over at my swim partner, Rodney. He seemed to be thinking what I was: *Damn, we got to do this for one more day. OK, you've been screwing us for this long, stick us in the ass for one more day.*

Somebody else, I don't remember who, wasn't going to do an extra day. He would rather quit. Fortunately, he didn't have to.

"Turn around and look at me when I'm talking to you!" Instructor Stoneclam said.

Like a platoon of zombies, we turned about-face.

There stood our commanding officer, Captain Larry

Bailey. He had led one of the first SEAL Team Two platoons in Vietnam. He also helped create the SEAL Team Assault Boat (STAB). "Congratulations, men. I am securing Hell Week."

Some of the others jumped for joy—I was hurting too bad for that kind of celebration. Randy Clendening cried tears of relief; he'd made it through with walking pneumonia. I stood there with a dumb look on my face. *What am I doing here?* I looked around. *Where did everybody go?* We'd started with ten or twelve boat crews, six to eight men in each. Now we only had four or five boat crews. *Why did those guys even start Hell Week if they knew they didn't want it?* They didn't know they didn't want it.

Medical personnel took Randy directly to the infirmary to ventilate him. They screened the rest of us. Some of the guys had cellulitis—infection had traveled from cuts to deep inside the skin. Others had damaged the band of tissue over their pelvis, hip, and knee, causing iliotibial band syndrome. All of us were swollen. The physician reached down and squeezed my calves. As he pulled his hands away, I saw the indentation of his hands imprinted on my legs. They also examined us for "flesh-eating bacteria" (actually, the bacteria release toxins that destroy skin and muscle rather than eating them). Since trauma covered our bodies from head to toe, we were meals on wheels for the killer bacteria.

I took a shower, then drank some Gatorade. In the barracks, on the top rack of the bunk bed, lay my brown T-shirt. A friend had given it to me as a post–Hell Week present. We bought our own underwear using our clothing allowance, but only guys who finished Hell Week were allowed to wear the brown T-shirts. Having it made me so happy. I lay down and went to sleep. People kept watch on us while we slept to make sure we didn't swallow our tongues, drown in our spit, or simply stop breathing due to fatigue.

The next day, I rolled over on the top rack of my bunk bed and jumped off the way I always did, but my legs weren't working. My face hit the deck, giving me a bloody nose and lip. I tried to call Laura collect, to let her know I made it through Hell Week, but when the operator came on the phone, my voice wasn't working. It took a few hours for my voice to come back.

A driver took us over to the chow hall in a van. People helped us get out of the vehicle. As we hobbled into the chow hall, all eyes seemed to be on us. We were the ones who had just made it through "the week." It had been the coldest week in twenty-three years; hail had actually rained down on us at one point. While eating, I looked over at the tables where the guys who had quit during Hell Week sat. They avoided eye contact.

I had begged one of them not to ring out, but he abandoned Mike and me to carry that boat by ourselves. *Could've at least waited to quit until after we got that boat back to the barracks.* He walked over to my table. "I'm sorry, man. I know I let you guys down, but I just couldn't do it anymore."

I looked up at him. "Get out of my face."

Training resumed slowly, starting with a lot of stretching exercises. Then it picked up speed. Time limits tightened. Distances increased. More swims, runs, and obstacle course trials. Academic tests continued. Pre–Hell Week, we had focused on topics such as first aid and boat handling. Now we focused on hydrographic reconnaissance. Enlisted men like me had to score 70 percent or higher. Although we had lost all our officers, officer standards were 80 percent or higher.

A new evolution we had to pass was the 50-meter underwater swim. At the pool, Instructor Stoneclam said, "All of you have to swim fifty meters underwater. You'll do a somersault into the pool, so no one gets a diving start, and swim twenty-five meters across. Touch the end and swim twenty-five meters back. If you break the surface at any time, you fail. Don't forget to swim along the bottom. The increased pressure on your lungs will help you hold your breath longer, so you can swim farther."

I lined up with the second group of four students. We cheered the first group on. "Go for the blackout," some of us said. It was a new way of thinking that would influence future activities—pushing the body to the edge of unconsciousness.

When it was my turn, I hyperventilated to decrease the carbon dioxide in my body and decrease the drive to breathe. During my somersault into the pool, I lost some breath. I oriented myself and swam as low as I could. After swimming 25 meters, I neared the other side. During my turn, my foot touched the wall, but I didn't get a great push-off.

My throat began to convulse as my lungs craved oxygen. *Go for the blackout.* I swam as hard as I could, but my body slowed down. The edges of my vision began to gray until I found myself looking at my destination through a black tunnel. As I felt myself begin to pass out, I actually felt peaceful. If I'd had any lingering thoughts about drowning, they were gone now. I tried to focus on the wall. Finally, my hand touched it. Instructor Stoneclam grabbed me by the waistband of my swim shorts and helped pull me out. I passed. Others were not so lucky. Two failed their second chance and were expelled from training. (NOTE: Do not practice underwater swimming or breath holding at home because it *will* kill you.)

Another important post–Hell Week evolution was underwater knot tying. Wearing only our UDT shorts, my class climbed the outside stairs to the top of the dive tower and entered. Inside, I lowered myself into the warm water. The depth was 50 feet. I would have to dive down 15 feet and tie five knots: becket bend (sheet bend), bowline, clove hitch, right angle (rolling hitch 1), and square knot. These included some of the knots we would have to use for demolitions. For example, the becket bend and square knot can be used for splicing the end of detonating (det) cord. We had practiced these knots during the few breaks we had, so I experienced no problem tying them, but this was the first time doing the knots at 15 feet underwater.

We could tie one knot for each of five dives, but I thought that five dives would be too tiring. Or one dive with five knots—I didn't think I had the lungs for that. Or any combination we wanted. I greeted Instructor Stoneclam, who wore scuba gear. "Respectfully request to tie the becket bend, bowline, and clove hitch." He gave me the thumbs-down, giving me permission to descend. I mirrored his thumbs-down, showing him that

I understood. Stoneclam gave me the sign again, and I did my combat descent 15 feet below, where I had to tie into a trunk line secured to the walls. I tied the three knots. Then I gave the instructor the OK sign. He checked the knots and gave me the OK sign. I untied them and gave him the thumbs-up. He acknowledged, pointing his thumb up—giving me permission to ascend.

On my second dive, I tied the last two knots and gave Instructor Stoneclam the OK sign. He didn't even seem to look at the knots, staring into my eyes. I saw he was going to give me trouble. I gave him the thumbs-up sign to ascend, but he just kept staring. The depth put pressure on my chest, and my body craved air. I knew what he was looking for, and I wouldn't give him the satisfaction. The SEAL instructors had taught me well. *I can ascend myself, or you can drag my body to the surface when I pass out. Either way.* He smiled and gave me the "up" signal before I even came close to passing out. I wanted to shoot to the top, but I couldn't show panic, and shooting to the top isn't tactical. I ascended as slowly as I could. Pass. Not all of my classmates were as lucky, but they would get a second chance.

In Second Phase, Land Warfare, we learned covert infiltrations, sentry removal, handling agents/guides, gathering intelligence, snatching the enemy, performing searches, handling prisoners, shooting, blowing stuff up, etc. As a child, I learned attention to detail—making sure that not one single pecan remained on the ground when my dad came home saved my butt from getting whipped. Now, that same attention to detail would save my butt from getting shot or blown up. Attention to detail is why I would never have a parachute malfunction.

We became the first occupants of the new barracks building, just down the beach from the multimillion-dollar Coronado condos. One Saturday afternoon, I sat in my room shining jungle combat boots with Calisto, one of the two Peruvian officers going through BUD/S with our class. They had our training schedule, complete with days and times. Both of them had been through Peru's BUD/S, which was a mirror image of our training. Calisto and his buddy had been operating for nearly ten years as SEALs, including real-world ops. We received a lot of intelligence about training from them.

I asked him, "If you're already a Peruvian SEAL, why are you doing this again?"

"Must come here before become Peru SEAL instructor."

"I understand you'll get more respect and all . . ."

"Not respect. More money." His family had come with him, and he stayed with them on weekends in an apartment downtown. They bought a lot of blue jeans and sent them home. He explained that the amount of money they would receive would change their lives.

They were the only officers remaining in our class, but because they weren't American, they couldn't lead us. Mike H., an E-5, led our class. He and I shared the same rank, but he was senior to me. We didn't have any cake-eaters (commissioned officers). The enlisted instructors seemed to enjoy it.

Out at San Clemente Island, I served as a squad leader and once led my squad to assault the wrong target. Calisto led us the next time. He was an excellent land navigator. We assaulted the instructors while they were still sitting around the campfire jacking their jaws. Our squad hit them so fast that they didn't even have their M-60s set up yet. They were not happy. The instructors changed our exfil route and made us go out through a field of cacti. Later, the corpsman had to come around with pliers to pull the needles out of our legs.

During the debrief, the instructors explained, "Sorry we had to send you out another way, but the exfiltration route was compromised." The instructors always had the last laugh.

We ran before each meal on even days. On odd days, we did pull-ups before each meal. One day, the number of pull-ups had just changed from nineteen to twenty. I must've had a brain fart because I dropped off the bar after nineteen pull-ups.

"Wasdin, what the hell are you doing?" an instructor asked. "That was only nineteen."

I didn't understand what he was asking me.

"The pull-up count is twenty. Just to make sure you know how to count to twenty, drop down and give me twenty."

I did twenty push-ups.

"Now get back up on the bar and give me my twenty pull-ups."

That wasn't happening. He got maybe three or four more out of me before my arms gave out.

"Get your MRE and hit the surf."

I got to sit down in the chilly ocean and eat a cold Meal, Ready-to-Eat (MRE). Randy Clendening and some others joined me. We were shivering our petunias off.

Randy had a smile on his face.

"What the hell are you smiling about?" I asked. "We're up to our nipples in freezing water eating cold MREs."

"Try doing this every other day." Randy always made the timed sprints but failed the pull-ups. Every other day he sat in the ocean with water up to his chest and ate his cold MRE for breakfast, lunch, and dinner. He wanted the program way more than I did.

After that, I risked trouble with the instructors to sneak food into the barracks for him on odd days. Other guys snuck him food, too. I have the greatest respect for guys like Randy who work harder than everyone else and somehow manage to finish BUD/S. More than the gazelles running ahead, more than the fish swimming in front, more than the monkeys swinging through the O-course—these underdogs were hardcore.

One of the most famous of these underdogs was Thomas Norris, BUD/S Class 45. Norris wanted to join the FBI but got drafted instead. He joined the navy to become a pilot, but his eyesight disqualified him. So he volunteered for SEAL training, where he often fell to the rear on runs and swims. The instructors talked about dropping him from the program. Norris didn't give up and became a SEAL at Team Two.

In Vietnam, in April 1972, a surveillance aircraft went down deep in enemy territory where over thirty thousand NVA (North Vietnamese Army) were preparing for an Easter offensive. Only one crew member survived. This precipitated the most expensive rescue attempt of the Vietnam War, with fourteen people killed, eight aircraft downed, two rescuers captured, and two more rescuers stranded in enemy territory. It was decided that an air rescue was impossible.

Lieutenant Norris led a five-man Vietnamese SEAL patrol and located one of the surveillance aircraft pilots, then returned him to the forward operating base (FOB). The NVA retaliated with a rocket attack on the FOB, killing two of the Vietnamese SEALs and others.

Norris and his three remaining Vietnamese SEALs failed in an attempt to rescue the second pilot. Because of the impossibility of the situation, two of the Vietnamese SEALs wouldn't volunteer for another rescue attempt. Norris decided to take Vietnamese SEAL Nguyen Van Kiet to make another attempt—and failed.

On April 12, about ten days after the plane had been shot down, Norris got a report of the pilot's location. He and Kiet disguised themselves as fishermen and paddled their sampan upriver into the foggy night. They located the pilot at dawn on the riverbank hidden under vegetation, helped him into their sampan, and covered him with bamboo and banana leaves. A group of enemy soldiers on land spotted them but couldn't get through the thick jungle as fast as Norris and his partner could paddle on the water. When the trio arrived near the FOB, an NVA patrol noticed and poured heavy machine-gun fire down on them. Norris called in an air strike to keep the enemy's heads down and a smoke screen to blind them. Norris and Kiet took the pilot into the FOB, where Norris gave him first aid until he could be evacuated. Lieutenant Thomas Norris received the Medal of Honor. Kiet received the Navy Cross, the highest award the navy can give to a foreign national. That wasn't the end of Norris's story, though.

About six months later, he faced the jaws of adversity again. Lieutenant Norris chose Petty Officer Michael Thornton (SEAL Team One) for a mission. Thornton selected two Vietnamese SEALs, Dang and Quon. One shaky Vietnamese officer, Tai, was also assigned to the team. They dressed in black pajamas like the VC and carried AK-47s with lots of bullets. The team rode a South Vietnamese Navy junk (U.S. Navy ships were unavailable) up the South China Sea, launched a rubber boat from the junk, then patrolled on land to gather intelligence. Norris walked the point with Thornton on rear security and the Vietnamese SEALs between them. The junk had inserted them too far north, and during their patrol, they realized they were in North Vietnam. While hiding in their day layup position, the Vietnamese SEAL officer, without consulting Norris or Thornton, ordered the two Vietnamese SEALs to do a poorly planned prisoner snatch on a two-man patrol. The Vietnamese SEALs wrestled with the two enemy.

Thornton rushed in and knocked out one of the enemy with his rifle butt, so he couldn't alert the nearby village. The other enemy escaped and alerted about sixty North Vietnamese Army troops. Thornton said, "We've got trouble." The SEALs bound the knocked-out enemy, then had Dang interrogate him when he became conscious.

Norris and Dang fired at the approaching enemy. Between shots, Norris used the radio on Dang's back to call for naval gunfire support: coordinates, positions, types of rounds needed, etc. The navy operator on the other end (his ship under enemy fire in a separate battle) seemed new at his job, unfamiliar with fire support for ground troops. Norris put down the phone to shoot more enemy. When he got back on the radio, his call had been transferred to another ship, which was also under enemy fire—and unable to help. Norris and Dang moved back while firing at the enemy.

Thornton put the Vietnamese lieutenant in the rear while he and Quon defended the flanks. Thornton shot several NVA, took cover, rose in a different position, and shot more. Although Thornton knew the enemy popped up from the same spot each time, they didn't know where Thornton would pop up from or how many people were with him. While maneuvering back, Thornton shot through the sand dune where the enemy heads had ducked, taking them out.

After about five hours of fighting, Norris connected with a ship that could help: the *Newport News*.

The enemy threw a Chinese Communist grenade at Thornton. Thornton threw it back. The enemy threw the same grenade back. Thornton returned it. When the grenade came back the next time, Thornton dove for cover. The grenade exploded. Six pieces of shrapnel struck Thornton's back. He heard Norris call to him, "Mike, buddy, Mike, buddy!" Thornton played dead. Four enemy soldiers ran over Thornton's position. He shot all four—two fell on top of him, and the other two fell backward. "I'm all right!" Thornton called. "It's just shrapnel!"

The enemy became quiet. Now they had the 283rd NVA battalion helping them outflank the SEALs.

The SEALs began to leapfrog. Norris laid down cover fire so Thornton, Quon, and Tai could retreat.

Then Thornton and his team would do the same while Norris and Dang moved back. Norris had just brought up a Light Antitank Weapon (LAW) to shoot when an NVA's AK-47 shot him in the face, knocking Norris off a sand dune. Norris tried to get up to return fire but passed out.

Dang ran back to Thornton. Two rounds hit the radio Dang carried on his back.

"Where's Tommy?" Thornton asked.

"He dead."

"You sure?"

"He shot in head."

"Are you sure?"

"See him fall."

"Stay here. I'm going back for Tommy."

"No, Mike. He dead. NVA coming."

"Y'all stay here." Thornton ran 500 yards to Norris's position through a hail of enemy fire. Several NVA neared Norris's body. Thornton gunned them down. When he reached Norris, he saw that the bullet had entered the side of Norris's head and blown out the front of his forehead. He was dead. Thornton threw the body on his shoulders in a fireman's carry and grabbed Norris's AK. Thornton had already used up eight grenades and his LAW rockets and was down to one or two magazines of ammo. It looked like the end for him, too.

Suddenly, the first round from the *Newport News* came in like a mini Volkswagen flying through the air. When it exploded, it threw Thornton down a 30-foot dune. Norris's body flew over Thornton. He picked himself up and walked over to pick up Norris.

"Mike, buddy," Norris said.

"You sonofabitch. You're alive!"

Thornton felt a new burst of energy as he picked up Norris, put him on his shoulders, and took off running. Dang and Quon gave cover fire.

The *Newport News*'s artillery round had bought them some time, but that time was now up. Enemy rounds rained down on the SEALs again.

Thornton reached Dang and Quon's position. "Where's Tai?"

When Thornton went back to get Norris, the shaky Vietnamese lieutenant had disappeared into the water.

Thornton looked at the two Vietnamese SEALs. "When I yell *one,* Quon, lay down a base of fire. When I yell *two,* Dang, lay down a base of fire. *Three,* I'll lay down a base of fire. And we'll leapfrog back to the water."

Shooting and retreating, as Thornton reached the water's edge, he fell, not realizing he'd been shot through his left calf. He picked up Norris and carried him under his arm. In the water, he felt a floundering movement—he had Norris's head under the water. Thornton got his buddy's head above water. Norris's life vest was tied to his leg, standard operating procedure for Team Two. So Thornton took off his own vest and put it on Norris, using it to keep both of them afloat.

Quon fluttered in the water, the right side of his hip shot off. Thornton grabbed him, and Quon hung onto Norris's life preserver. Dang helped as they kicked out to sea. Thornton could see bullets traveling through the water. Thornton prayed, *Good Lord, don't let any of those hit me.*

Norris came to. He couldn't see the Vietnamese

officer. "Did we get everybody?" Pushing down on Thornton, immersing him, Norris rose high enough to see the Vietnamese officer, swimming far out to sea. Norris blacked out again.

After swimming well out of the enemy's range of fire, Thornton and the two Vietnamese SEALs saw the *Newport News*—then saw it sail away, thinking the SEALs were dead.

"Swim south," Thornton said. He put two 4″×4″ battle dressings on Norris's head, but they couldn't cover the whole wound. Norris was going into shock.

Another group of SEALs, manning a junk searching for their buddies, found the Vietnamese lieutenant and debriefed him. Then they found Thornton, Norris, Dang, and Quon. Thornton radioed the *Newport News* for pickup.

Once aboard the *Newport News,* Thornton carried Norris to medical. The medical team cleaned Norris up as best they could, but the doctors said, "He's never going to make it."

Norris was medevaced to Da Nang. From there, they flew him to the Philippines.

For Thornton's actions, he received the Medal of Honor. It is the only time a Medal of Honor recipient has rescued a Medal of Honor recipient. Years later, Thornton would help form SEAL Team Six and serve as one of its operators.

Norris survived, proving the doctor wrong. He was transferred to the Bethesda, Maryland, Naval Hospital. Over the next few years, he underwent several major surgeries, as he had lost part of his skull and one eye. The navy retired Norris, but the only easy day was yesterday. Norris returned to his childhood dream: becoming an FBI agent. In 1979, he requested a disability waiver. FBI Director William Webster said, "If you can pass the same test as anybody else applying for this organization, I will waiver your disabilities." Of course, Norris passed.

Later, while serving in the FBI, Norris tried to become a member of the FBI's newly forming Hostage Rescue Team (HRT), but the FBI's bean counters and pencil pushers didn't want to allow a one-eyed man on the team. HRT founder Danny Coulson said, "We'll probably have to take another Congressional Medal of Honor winner with one eye if he applies, but I'll take the risk." Norris became an assault team leader. After twenty years with the FBI, he retired. He was last on the runs and swims at BUD/S, and he only had one eye when he went to the FBI Academy, but Norris had fire in the gut.

Some legends are passed down to BUD/S trainees, but I wouldn't learn about Norris until after I became a SEAL. In such a small, tight-knit community, a SEAL's reputation, good or bad, travels fast. That reputation begins at BUD/S. Norris remained the underdog throughout his careers in the Teams and the FBI. Now I had to forge my own reputation.

During one of our long runs, halfway through training on the island, we ran behind a truck while music played. I actually visualized myself wearing the SEAL trident. *I'm either going home in a coffin or I'm going home wearing the trident. I'm going to make it through training.* It felt like a vision had opened up in my mind. It was the first and only time I got a runner's high. Some guys got that runner's high repeatedly. For me, it sucked every time I ran.

In Third Phase, Dive Phase, we learned underwater navigation and techniques for sabotaging ships. Some of my classmates had trouble with dive physics and pool competency (pool comps). I had difficulty treading water with tanks on and keeping my fingers above the water for five minutes. An instructor would yell, "Get that other finger up, Wasdin!" So I would.

BUD/S prepares us to believe we can accomplish the mission—and to never surrender. No SEAL has ever been held prisoner of war. The only explicit training we receive in BUD/S is to look out for each other—leave no one behind. A lot of our tactical training deals with retreats, escape, and evasion. We are taught to be mentally tough, training repeatedly until our muscles can react automatically. Looking back, I now realize that my mental toughness training started at an early age. Our planning is meticulous, which shows in our briefings. In my encounters with the army, navy, air force, and marines, I've only seen Delta Force brief as well as we do.

A SEAL's belief in accomplishing the mission transcends environmental or physical obstacles that threaten to make him fail. Often we think we're indestructible. Forever the optimists, even when we're outnumbered and outgunned, we still tend to think we have a chance to make it out alive—and be home in time for dinner.

Nevertheless, sometimes a SEAL can't find his way back to Mother Ocean and must make a choice between fighting to the death or surrendering. For many brave warriors, it's better to roll the dice on surrendering in order to live to fight another day—SEALs have incredible respect for those POWs. As SEALs, though, we believe our surrender would be giving in, and giving in is never an option. I wouldn't want to be used as some political bargaining chip against the United States. I wouldn't want to die in a cage of starvation or have my head cut off for some video to be shown around the world on the Internet. My attitude is that if the enemy wants to kill me, they're going to have to kill me now. We despise would-be dictators who wish to dominate us—SEALs steer the rudders of their own destinies. Our world is a meritocracy where we are free to leave at any time. Our missions are voluntary; I can't think of a mission that wasn't. Ours is an unwritten code: It's better to burn out than to fade away—and with our last breaths we'll take as many of the enemy with us as possible.

Laura and Blake, who was just a toddler, flew out for my graduation. Blake rang the bell for me. I told him, "Now you never have to go to BUD/S, because you've already rung out." In his teenage years, he would want to become a SEAL, but I would talk him out of it. Half a dozen people in my hometown would have kids who wanted to go to BUD/S. I would talk every single one of them out of it. If I'm able to talk someone out of it, I'm just saving them time, because they really don't want it anyway. If I can't talk them out of it, maybe they really want it.

After BUD/S, we went directly to airborne training at Fort Benning, Georgia, home of the army's airborne and infantry schools. The summer was so hot that they had to run us through the sprinklers two or three times a day to cool us off. Even so, people still fell out from heatstroke and heat exhaustion. Some of the soldiers talked as if the training were the hardest thing in the world. They thought they were becoming part of some elite fighting force. Coming from BUD/S, airborne training was a joke.

"This isn't hard," I said. "You've got women here making it through the training." I felt like we could have done their two weeks of "intensive training" in two days.

Army regulations didn't allow the instructors to drop anyone for more than ten push-ups. One airborne instructor was a "good old boy" who always had a wad of Red Man chewing tobacco in his mouth. We tadpoles screwed around with him wanting more push-ups.

"Give me ten, Navy," he said.

We did ten push-ups, then stood up.

"Hell no." He spit his tobacco. "Too damn easy."

We dropped down and did ten more.

"Hell no. Too damn easy."

We did ten more.

At night, we went out drinking until late. For us, airborne training was a holiday.

West Point gave its seniors a choice of what army school to attend during summer. Some of the officer candidates chose airborne school. Two or three would polish our boots if we told them BUD/S stories. I felt like a celebrity. Seems strange thinking back on it now. They were officer candidates from the army's most prestigious school, and they were polishing my E-5 enlisted boots just so I would tell them about BUD/S. I wasn't even a SEAL yet and had never seen combat. The West Point guys were mesmerized by our tales. Soon we had to leave our rooms for a bigger area because there were so many guys who wanted to hear us.

By the end of airborne training, we had completed five static-line "dope on a rope" jumps, meaning the parachute automatically deploys immediately after leaving the plane and there is no need to pull a ripcord. It was real, and it was fun—but now the real fun would begin.

6.
SEAL TEAM TWO

After airborne training, I reported to my SEAL Team. The odd-numbered Teams (One, Three, and Five) were on the West Coast at Coronado, California, and the even-numbered Teams (Two, Four, and Eight) were on the East Coast at Little Creek, Virginia. Although the Top Secret SEAL Team Six existed, I knew nothing about it. I reported to SEAL Team Two in Little Creek.

During a Wednesday run on the obstacle course, a nearly sixty-year-old SEAL, still on active duty, ran with us—Rudy Boesch. I thought I could take it easy—no instructors around yelling at us. At the end of the course, Rudy pulled aside all of us who finished behind him. "Meet me back up here this afternoon."

That afternoon, the slowpokes and I ran the O-course again. It was a wake-up call. Even in the Teams, it paid to be a winner. Later, I would become one of the fastest men on the O-course at Team Two.

Rudy soon served as the first senior enlisted adviser of the newly formed United States Special Operations Command (USSOCOM), commanding navy, army, air force, and marine special operations units, including those in JSOC such as SEAL Team Six and Delta. After more than forty-five years in the navy, most of it as a SEAL, Rudy retired. When he reached his seventies, he competed on the reality TV series *Survivor.*

Some Team Two guys returned from deployment on an oil barge called the *Hercules,* one of two in the Persian Gulf. They were a part of Operation Praying Mantis. When an Iranian mine damaged the USS *Samuel B. Roberts*, one of the SEALs' missions was to capture an Iranian oil platform that had been launching attacks against ships in the Gulf. The SEALs planned for a navy destroyer to shoot up the platform with armor-piercing ammo in order to keep the Iranians' heads down. Then the SEALs would land on the helipad and take down the platform. Unfortunately, someone on the destroyer loaded incendiary and high explosive rounds instead. When the destroyer opened fire on the platform, it literally opened fire. Instead of keeping their heads down, the Iranians promptly jumped off the burning platform. The barge burned so hot that the SEALs couldn't land their helo on it. The barge melted into the sea. Oops.

Dick, Mike H., Rob, and I hadn't participated in that op because we still had more training to do, but that didn't stop us from wanting to celebrate the guys' safe return. After work, we left the SEAL Team Two compound, exited the Little Creek base's Gate Five, and headed to a little strip club called the Body Shop. Because the Body Shop was in such close proximity to the SEAL Team Two compound, a number of us had spent some time there. The bouncer was a new guy, sitting in for Bob, a SEAL Team buddy. One of us asked him, "A group of our guys just got back from the Persian Gulf. Can you give them a congratulations over the PA?"

So he did. "Let's send out a big thank-you to our American fighting men who just returned from the Persian Gulf."

Applause and cheers filled the room.

We high-fived each other, buying beers.

From the back of the room where a table of four Tunisian men sat, one said in fluent English, "Why doesn't America mind its own damn business?"

Dick didn't go around the runway where the girls were dancing. He went straight over it. By the time I ran around it and got to the four men, Dick had the loud-mouth in a choke hold. During our brief altercation, the three buddies of the loudmouth shouted expletives at their comrade. The four of us left the four Tunisians in a pile.

As we attempted to leave, the new bouncer tried to stop us. "You just had a fight in here. You're not going anywhere."

We catapulted him over the bar.

At the front door, a police officer showed up. He must've been right around the corner, because it had only been five minutes since the fight had started.

"Come on, gentlemen, let's just sit down for a minute."

So we did. *This guy seems cool.*

The bouncer had picked himself up and cut in. "These guys are Navy SEALs. They just came in here and were tearing up the place."

Oh, no. He said the S-word.

The officer panicked, calling on his radio. "Navy SEALs are tearing up the place, and I need backup!"

We were sitting down calmly talking to him. That was enough. We stood up to leave.

"Wait, you can't go anywhere."

Ignoring him, we walked to the front door. Outside, a sea of blue lights flashed at us from the parking lot. The backup included a large police van with K-9 UNIT written on the side. The first officers stepped out of their vehicles.

We started to explain.

The policeman from inside cut off our explanation, suddenly becoming brave. "I'm sorry, but you're going to have to come with me." He grabbed Mike by the shirtsleeve.

Dick caught the policeman in the chin with a square blow, dropping him straight down.

Now police officers with batons faced the four of us with our bare hands. We fought for what seemed like ten or fifteen minutes. On TV, batons might drop people to the pavement, but these batons were bouncing off of us. The police dog jumped up and bit Dick. He grabbed the dog by the head, bent it over, fell down on top of it, and bit a plug out of the dog. The dog yelped and ran away.

I was fighting the two cops in front of me when I felt a little thud on my back. Turning around with my fist cocked back, I saw that a small female police officer had just hit me with her baton. It felt like a mosquito bite compared to the whacks the other cops were delivering. Realizing she was a woman, instead of punching her, I picked her up and pushed her onto the hood of her car.

Now there were nearly thirty cops against the four of us. We finally lost. They handcuffed us. We told them our story. The Tunisian guys had walked out of the Body Shop and resumed talking their anti-American rhetoric. Now the police were mad at the first officer. "What were you thinking? Are you crazy?"

What was done was done. We had assaulted cops. They separated us and loaded us into the back of the patrol cars. The female police officer stuck her phone number in the pocket of my shirt and said, "Hey, give me a call sometime."

At the station, they processed us and gave us a court date. They contacted our command at SEAL Team Two. The police wouldn't let us leave until SEAL Team Two sent a driver to pick us up.

When our court date came, I feared for my job. We were all new to the SEAL Teams and expected our careers to be ruined. On the front row of the courtroom sat police officers wearing neck braces. One had his arm in a cast. Another had a cane. They looked like fertilizer. In our dress blue uniforms, we looked like a million bucks.

Voted by my Teammates to be spokesman, I told the judge our side of the story. The people in the courtroom seemed sympathetic toward us because of what happened and how it happened.

The judge asked, "Why were three of these men taken to jail and immediately released, and Petty Officer [Dick] wasn't released until later?"

The K-9 officer explained, "The dog bit him, and we had to take him to the doctor for a shot."

"How long could that have taken?" the judge asked.

"Well, Your Honor, he took a bite out of my dog, so I had to take my dog to the vet for a shot."

The courtroom behind us erupted in laughter.

The K-9 officer explained, "Your Honor, it really isn't funny. It took me months to train him, and I still spend sixteen hours a month training him. But since Petty Officer [Dick] bit the dog, it won't do the job anymore."

The laughter rose to sheer pandemonium.

Down came the judge's gavel. "Order. Order in the court!"

Except for a couple of snickers in the back of the courtroom, the noise calmed down.

"Now, the four of you need to step forward to the bench," the judge said.

Oh, man. Lose our careers. Go directly to jail. Do not collect two hundred dollars. We were scared.

The judge leaned forward and then spoke quietly and calmly. "Gentlemen, I'm going to write this off to youthful vigor and patriotism, but don't ever let me see you in this courtroom again."

I heard applause from the courtroom behind us.

Turning around, I saw the cops in the front row. They looked like thieves had just robbed their houses. On our way out, I passed the cop in a neck brace and the one with a cane. As I passed the police officer with his arm in a cast, I winked at him. We left the courtroom.

Back at SEAL Team Two, we reported what happened

to the Team Two skipper, Norm Carley, a short Irish Catholic guy from Philadelphia, graduate of the Naval Academy, and the first executive officer (second only to the commanding officer) of SEAL Team Six. Recently, the SEAL Team Two skipper had returned from Operation Praying Mantis in the Persian Gulf. He looked at us for a moment. "There was a time when we used to go out and fight the cops a lot. Those days are coming to a rapid end. The military is changing."

He let us go, and his prophecy came true—the modern military has changed. On March 31, 2004, Ahmed Hashim Abed, an Iraqi al Qaeda terrorist, orchestrated the ambush of empty trucks picking up kitchen equipment from the army's 82nd Airborne. Abed's terrorists killed four Blackwater guards, then burned the corpses, mutilated them, dragged them through the streets, and hung two of the bodies from the Euphrates Bridge. One of the four guards was former SEAL Scott Helvenston. On September 1, 2009, the SEALs captured Abed. Then three other SEALs received courts-martial for allegedly giving him a bloody lip. Although the three SEALs were eventually found not guilty, such charges never should have risen to the level of courts-martial. If the SEALs had simply killed Abed, nothing could've been said. It's hard to lawyer up when you're dead.

In the same building as the Body Shop was a 7-Eleven. My house was two miles away. One evening after dinner, when Blake was still four years old, I drove with him to the 7-Eleven around seven o'clock to get some milk and bread. At the same time, Smudge pulled up in his Ford Bronco pickup truck jacked up on big wheels and big suspension. We had become friends after I joined him in Foxtrot Platoon at SEAL Team Two. Smudge walked over and, as usual, picked up Blake and gave him a hug.

As he held Blake, I said, "I'm just going to run in and get some milk and bread. I'll be right out." When I came back out with the groceries, they were gone. I looked at the Body Shop. Smudge's girlfriend was a stripper there. *Oh, no, he didn't.* When I hurried in, the bouncer greeted me, "Evening, Howard."

"Hey, Bob," I said. "Need to see if my son is in here."

He smiled, letting me pass without paying the cover charge.

Walking into the club, it was mostly dark except for light coming from the center stage where a dancer shook her assets. Smudge sat at a table with his foot up on the stage while Blake sat on his lap. Smudge's topless girl-friend stood next to them, bent over, running her fingers through Blake's hair and stroking his cheek. "You're such a cutie." Her breasts were so huge, it's a wonder she didn't put my son's eyeballs out.

I grabbed Blake, yelling at Smudge as I left, "Man, are you crazy? You're going to get me killed."

He couldn't see what the problem was. "I just wanted to introduce him to Cassandra."

I helped Blake into the car and tried to debrief him on our way home. *This is going to be it. Smudge is one of my good friends, and he loves Blake—but if Laura finds out, I'll never be able to have Smudge around my child again.*

At home, luckily Laura was busy working in the kitchen. I took Blake to his room and occupied him with his Nintendo Duck Hunt game. Then I put away the milk and bread I picked up from the 7-Eleven. I went into the living room and studied some op orders and SEAL training manuals as I often did, but I had my eye on the clock, waiting for Blake's bedtime. If I could get him to bed, I'd be in the clear at least until morning. Usually, I was the one to tuck him in for the night, and when his bedtime came that evening, I made a point of walking to his room and tucking him in. Days later, Laura, Blake, and I drove by the Body Shop on the way to SEAL Team Two. *Holy crap, is seeing the place going to trigger Blake to say something to Laura? "Hey, I saw some big boobies in there."* Even for a couple of weeks after, I still worried. Fortunately, Blake never said another word about it until he was twelve or thirteen years old. And I never went back to the Body Shop again.

The first time Blake had a sip of beer, a Team guy gave it to him. When he got older, we all played golf together. Blake's first driving lesson came on a golf cart with one of my drunken buddies—bouncing off of trees. Blake would later tell me, "Some of my best memories of Virginia are hanging out with the different guys." They were his SEAL Team uncles who listened to Thin Lizzy's "The Boys Are Back in Town" and sometimes let him do things he shouldn't do.

After a few months of limbo, doing odd jobs around the SEAL Team Two compound, I finally made it to advanced training in sea, air, and land warfare, known as SEAL Tactical Training (STT). While BUD/S focused on screening out people *and* training the survivors, STT mostly focused on training. During the six months of STT, only two people were dropped because of poor performance. We learned advanced levels of diving and land warfare, including close-quarters combat (CQC). (For more on advanced training after BUD/S, see Dick Couch's *The Finishing School*.)

When I completed STT, the SEAL Team Two skipper, Norm Carley, came out with tridents and pinned one on me. The trident consisted of an eagle clutching a U.S. Navy anchor, trident, and pistol. Because it looked like the old Budweiser eagle, we often called the trident "the Budweiser." Both officers and enlisted wore the same gold badge, rather than following the common navy practice of making enlisted men wear silver. It is still one of the biggest, gaudiest badges in the navy. With his fist, Skipper gave it a smack on my chest. Then each member of my platoon came by and punched it in. The trident literally stuck so deep into my chest that the leading petty officer had to pull it out of my skin. The marks remained on me for weeks. Now I could officially play with the big boys.

My first platoon commander was Burt. In the navy, a "sea daddy" is someone who takes it upon himself to mentor a sailor. I never really had a sea daddy because I took advice, both tactical and personal, from a number of people, but I owed gratitude to Burt for drafting me into his winter warfare platoon right out of STT. SEALs were supposed to have served in a regular platoon before working in a winter warfare platoon, but Burt showed an early confidence in me.

Like nearly 50 percent of SEAL officers, an extremely high percentage in the military, Burt had been an enlisted man before becoming an officer—what we call a mustang—which is probably why I liked him so much. Never asked us to do anything he wouldn't do himself. He was big on doing proper mission briefs, thoroughly evaluating the brief and the resulting op. The man was a great facilitator and diplomat. Burt loved the winter environment—skiing, snowshoeing, and the rest—and leading the Teams in high-tech winter warfare gear. For example, we tested and evaluated expeditionary weight Gore-Tex.

Burt's second in command was Mark, who stood over six feet tall. Mark's parents emigrated from a Russian satellite country. Low-key, he didn't tell people he was an MIT graduate who spoke Russian, Czechoslovakian, Polish, and German. His security clearance took forever. Although highly intelligent and multilingual, he never talked down to us. Mark devised great plans, and he could explain them simply and clearly enough so everyone could understand. He spoke with a slight lisp, though, which we mimicked during his mission briefs, screwing with him. After work knocked off, give him a couple of drinks and a pretty girl on each side, and Mark's speech would become incomprehensible.

At SEAL Team Two, one day a week, we did Team physical training. Wednesday was O-course day. The other days, we ran our own PT. Some guys used those days as time to play basketball or goof off, but Mark insisted we bust our chops doing a long run-swim-run or some other torture. He ran like a gazelle and swam like a fish—making those of us who couldn't keep up with him hate life, although we enjoyed working with Mark.

* * *

At SEAL Team Two, I started to hear whisperings about a Top Secret SEAL Team Six. After the 1980 failed attempt to rescue American hostages at the U.S. Embassy in Iran, the Navy asked Richard Marcinko to create a full-time counterterrorist team. As its first commanding officer, Marcinko named the new unit SEAL Team Six. He recruited heavily from the SEALs' two counterterrorist units: Mobility Six (MOB Six) at SEAL Team Two on the East Coast and Echo Platoon at SEAL Team One on the West Coast. They wore civilian clothes and longer haircuts and were allowed to grow nonregulation beards and mustaches. Officers and enlisted men addressed each other by first names and nicknames, not using military salutes. They specialized in rescuing hostages from ships, oil rigs, and other maritime locations. In addition, they assisted with military base and embassy security. On top of all that, Team Six also supported CIA operations.

Team Six's baptism of fire came in 1983. After Communists allied with Cuba and the Soviet Union overthrew the government of Grenada in a bloody coup d'état, the United States launched Operation Urgent Fury to restore Grenada's government. In support of the operation, twelve shooters from SEAL Team Six would parachute-drop off the coast of Grenada. This first mission was a goat-screw for at least three reasons. First, although SEAL Team Six had trained intensively in numerous counterterrorist tactics, they had not trained in nighttime water drops—which is even more difficult with boats. A mission that probably should've gone to SEAL Team Two, who were standing by, went to SEAL Team Six instead. Second, intelligence was crap. The mission was planned without taking into account daylight saving time; as a result, that hour difference made a daytime drop turn into a nighttime drop. Not even the moon was out. No one told the Team Six guys about the ten-foot ocean swells, high winds, and hard rain. Third, probably because the air force pilots weren't experienced with water drops, the second plane dropped the SEALs in the wrong spot, far from everyone else.

As a result, when the twelve men hit the water, the wind continued blasting their parachutes, dragging them. With too much equipment and not enough buoyancy, some of the SEALs were sinking. Although they had practiced with high-tech parachutes, now they were using old MC-1 chutes. The guys fought for their lives to keep the parachutes from dragging them to watery graves. Without lights, gathering everyone together became impossible. One SEAL kept shouting and fired three shots into the night—but no one could reach him. A total of four SEALs disappeared. The survivors searched, but they never found their Teammates: Kenneth Butcher, Kevin Lundberg, Stephen Morris, and Robert Schamberger. Although heartbroken, the other SEALs still had a mission to do.

Black Hawk helicopters raced for an hour through the early-morning darkness to the governor-general's mansion to rescue Governor-General Paul Scoon. Soviet aircraft rounds carved green lines into the sky. Aboard one of the helos, the fifteen SEALs crammed inside appeared calm—until enemy fire started punching holes in the helo. Denny "Snake" Chalker and the others who had never been in combat dropped their poker faces. Vietnam veteran SEALs officer in charge Wellington T. "Duke" Leonard, Bobby L., Timmy P., and JJ smiled. "How's it feel getting shot at?" After a tense moment, Denny and the others smiled—what else could they do? The command helo, carrying SEAL Team Six's commanding officer, Bob Gormly (Dick Marcinko's replacement), took the heaviest fire and had to break off from the others in order to limp back to the aircraft carrier before the wounded helo fell out of the sky.

Duke and Denny's chopper flared its nose up to a stop 90 feet in the air in front of the mansion while the other helo took the rear over the tennis court. One of the pilots was shot, but he continued flying. AK-47 fire popped at them from the mansion. A SEAL leaned out and fired back. Rich had been hit, but he was so pumped on adrenaline that he didn't notice. Denny kicked out the rope and fast-roped to the back of the mansion, crashing through pine tree limbs on his way down. Duke and the others followed close behind—hitting the limbs Denny hadn't already broken.

As Denny neared the mansion, an AK-47 poked out from a door in his direction. Denny held fire with his CAR-15 (forerunner of the M-4) assault rifle until he could identify the target—it was Governor Scoon. Duke, carrying a shotgun, relieved the governor of his weapon. The guys cleared the mansion, but only the governor, his family, and staff were inside. They set up a perimeter. RPGs—rocket-propelled grenades—skipped across the top of the roof without exploding.

Their satellite communication (SATCOM) radio

had flown off in the wounded command bird, limiting communications, so they had to conserve the batteries in their handheld radios.

Duke told everyone, "Don't challenge anyone unless they enter the compound." They didn't want to start a fight they couldn't finish. Rescuing the governor was the priority.

As night began to fall, thirty enemy fighters and four Soviet eight-wheeled armored personnel carriers (BTR-60PBs) circled the mansion. Duke used his little MX-360 handheld radio to contact Master Chief Dennis Johnson at Port Salines airfield. The master chief relayed Duke's message to an AC-130 gunship flying overhead. "Do a 360-degree firing run around the mansion." The Spectre fired its 40 mm gun: *bloop, bloop.* The resulting explosions took out the surrounding enemy except for two that ran. Soon the little MX-360 radios ran out of power. Duke used the governor's telephone to maintain communications.

Two Cubans armed with AKs walked up the driveway. The Cubans raised their weapons. So the guys fired: shotgun, CAR-15s, Heckler & Koch 21 light machine gun, M-60 machine guns, and a .50 RAI 500 (Research Armament Industries Model 500) sniper rifle. One Cuban tried to escape over a wall, but he and his comrade were literally cut down.

The next morning, Force Recon Marines helped the SEALs, the governor, and his family out. They saw the charred remains of burned-out trucks, weapons, and blood where the Spectre had fired—someone had removed the bodies. On their way out, the SEALs found a Grenadian flag, so they replaced it with a SEAL Team

Six flag, which someone always carried for such an occasion. Later, the guys would hang the Grenadian flag up at SEAL Team Six when they returned. The entourage proceeded to a helicopter landing zone where a helicopter extracted everyone.

On a separate mission in Grenada, twelve SEALs, led by Lieutenant Donald Kim Erskine, flew in a helo to the radio station, which they were to secure until Governor Scoon could come in and broadcast a message to the people on the island. While in the air, they received some small-arms fire, but when they landed, the enemy had deserted the radio station. Erskine's men had radio problems and couldn't make contact with the command post—someone had changed the frequencies without informing the SEALs.

They set up a defensive perimeter. Before long a truck arrived loaded with twenty enemy soldiers. The SEALs ordered them to drop their weapons, but they didn't. So the guys opened up on them, using about a third of their ammo, and killed ten of the enemy. They took the surviving ten as prisoners and used up most of their first aid supplies patching them up in the radio station. None of the SEALs were wounded.

A BTR-60PB and three trucks climbed up the hill to the station. Forty to fifty enemy soldiers poured out of the vehicles. The Cuban officer swatted his men on the butts with a command stick: "Attack." Erskine and his guys defended from the building. The enemy tried to outflank them while their BTR rolled up toward the front door and unleashed its 20 mm cannon. The cannon blasted holes through the building's concrete like it was paper.

One of the SEALs mounted a Rifleman's Assault Weapon (RAW), a rocket-propelled grenade, onto the barrel of his CAR-15 and pulled the rocket's safety. He aimed at the BTR and pulled his rifle trigger, the shot launching the rocket. Two pounds of high explosives scored a direct hit on the BTR.

Running out of ammunition in the face of overwhelming enemy firepower, Erskine and his SEALs set their explosives on the station and ran out the back door. They all thought they were dead, but the SEALs dashed across the meadow behind the station. With enemy closing in on their rear and both sides, Erskine calmly led his men in a leapfrog across a wide-open kill zone to the beach. He and half his men fell to the ground and fired at the enemy while the other half retreated. Then the retreating men dropped and fired at the enemy while Erskine and his shooters retreated. Bullets hailed down on them, one blowing Erskine's canteen off; even though Erskine stood taller than six feet and weighed over 200 pounds, the shot knocked him to the ground. His squad members hit the dirt with him. They turned around and fired while the other squad retreated. As the guys continued their leapfrog, another round tore off Erskine's boot heel, sending him to the earth. The next time he got up and ran, a shot ricocheted off the ammo magazine on his belt, whacking him down again. Bullet number four was less kind. It ripped out a chunk of Erskine's right elbow, literally picking him up off the ground before slamming him into the dirt. He felt like his entire arm had been blown off. At the end of the meadow, the guys cut through a chain-link fence and crawled through. As Erskine counted his men, he realized a SEAL leader's worst nightmare—he was missing a man. Then the SEALs saw their missing Teammate. Erskine and his men fired at the enemy as the radioman lugged the useless SATCOM radio across the field.

"Drop the radio!" Erskine yelled.

The radioman took off the radio and fired several rounds from his SIG SAUER 9 mm sidearm into its cryptographic parts. Then he sprinted to join his buddies.

They ran into a jungle of vegetation, which hid them from the enemy. Even though they had killed some of the opposition, the SEALs were still outnumbered and had almost no ammunition left in their rifles. The men continued down a path and embraced Mother Ocean. Swimming straight out to sea would make them targets for the enemy. Erskine told the guys, "Ditch everything except your primary gear and swim parallel to the beach." They shed their rifles, backpacks, and nearly everything except pistols, pistol ammo, and E&E (escape and evasion) kits. The SEALs swam parallel to the beach and found shelter in the cliffs, where an overhang concealed them from the enemy above.

Friendly forces, not knowing they were still alive, blasted the bad guys near their position. The SEALs waited until the enemy had gone, then at 0300 swam out to sea. The SEALs floated in the ocean for six hours until a rescue plane saw them and called in a navy ship to pick them up. The guys had been awake for forty-eight hours. After making sure he had all his men on the ship, Erskine passed out. He later recovered. The navy awarded him the Silver Star Medal.

In 1985, PLO (Palestine Liberation Organization) terrorists hijacked the cruise ship *Achille Lauro* and killed passenger Leon Klinghoffer. The terrorists sought shelter in Egypt, and when Egypt tried to sneak them out on a flight to the PLO headquarters in Tunisia, U.S. Navy fighter planes forced the plane down at the NATO base in Italy. SEAL Team Six surrounded the terrorists on the runway, but the Italians stopped the SEALs from taking the plane down, demanding the five terrorists be turned over to them. After a brief showdown of SEALs vs. Italian military and law enforcement, America agreed to turn over the terrorists to Italy. Unfortunately, the Italian government freed the leader, Abu Abbas (who was later captured in Iraq in 2003). Although the other terrorists went to jail, one was granted furlough and escaped (he was recaptured in Spain). Another terrorist disappeared from Italy while on parole.

In 1989, SEAL Team Six went to Panama to capture drug-dealing dictator Manuel Noriega. Noriega tried to hide out in a Catholic church, but with no way out of the country, he finally surrendered.

Grenada, the *Achille Lauro,* and Panama were just three of the many operations SEAL Team Six performed before I joined them.

I took my first deployment with SEAL Team Two to Machrihanish, Scotland—land of my mother's Kirkland ancestors, who changed their name to Kirkman when they immigrated to the United States. The Scottish locals gave Smudge his nickname, taken from a famous English soccer athlete. We went with some of the guys to a tartan museum in Edinburgh, where I found that my clan had come from the Highlands.

Smudge teased me about finding my tartan. "Wow, Howard's the Highlander."

"Yeah, there can be only one!" I exclaimed.

From Scotland, we trained alongside or interacted with a number of foreign special operation units: the British Special Boat Service, French Commando Hubert, German Combat Swimmers (Kampfschwimmer), Swedish Coastal Rangers (Kustjägarna), Norwegian Navy Ranger Command (Marinejegerkommandoen), and others. During a harbor penetration exercise in Germany, I exchanged a case of my MREs with the rations of a Commando Hubert. His commando frogman unit had received much help in its creation from a World War II naval officer named Jacques-Yves Cousteau, whom many came to know because of his TV series about the underwater world. The French rations included bottles of wine, cheese, and pâté. It amazed me how much they liked our freeze-dried food and Maxwell House coffee—just add water. When I returned to the barracks in Scotland, nearly everyone begged me for some of my wine, cheese, and pâté.

For winter warfare training, I enjoyed over a month of fun with the Swedish Coastal Rangers, who perform long-range reconnaissance, sabotage, and assaults against enemies invading Sweden's coast. Although all young Swedish males must serve in the military for one year, some of them attempt to become Coastal Rangers. During the Cold War, Russia was their biggest threat.

Burt, DJ, Steve, and I flew into Stockholm, the capital of Sweden. Historic churches, palaces, and castles mixed with green parks and waterways, making it a Venice of the North. Newer buildings blended ecological designs with high tech and functionalism. Our hosts put us up in a wonderful hotel. One evening, as we returned from training, a short, skinny guy with spiky hair sat in the lobby, a long-legged woman sitting on each leg and one in his lap. *Who is that?* Two of us walked in closer to see who it was: Rod Stewart. There's hope for ugly guys everywhere—become a rock star.

In the morning, Burt drove us in a rental car to a ferry, which shuttled us across the water, so we could drive to the Coastal Rangers' base, located in Berga at the Swedish Amphibious Corps, First Marine Regiment (Första Amfibieregementet, AMF1). Our first operations began in the Stockholm archipelago. With thousands of islands, it is one of the largest archipelagos in the Baltic Sea. My counterpart and I pushed off in a light, two-man, nonmetallic folding kayak to search for Soviet submarines. I wore Vuarnet sunglasses, named after the French Olympic gold medalist Alpine ski racer, to shield my eyes from the sun. We landed on islands and searched them for any human activity—a cat-and-mouse game with the Soviets. Kayaking from island to island while carrying all our equipment was cold, hard work.

After nearly a week, we loaded up with the Coastal Rangers on several charter buses. They brought bags of food on the bus. "How far are we going, again?" I asked.

"Sixty-one miles." The Coastal Rangers spoke good English.

"Why all the food?"

"Long trip."

Only sixty-one miles—I could do that standing on my head.

After three hours on the road, I said to another Coastal Ranger, "I thought this was only going to be sixty-one miles."

"Yes, sixty-one miles."

"We've gone over sixty-one miles."

Another Coastal Ranger smiled. "Sixty-one Swedish miles."

I frowned. "How far is that?"

"Oh . . . about three hundred and eighty American miles."

You've got to be kidding me. I was glad I hadn't offered to go on any 4-mile runs with them.

We passed a MOOSE CROSSING sign before arriving in a small snowy town called Messlingin, next to Messlingin Lake, which was frozen over. Not found on any tourist maps, Messlingin is located 134 miles southwest of Östersund in central Sweden. The four of us checked into a wooden hotel with a sloping roof and overhanging eaves that looked like a chalet. Soon the Coastal Rangers took us for a dip in an ice hole. Although optional for us, everyone jumped into the nearly frozen water. We led by example—one of the stupid SEAL Team "kick me in the nuts I can take it" traditions. Around our necks we wore a cord with an ice pick dangling off it at chest level. The wooden handle was hand-sized, and the pick was an inch long. We had to jump into the ice hole, calm down, and request permission to get out of the water. Then we could reach forward, stab the ice with the pick, and pull ourselves out. On the first try, my vocal cords didn't even work, it was so cold—I just jumped out. During the third attempt, I calmed down and allowed my vocal cords enough time to function. My voice squeaked, "Request permission to get out." After exiting the water, getting warm became the priority.

I thought back to winter warfare training in Alaska. Kevin and I became partners. He was a big, easygoing SEAL with dark hair and dark eyes. Trained as a hospital corpsman, he could handle most combat medical emergencies until the injured could be transported to a hospital (later, I heard he left the SEALs and became a doctor for the navy, stationed in Spain). Kevin and I skied a deception trail—skiing past the area where we would pitch our tent. Then we'd do a fishhook back to our tent. This way we could hear someone coming before they reached us. We pitched a North Face two-man tent, put our rucksacks under the front of it, and piled snow outside the entrance, so we could melt it later for drinking water, including what we'd use on our ski the next day; people actually dehydrate more in the winter because their lungs use a lot of moisture to heat up the air. We'd also add it to our freeze-dried meals. Inside the tent vestibule, we stripped off wet clothing down to our polypro underwear. We lit the MSR WhisperLite stove to make water. The heat it put out warmed up the tent fast. Kevin's feet were huge—his overboots wouldn't fit over his ski boots. While we waited for the snow to melt, Kevin would take off his boots, and I'd put his toes under my armpits to prevent them from getting frostbite. Other guys looked forward to getting in their tents, but not me. Every night for ten days, I warmed those damned ice cube toes under my armpits. Then I could jump into a sleeping bag on my ground pad.

Fortunately, in Sweden, only 50 yards away from the ice hole, they had a sauna—and beer.

Also in Sweden, I experienced a snowcat for the first time—an armored personnel carrier on tracks that runs on the snow. Troops can shoot at the enemy from inside. They would attach a tow rope to the back of the snowcat and tow ten or twelve soldiers on skis. Hooking a ski pole into the rope, I held onto the handle as it towed me. Many of the Coastal Rangers had grown up skiing. One of them was an Olympic athlete in the ski jump event. Of course, there were no ski slopes in South Georgia, where I grew up. I'd fall down, and the Coastal Rangers behind would try to maneuver around me. Four of them ended up going down with me. After a while, they started arguing. I couldn't understand the words, but I knew they were fighting over who would have to ski behind me. My three Teammates and I fell down so many times, taking the Coastal Rangers down with us like dominoes, that they respectfully moved us to the tail of the rope. If we could've videotaped our SEALs on Ice Show for *America's Funniest Home Videos,* we probably would've won.

Because we were there as cadre to help train the young conscripts, the conscripts treated us like officers, cleaning and waxing our skis while we ate dinner. In the evening, if we left our boots outside the door, they'd clean and polish them before the next morning. The recruits would even clean our weapons for us.

Another cool thing we did was learn how to make a

snow cave. My Coastal Ranger counterpart stood tall
and slim. He could effortlessly ski circles around me.
We dug horizontally into the side of a snowdrift, up,
and horizontally inward, creating a plateau for the heat
to rise to while the cold air dropped to the lower level.
The Coastal Ranger and I put our packs in the entrance
to block the wind and kept our ice axes inside, just in
case we might have to dig ourselves out. From the plateau, we shaped the roof into a dome, so it wouldn't
drip directly on us.

We took off our overboots before entering the plateau area. With only four SEALs serving as cadre, my
partner seemed honored to be paired up with me. He
tried to clean off my boots.

"No, it's OK. I'll take care of it," I said.

He gave me a strange look. Later, he appreciated not
having to be my servant.

One or two candles were sufficient to heat the cave.
Outside, the temperature was −40° F. Inside, I sat on a
sleeping bag wearing just my navy blue polypro long un-
dergarments. We didn't want to heat up the interior temperature much higher than 32 degrees, or our snow cave
might unfreeze, start raining, and then collapse on top of
us. The difference between the temperature outside and
inside, 70 degrees, made it feel like living in the Baha-
mas. The interior heat softened the walls and ceilings, so
we patted them until they became hard again.

After living in the same snow cave for two weeks, using it as a base to run ops from, we had patted the walls
and ceilings so much that the interior space seemed on
its way to becoming a snow house. The Swedes knew
how to fight a war—their rations included cognac and

the best hot chocolate mix I'd ever had, plus meals like pasta Bolognese with rye bread. To my amazement, my Swedish counterpart wanted to trade his rations for my MREs. Guess he got tired of the same meals all the time. We enjoyed eating each other's food in our snow cave.

In fact, part of the fun training with foreign special ops units was the gear exchange. From the States, I had brought some big beef sticks, no spicy flavors, to slice up and put on my rations for extra energy in the cold weather. The Coastal Rangers loved the beef sticks. I had also brought a Zippo lighter, for which one of the Coastal Rangers traded his beautiful Laplander knife. It had a wooden handle with a slightly curved blade plus a leather sheath that had two strands of rawhide string to tie it onto my pack. The Zippo lighter is more reliable in the cold than a butane lighter, but I liked the knife better.

On the last day, my partner and I applied white face paint on the parts of our faces that naturally formed shadows and gray on the prominent features: forehead, cheeks, nose, brow, and chin. All of us left our snow caves for the big op. Somewhere between one hundred and one hundred and fifty of us hooked up to the ropes behind our snowcats, which pulled us to our objective area. We skied in as far as we could, then removed our skis and backpacks inside the tree line, 300 yards away from our objective.

I put on my big clunky NATO snowshoes. The Coastal Rangers had nice small composite metal snow-shoes that they could run with. *Wow, you guys are way more high-tech in winter warfare than we are.* For a pair of them, I traded my old Swiss Army knife and the snapped leather holder I used to carry it on my belt. It was too bulky to carry in my pocket. One of the black plastic sides of my knife had broken off, but it still had tools: saw, fish scaler with hook remover, leather punch with threader, magnifying glass, long blade, short blade, scissors, small pliers, corkscrew, toothpick, and tweezers. One would think that because Sweden is closer to Switzerland than the United States is, a Swiss Army knife would be in less demand there, but not so. The Coastal Ranger even threw in a bottle of schnapps to go with the snowshoes. He was so happy, he practically worshipped me for making the trade. Then the Coastal Ranger went and told all his buddies. They chewed him out for taking advantage of me. If he'd brought those snowshoes when I was doing winter warfare in Alaska, I would've traded five Swiss Army knives. When I returned to the U.S., I would buy a new one.

We patrolled forward in a wedge formation with a man in the middle and a wing on each side. Another element approached the objective area from the left flank. Shooting blanks, the left flank and our front wedge simultaneously assaulted through a mock fortification of ten buildings. Normally the basic SEAL unit is made up of a boat crew, only seven or eight men. In this company-sized assault of over a hundred soldiers, we just had to go with the flow.

The Swedish Coastal Rangers and other Northern European units such as Norway's Navy Rangers spend more time on skis and operating in the winter environment than Americans do, giving them a distinct advantage. However, America's technology helps level the playing field. It doesn't matter how good you are on those skis if I can catch you in my night-vision scope from 400 yards away. Ski on that.

I heard that while I'd been away training in Sweden, Laura had been out until late most nights partying hard with some other SEAL wives. When I asked her about it, she said, "Oh, it was only one or two times. I just got bored." I took her word for it because I believed her—I didn't want to believe anything else. We went to church on Sundays, and everything seemed OK.

My son, Blake, really liked hanging out with the SEAL Team guys, and they loved him, too, especially after a particular incident when Blake was four years old. One day after work, I returned home to find Laura in the kitchen, out of her mind.

"What's going on?" I asked.

"Little Debbie was over, and they got into Blake's wading pool. Naked!" Little Debbie was a neighbor's six-year-old daughter.

"Oh."

"I called her mama and told her. She thought it was funny. You better talk to him."

So I walked down the hall to his room.

Blake was playing Duck Hunt on the Nintendo, shooting flying ducks with his Nintendo Zapper Light Gun.

"Hey, buddy, how was your day?"

"Good," he said.

"What'd you do today?"

"Played."

I left him to his game and returned to Laura in the kitchen. "He's fine. Didn't even bring it up. Must not be such a big deal."

"Oh, no. You have to make him talk about it. He's probably traumatized."

So I returned to Blake's room. A dog on the TV monitor sniffed out the dead ducks in the grass and congratulated Blake.

I became more direct with my questioning. "Did you go swimming today?"

"Yep."

"Well, did anyone go swimming with you?"

"Yep, Debbie went swimming with me."

"Did you and Debbie take y'all's clothes off while you were in the wading pool?"

"Debbie took her bathing suit off, and told me to take my bathing suit off."

"Do you know you're not supposed to let people see your pee-pee?"

"Yes, Mom told me not to let people see my pee-pee."

"Well, did Debbie see your pee-pee?"

"Yep, Debbie saw my pee-pee." He laughed.

"Did you see Debbie's pee-pee?"

He stopped playing his game and put down the gun. There was a hint of concern in his voice. "You know what, Dad? Debbie doesn't have a pee-pee." He seemed to feel sorry for her. "She's got a front-butt."

It was all I could do to keep from laughing my head off. I called up Smudge, and he nearly busted a gut.

The next day, in the afternoon, Blake joined me in the SEAL Team Two Foxtrot Platoon Ready Room. We started talking about the front-butt story, and everyone cracked up.

Years later, one of the guys would say, "Hey, you know what? Think I'm going to head out into town tonight and try to find me a little front-butt." My son had become a Team legend.

While I was at SEAL Team Two, my uncle Carroll died of a heart attack while fishing. My heart ached as I returned home for the funeral at the First Baptist Church—the same church where I had beaten the crap out of Timmy so many years earlier. Relatives, friends, and people I didn't know packed the inside of the church. At the front, Uncle Carroll lay in his casket. He had loved me, spent time with me, and helped me grow up to be a young man. The memorial service was a blur to me—hymns, prayers, readings from the Bible, words from Brother Ron, and a eulogy. Sitting on the pew, I just physically couldn't take it. I rose to my feet and walked outside the front door of the church. I stood on the steps and cried, shaking uncontrollably. It was the hardest I had ever cried. Someone put his arms around me and hugged me. I looked up expecting to see Brother Ron, but the man with his arms around me wasn't Brother Ron. He was Dad. It was only our second hug. Not like the forced one before I got on the bus for college. "You know, Howard, I'm going to miss him, too. He always took the time with you because he was better at training you than I was. He had more patience. That's why Uncle Carroll always did that with you."

Later, I pulled myself together and followed the

funeral procession to the cemetery where Uncle Carroll was laid to rest.

On June 6, 1990, my daughter, Rachel, was born at a civilian hospital in Virginia Beach. My mother-in-law had arrived from South Georgia. I'd been up at Fort A. P. Hill, Virginia, one of the largest live-fire ranges on the East Coast. I drove 140 miles southeast to see Laura and my baby girl. Seeing Rachel made me extremely happy. Even so, as much as I loved her, part of me was preoccupied with the Team. Maybe some SEALs can balance God, family, and the Teams. I couldn't. The Teams were everything. After staying at the hospital for a day or two, I was gone again.

Whenever I returned home, she was Daddy's girl. She loved to be with me, and I loved being with her. Once, when she got older, Blake pushed her off the back deck.

"Blake, go in the closet and get a belt!"

He disappeared into the closet, then emerged with my biggest leather belt.

"Son, why'd you bring the biggest belt you could find?"

He looked in my eyes. "Dad, that was a bad thing I did. So I figured I deserved to get spanked with this big belt."

Maybe he was just playing me. Anyway, I didn't spank him that time. Or any time after. If anything, I was too lenient with Blake. I could probably count the number of times on one hand that I'd laid him on the bed and spanked him with a belt.

I let Rachel get away with more than Blake. She was my sweetheart, and he was my buddy.

I continued to hear more about SEAL Team Six, the secret counterterrorist unit. Guys said that Team Six was the Team to go to. Six was the tier-one unit, recruiting only the best SEALs—like the Pro Bowl of the National Football League. They did hostage rescue and got all the money. Operators went to whatever schools they wanted. Spend thousands of dollars to go to a two-week driving academy? No problem. Want to go to Bill Rogers's shooting academy? Again? No problem. They used top-of-the-line equipment. They got all the support—an entire helicopter squadron was dedicated to them. It was a no-brainer. I wanted to go to SEAL Team Six. As things turned out, I would go to war first.

7.
DESERT STORM

With Iraq's economy failing, President Saddam Hussein blamed Kuwait, invading the country on August 2, 1990, and taking Western hostages. The UN condemned the invasion, demanded a withdrawal, placed economic sanctions on Iraq, and formed a blockade. However, Hussein seemed poised to invade Saudi Arabia next.

On August 7, Operation Desert Shield began. U.S. aircraft carriers and other ships entered the Persian Gulf. Our troops were sent to Saudi Arabia. The UN gave Iraq an ultimatum to leave Kuwait by January 15, 1991, or be forcefully removed. We formed a coalition of thirty-four countries, with financial contributions from Germany and Japan.

My platoon readied our equipment and deployed to Machrihanish, Scotland. As we learned that Desert *Shield* was about to become Desert *Storm,* we flew to Sigonella, Sicily. Our Naval Air Station was located on the NATO base, serving as a hub to the Mediterranean. There we waited for our ship to arrive.

While waiting, I often went off base to eat at a nearby restaurant. Their manicotti was particularly delicious. One evening, I asked the waitress how to cook it. She disappeared into the kitchen, then came out and told me. After I'd eaten there a few more times and asked how to cook the dishes each time, she said, "You and chef talk." She escorted me back to the kitchen. I realized a family was running the place. The chef and I drank Chianti while he showed me how to do prep work and, after a number of visits, taught me how to cook Sicilian—homemade meatballs, sausages, baked ziti, and manicotti. He seemed pleased that I had taken an interest in assisting with the cooking. The most important part of cooking Italian is the sauce, which can take a couple of days to make. First, chop up the peppers, onions, garlic, tomatoes, and mushrooms. Then sauté them. Cook some herbs to a boil in tomato sauce, then put the heat on low and add the vegetables. Add wine. This would take a full day. Make meatballs and sausages while the sauce is slow cooking. Then add the meat to the sauce. Wake up in the middle of the night to put it in the refrigerator. Then take it out to eat the next day. Even now, I still cook Sicilian. My wife and I often invite friends and neighbors over to enjoy the same food and atmosphere I enjoyed while in Sicily. Occasionally I'll be outside walking the dog when a neighbor asks me, "Hey, Howard, when are you going to cook some Italian again?"

After several weeks had passed, I came back from the restaurant one evening and stopped by the air tower to watch some TV. On CNN, they showed the first shots of Desert Storm. I sprinted to the Explosives Ordnance

Disposal locker where my platoon slept in sleeping bags and woke them up. "Hey, the war has started."

Everybody jumped up, ready to get busy. Then we realized, *What the hell are we getting all excited for? We haven't been told what to do yet.* So I grabbed a sleeping bag and slept.

The next morning, we found out we were going to the *John F. Kennedy,* the same aircraft carrier where I'd done Search and Rescue. When the ship arrived from the Mediterranean Sea, it seemed to take forever to get all our equipment loaded: cases of 84 mm one-shot light antitank rockets (AT-4s), claymores, ammunition . . . We didn't know what specific missions we'd be tasked with, so we took everything.

The *John F. Kennedy* was 1,052 feet long and 192 feet tall from the waterline to the top of the mast. It could sail at 34 knots (1 knot equals roughly 1.15 miles per hour) carrying more than five thousand personnel. In addition to more than eighty aircraft, it was armed with two Guided Missile Launching System Mark-29 launchers for Sea Sparrow missiles, two Phalanx close-in weapon systems for attacking incoming missiles, and two Rolling Airframe Missile launchers that fire infrared homing surface-to-air missiles.

I saw a lot of my old buddies on board. Even some of the same pilots remained. *John F. Kennedy* sailed through the Suez Canal to the Red Sea, heading for the Persian Gulf. Most ships didn't have quarters for a SEAL contingent. We slept and held meetings wherever we could find a space. Fortunately, we had a great rapport with the ship personnel. Whenever the ship's crew saw us coming through the passageway wearing our camouflage uniforms and SEAL tridents, they said, "Make a hole, SEAL coming through." It felt like being a celebrity. We tried to treat them with respect, too.

At first no one approached us when we were in the chow hall. After a while, people started to join us. They asked us about BUD/S and other things. In the huge hangar bay, we did our physical training every morning. Some of the ship's personnel showed up and joined us.

We didn't follow the Dick Marcinko Charm School of arrogance and alienating people. Marcinko created SEAL Team Six, served time in jail for defrauding the government, wrote his autobiography, entitled *Rogue Warrior,* and made a video game. Although I respect that he created Team Six, Marcinko gave us a black eye by disrespecting people who weren't SEALs—and by disrespecting SEALs who weren't part of his clique. I was on a flight once with a pilot who was amazed at our behavior in comparison with the loud, obnoxious, gun-waving attitude of Marcinko's SEALs. Even worse, Marcinko cheated the government out of money, putting Team Six under a dark cloud of suspicion. He had been imprisoned for conspiring with a civilian contractor to overcharge the government for explosives and pocketing the money. For years, we had to overcome that legacy. Especially at SEAL Team Six, subsequent commanders worked hard to clean up the crap stains Marcinko left behind.

On the *John F. Kennedy,* we were visitors in someone else's home. They were the ones in charge. They were the ones who took care of it—making our stay as good or as bad as they wanted. If the ship sprang a leak, we depended on the ship's personnel to plug the hole. We treated the crew well, and they treated us like royalty.

I'm not saying we had to kiss everyone's butts, but we were all on the same team. The non-SEALs took the same navy oath as the SEALs to "defend the Constitution of the United States against all enemies, foreign and domestic." Treat people like crap who are in the same military and eventually it will come back and bite you in the butt. If I saw Marcinko on the street, I would respect him for creating SEAL Team Six, but if he said anything to me about how everything used to be better when he was commanding officer, I'd tell him, "Go play your video game and blow some more smoke up your own ass."

For over a week, pilots from our ship took off loaded up with bombs, leaving us behind to watch their payloads explode on CNN. Then we stood by as the pilots came back without their bombs. We had trained and trained for this moment. Especially in winter warfare, we skied in and set up a beacon to let the pilot in the aircraft see our location. Then we would "paint" the target with a laser, letting the bomb know where to go. *We're missing out.* Wearing Ray-Ban aviator sunglasses, I stood on the outer deck of the aircraft carrier feeling a breeze and looking across the shimmering calm ocean toward Iraq. I could see the USS *San Jacinto* (CG-56), a cruiser loaded with Tomahawk missiles. The USS *America* (CV-66) and USS *Philippine Sea* (CG-58) also sailed in our battle group. I was all dressed up with nowhere to go. My platoon and I weren't the only ones.

Although General Norman Schwarzkopf had utilized British special ops, the Special Air Service (SAS), at the beginning of the war, he didn't utilize American special ops. He clearly favored American conventional forces over American unconventional units like the SEALs or Delta. It sucked.

On a side note, although the SEALs had specifically rehearsed to protect the oil wells in Kuwait, Schwarzkopf didn't use us. Later, as Coalition military forces drove the Iraqi military out of Kuwait, Saddam's troops conducted a scorched earth policy, destroying everything they could—including setting fire to over six hundred of Kuwait's oil wells. Kuwait lost five to six million barrels of oil each day. Unburned oil formed hundreds of oil lakes, contaminating forty million tons of earth. Sand mixed with oil created "tarcrete," covering 5 percent of Kuwait. Putting out the fires cost Kuwait $1.5 billion. They burned for more than eight months, polluting the ground and air. Many Kuwaitis and Coalition troops developed respiratory difficulties. The thick billows of black smoke filled the Persian Gulf and surrounding areas. Wind blew the smoke to the eastern Arabian Peninsula. For days, the smoky skies and black rain saturated nearby countries. The environmental and human suffering caused by the fires continues to be felt to this day. If it hadn't been for Schwarzkopf's underestimating their ability to light fires, the belief among the Team guys was that, we could've eliminated many of the booger-eaters before they reached the six hundred oil wells, lessening the suffering.

One evening, we were awakened around midnight to muster in one of the jet fighter wing's ready rooms.

Intel told us that a cargo ship disguised under an Egyptian flag was laying mines in the Red Sea. Our mission would be to take the ship down. SEAL Team Six did this kind of mission with Black Hawk helicopters and state-of-the-art gear. As Team Two SEALs, we'd have to make do with the bumblebee-looking SH-3 Sea King helicopters and our wits.

We started our mission planning. How many helicopters? Who's going to be in what bird? Who's going to be in what seat? Which helicopter will hover over the ship first? Which helo is second? How will we set up sniper positions? Escape and evasion plans if we have to bail? Meanwhile we continued to get new intelligence, and the aircraft carrier moved us closer to striking position.

The ship's whistle blew—lunchtime. We ate, not knowing when we'd have a chance to eat again. Then we went to the intelligence center to update our intel and check out blueprints of the cargo ship we'd take down. How many decks? How many rooms? How many crew members? The amount of intel and planning that goes into a mission is mind-boggling.

As the air rep, I prepared the portable wire ladders (caving ladders) for climbing back up to the helicopter if we needed to, fast ropes, and other air-related gear. I attached a ninety-foot braided nylon rope to a clevis pin on a bar bolted to the interior roof of the SH-3 Sea King, a twin-engine antisubmarine-warfare helicopter. Not designed with our type of work in mind, the helo would later be replaced by the SH-60 Sea Hawk, the maritime version of the Black Hawk. SEAL Team Six had the Black Hawks, but we blue-water SEALs had to make do with what was available. I placed the coiled rope inside near the helo door.

We divided up other responsibilities. Serving as lead member of the prisoner handling team, I had to carry an additional ten pairs of flexicuffs in my backpack, in addition to the standard two pairs for the prisoners, and plan where to put prisoners as we took down the ship.

We geared up, wearing black BDUs. On our feet, we wore Adidas GSG9 assault boots. They're soft on the bottom and grip well, like wearing a tennis shoe with ankle support. You can get them wet and fins slip on easy over the tops. To this day, that's my favorite boot. Black balaclavas covered our heads, and paint covered our exposed skin. For our hands, we customized our green aviator gloves by dying them black, then cutting off two of the fingers on the right-hand glove: the trigger finger down to the second knuckle and the thumb down to the first knuckle. With the fingers cut out, it became easier to squeeze the trigger, change magazines, pull the pins on flashbangs, etc. Casio watches on our wrists kept time. On my belt, in the small of my back, sat a gas mask. During Desert Storm, everyone prepared for gas or biological weapons; Hussein was reported to still have chemical weapons that he wouldn't hesitate to use. I also took along two or three flashbangs.

I carried the Heckler and Koch MP-5 submachine gun with a SIG SAUER 9 mm on my right hip. I kept a thirty-round magazine in the MP-5. Some guys like to carry two magazines in the weapon, but our experience was that the double magazine limited our maneuverability, and it's hard to do a magazine change. I carried three magazines on my left thigh and an extra three in my backpack. We test-fired our weapons off the fantail, on the back of the ship.

Although we had sixteen guys in our platoon, one would remain as a sniper in each of the two circling helicopters. That left only fourteen of us to take down the entire ship—two more helos with seven assaulters in each. Mine would be the lead helicopter.

The helicopter crew members were familiar faces— I'd served with their squadron, SH-7, during my earlier navy days as a SAR swimmer. As ropemaster, I sat inside the helo door in the middle of the coil of the rope with my left hand on the part leading up to the hoist mount sticking out of the helo. When we became airborne, I felt the outside wind try to pull the rope away from me. I closed my eyes and took a rest.

"Fifteen minutes." The air crewman's voice came into my headset, relaying information from the pilot.

I opened my eyes and relayed the message to my Teammates. "Fifteen minutes!" Then I closed my eyes again.

"Ten minutes."

I was used to the routine.

"Five minutes."

Getting close now.

"Three minutes."

We had approached the ship from the rear, slowing from 100 knots to 50 knots.

"One minute."

Flaring the helo's nose up at an angle, the pilot put on the brakes. As we leveled out to a hover over the ship, I had enough daylight left to see the deck. We were in position. I kicked the 90-foot rope out the door and called, "Rope!" It hit the fantail on an area too small to land a helicopter.

"Go!" Wearing thick wool inserts in my gloves, I grabbed the rope and slid down it like a fireman's pole. With more than 100 pounds of gear on my back, I had to grip the rope tight to prevent myself from splattering onto the deck. Of course, with six guys behind me waiting in the helicopter, one big hovering target, I didn't want to descend too slowly, either. My gloves literally smoked on the way down. Fortunately, I landed safely.

Unfortunately, our pilot had a hard time holding his position over the ship in rough seas with darkness falling and gusts of wind blowing. To add to the difficulty, the pilots weren't used to hovering over a target while a 200-pound man and his 100 pounds of gear come off the rope—causing the helo to suddenly gain altitude. The pilot would have to compensate by lowering the helo for each man who dismounted the rope. We had practiced with the pilots earlier, but it was still a tricky maneuver. Without the pilot's compensation, the first operator would slide off the rope with three feet of rope on the deck, the second guy with only a foot, and the third guy with the rope off the deck—it wouldn't take long before some poor bastard dropped ten feet through the air with nothing to hold on to, the metal deck giving a lot less cushion than dirt. Even for the more experienced Black Hawk pilots, it's a tricky maneuver. The helicopter pulled away. *Crap.* There I was, in the middle of a war, in the middle of the Red Sea, on a strange enemy ship by myself. I felt naked. *If this goes really bad, I can fight my way through it. If this goes really,*

really bad—Mother Ocean is right there. Kick, stroke, and glide. The helicopter had to circle around, reestablish visual, make another approach, and hover again. It probably only took two minutes, but it felt like two hours.

I scanned the area with the muzzle of my MP-5 while my platoon fast-roped down. Once we were all together, we set our perimeter. Mark, who was our team leader, and DJ, our communications (coms) guy, took a group to the wheelhouse for command and control. Two shooters went to after steering to disable the ship—making it dead in the water. My team went to the cabins to get the crew.

Inside the ship, we approached the first cabin. *You're soft until you're hard.* Stay quiet for as long as possible. If I'd heard a shot or a flashbang, I'd be thinking, *Aw, crap. Here we go.* From then on out I'd be hard. Kick in every door and flashbang every room. Manhandle everyone. Violence of action turns up exponentially. We try to match the level of violence to the level required for the situation. No more, no less.

I opened the door, and four of us slipped in quietly while two stayed behind in the hallway to cover our rear. Speed is key, as is moving together. Two of us cleared left and two cleared right. The two crew members inside froze. We dominated the area. They couldn't speak English, but we knew some Arabic: *Down.*

They assumed the position.

Another SEAL and I stood next to the wall covering while two SEALs said, "Moving."

"Move," I answered, controlling the room.

They cuffed the two crew members on the deck.

I shouted, requesting to know if the hall outside was secure for us to come out. "Coming out?"

"Come out," came a reply from the hall.

We took our prisoners out into the hallway and moved on to the next door. Most rooms averaged two crew members. Some rooms were empty.

In one room, we went in and cuffed the crew. I said, "Coming out?"

"No," the two shooters in the hall replied.

The four of us stayed put with our two prisoners—waiting. I could hear arguing in the hall.

"Wasdin," one of the guys in the hall called.

I stepped into the hallway and saw a crew member standing in a T-intersection at the end of the hall. In his hand was a fire extinguisher. One of our shooters was about to cap him for noncompliance.

"What's going on?" I asked.

"This guy won't listen," the shooter said.

Maybe he thinks we're sabotaging the ship. "Down," I said in Arabic.

The crew member spoke Arabic. "No."

I looked in his eyes. He seemed confused, not like he was being hostile for the sake of being hostile. Thinking it was simple miscommunication, I lowered my MP-5 submachine gun a little.

He lunged at me with his fire extinguisher.

Damn.

I sidestepped just as the fire extinguisher glanced off the side of my head. Back then, we weren't wearing assault helmets. If I hadn't sidestepped, the blow would've caught me straight in the face.

Wow. He almost killed me with a fire extinguisher. How would that look? Try to be nice and get taken out with a fire extinguisher. I was furious. I caught him sideways and buried the muzzle of my MP-5 under his right ear, pushed him back, then gave him a butt stroke for good measure.

One of Mr. Fire Extinguisher's buddies, a skinny little man, put up his hands as if to take me on.

My Teammate was about to cap him.

"No, I got it." With my left hand, I gave Fire Extinguisher's buddy a karate chop just below his nose, backing him off. I put enough force into it that he probably needed to get his teeth retightened. He quickly became compliant, not wanting any more.

Then Fire Extinguisher got cuffed the *hard* way: arm bar, knee behind the neck, grabbing a handful of his hair, lifting him up by the cuffs until his arms almost came out of their sockets, and kicking him in the ass down the hallway. Our guys took him and the other prisoners to the holding area.

Blood trickled from my head down into my ear. Now I was really pissed. *Try to be a nice guy, and that's what happens.* In retrospect, Fire Extinguisher should've gotten two to the body and one to the head. He's a lucky sonofabitch.

We found most of the men in the crew's quarters, which doubled as a chow hall—interrupting their Turkish tea and cigarettes.

We cleared nearly every inch of the ship, top to bottom, stern to bow. SEAL Team Six would take the same ship down with thirty assaulters. Since we had fewer guys and were not as specialized as Six, it took us two hours. My team stayed on the bow with the prisoners in the darkness. Mark commanded our platoon from the wheelhouse while DJ ran coms next to him. Nobody got hurt. Other than me being an idiot. Now the ship belonged to us. Warships surrounded us as we sat dead in the water. Rigid Hull Inflatable Boats (RHIBs) floated beside us carrying Coast Guard Law Enforcement Detachment (LEDET), the lead agency for apprehending drug traffickers on the high seas. To a large degree, the dangerous part was over.

We mustered the prisoners. The ship's captain, up in the wheelhouse with Mark, sent his master-at-arms down to do a head count. We found out we were missing one of the ship's crew. *Somebody's hiding.*

We asked the prisoners if they knew where he was.

Nobody knew nothin'.

So we had to clear the whole freaking ship again. Leaving four men to guard the prisoners, we went back to after steering and started over. We were beyond pissed, tearing through every inch of the ship we thought we'd already searched. Halfway through clearing the ship, I got a call that we'd found the guy. He had been hiding tucked up between some pipes in an engine compartment—scared.

We took him to join his comrades on the bow, and we cut the flexicuffs off all the prisoners. Except Fire Extinguisher. I made him sit on the capstan, which looks like a giant motorized thread spool, the most uncomfortable seat on the bow.

Meanwhile, Mark spoke through DJ to an interpreter on one of the ships in order to communicate to the captain standing next to Mark.

"Were you laying mines? Where were the mines? Where are you going? Where are you coming from?"

"We're not laying mines."

"If you're not, why don't you have any cargo? Why are you on a course going away from Egypt when you should be going home?"

These guys were not giving us the right answers. Something was definitely fishy.

Fire Extinguisher complained, "My butt hurts."

My head was still pounding. *Sonofabitch, you're lucky you can feel anything.*

One of the prisoners on the bow reached for the inside of his jacket, going for a gun in his shoulder holster. The snipers in the helicopter aimed their infrared lasers at him as the rest of us clicked the safeties off our MP-5s, about to blow him away—but there was neither gun nor holster, just a white pack of cigarettes.

"No, no, no, no," pleaded the prisoner. His eyes looked like two fried eggs. He was lucky we had such tight trigger discipline—not like the four policemen in New York who shot Amadou Diallo forty-one times reaching for his wallet.

One of the crew spoke English, and we translated through him. "No sudden movements. Don't be reaching inside your clothes for anything."

Fire Extinguisher whined, "My butt hurts."

I hope you give me a reason to shoot you.

Later, a teenager burst onto the bow running. We took him down rudely and abruptly. After calling Mark, we found out the kid was the captain's messenger coming to get the keys to something. Maybe whenever the captain gave him an order, he was supposed to haul ass, but we made it clear to him: "No fast movements, and no running." I felt sorry for the poor kid because we took him down so hard.

The captain and crew still weren't giving us the right answers, so LEDET, armed with shotguns, came aboard and high-fived us, and we turned over the ship and prisoners to them. They would sail the ship to a friendly port in the Red Sea, where it wouldn't be the end of the story for the prisoners by any means.

Fire Extinguisher still had his cuffs on as LEDET took over. I hope he still has them on to this day.

Our job was done. The weather worsened, so we couldn't take a helicopter out. Instead, we lowered ourselves on caving ladders and left the vessel on LEDET RHIBs. The RHIBs took us to the LEDET's amphibious ship.

We boarded the amphibious ship in the early morning, having been awake for more than twenty-four hours. The last time we'd eaten was lunch the day before. Add to that the physical exertion and adrenaline dump—we were starving to death. In the chow hall, even though it was before breakfast hours, they brought out an amazing meal for all sixteen of us. I don't remember exactly what they fed us, but it seems like they fed us breakfast and dinner: quiche, grilled ham, buttermilk pancakes with blueberry topping, orange juice, hot coffee, steak, creamed asparagus soup, steamed cabbage and white sauce, mashed potatoes, and hot apple pie.

The head cook came out and shook each of our hands. "I've made some of my secret recipes. Hope you like it."

"Incredible," I said.

"We just found out you guys were coming, and this is all we had time for."

The debrief took place while we ate. All the officers on the ship seemed to be present. They treated us like kings. It seemed like everyone who could cram into the chow hall had come. People just wanted to meet, talk to, and be a part of us. Their hospitality meant a lot to me. Made me feel important.

Near early afternoon, our birds landed on the fantail of the amphibious ship, we waved good-bye, and flew back to the *Kennedy.*

Later I would receive the Navy Commendation Medal, which read:

The Secretary of the Navy takes pleasure in presenting the Navy Commendation Medal to Hull Technician First Class Howard E. Wasdin, United States Navy, for services set forth in the following citation: For professional achievement and superior performance of his duties while serving as air operations specialist for SEAL Team Two Foxtrot Platoon while deployed to the Red Sea in support of Operation Desert Storm from 17 January to 28 February 1991. During this period, Petty Officer Wasdin consistently performed his demanding duties in an exemplary and highly professional manner. As the air operations specialist responsible for all SEAL helo fast-rope operations his consistent hard work was instrumental in maintaining the assault team's capability to conduct rapid and efficient insertions onto designated targets. During one SEAL mission, he expertly directed the insertion and was the first man on deck to provide critical cover for his shipmates. He continued as lead member of a prisoner securing element displaying superior war fighting skills which proved critical to mission success. Petty Officer Wasdin's exceptional professional ability, initiative, and loyal devotion to duty reflect great credit upon himself and the United States Naval Service.

"I've been asked to select three men for a classified op, but Intel won't tell me what it's about until I select the men," Mark said.

Outside the Carrier Intelligence Center (CVIC), Smudge, DJ, and I stood in the passageway as Mark disappeared inside for a moment. Mark reappeared and said, "OK."

We walked in. There was a small break room off to the right with a coffee machine and a refrigerator. The left opened up into the main room with a conference table and chairs around it. On one wall hung a whiteboard, and in front of another stood a TV and video player. A couple of dark leather couches sat off to the side. In the middle of the room stood the ship's intelligence officer. Beside him was a man we'd never seen before. I didn't know if he was a spook or what. Without identifying himself, the man said, "Morning, gentlemen."

"Good morning, sir." We didn't know his rank, but it was safer to be overly polite than disrespectful.

"A Tomahawk missile was fired that missed its target and did not detonate. It landed in friendly territory, but there are enemy forces in the area. We need you to detonate the missile so the Iraqis cannot get the technology, which is invaluable. Also, we don't want them converting the explosives into an IED [Improvised Explosive Device]."

We returned to the berthing, where our beds (racks), lockers, and a small lounge were located, and began gearing up. "What's up?" other guys excitedly asked.

"The four of us are going out on an op." It sucked not being able to tell them the details.

Their excitement level dropped once they knew the twelve of them wouldn't be included.

I'd be using my CAR-15, which had a telescopic buttstock and held thirty rounds of .223 (5.56 mm) ammo in the magazine. Inside the stock, I put a few hundred dollars. In my left thigh cargo pocket, I stuck my E&E kit: pencil flare, waterproof matches, compass, map, red-lens flashlight, space blanket, and MRE entrée. Into the right thigh cargo pocket went my blowout kit: 4″×4″ gauze bandage with tie straps, a cravat, and a Vaseline-coated dressing for a sucking chest wound—all vacuum sealed in plastic to be waterproof. This was a minimum kit, mainly for a gunshot wound/bleeding trauma. Although SEALs often dress differently and carry a variety of weapons, the location of our blowout kit is universal. This way, if one of our shooters goes down, we don't have to play a guessing game of where his kit is to patch him up. Of course, I could use my own blowout kit to patch up an injured Teammate, but later if the need arose for me to patch myself up, I would lack the materials to do it.

The four of us boarded the SH-3 Sea King with light

brown and sand-colored stripes and blotches painted on our faces. Smudge carried 4 pounds of the off-white colored modeling clay with a slight odor of hot asphalt—C-4 plastic explosives. I carried the blasting caps, fuse, and fuse igniters. The C-4 couldn't blow up without the smaller explosion of a blasting cap, which is why we separated the two. Smudge had the safer cargo. Although blasting caps alone aren't powerful enough to blow off a hand, they have been known to blow off a careless finger or two.

We traveled light because this would be a quick in-and-out. The helo flew a few miles before slowing down to 10 knots, 10 feet above the water. I stepped out the side of the bird with my swim fins pointed straight down, falling through the stinging ocean spray kicked up by the helicopter. I couldn't hear my splash over the sound of the rotor blades chopping the air overhead.

One by one, the guys jumped out the side door and into the ocean. Similar to fast-roping, when each man jumped, it lightened the helicopter's load, making the helo gain altitude—the pilot had to compensate. The last SEAL to die in Vietnam, Lieutenant Spence Dry, was doing a helo cast when the helo rose significantly higher than 20 feet while flying faster than 20 knots—breaking Dry's neck.

Treading water, I looked around. Everyone seemed to be in one piece. A light blinked from the shore—our signal. I started to feel cold. We formed a line and faced the signal. Swimming the sidestroke, I kicked long, deep, and slow, propelling myself quickly, trying to stay in formation with the others. The swim warmed me. As we reached water shallow enough to stand in, we stopped, watching the shore. No danger signs yet. I removed my fins and hooked them to a bungee cord strapped across my back. Then we slithered onto the beach. Smudge and DJ spread out to the left and right flanks. I covered Mark with my CAR-15 as he approached the light source, a pear-shaped Arab who was our agent. They exchanged bona fides. Mark pulled his left ear. The agent rubbed his stomach with his left hand. *So far, so good.* Turning the agent with his back to me, I cuffed him and searched his body for a weapon, a radio, or anything that didn't belong. Nothing seemed out of place. I cut off his cuffs.

Mark signaled Smudge and DJ to come in. After they joined us, I handled the agent while we patrolled inland. If he became unusually fidgety as we neared the objective, I'd know he might be leading us toward a possible ambush. If he succeeded in leading us into an ambush, I'd be the first to put a bullet in his head. I haven't heard of a double agent living to tell about leading SEALs into an ambush. Behind the agent and me followed our leader, Mark. Next came DJ with the radio. Smudge brought up the rear.

After patrolling for half a mile through the sand, we stopped 100 yards away from a dirt road and went prone while the agent picked up a large rock, walked forward, and laid the rock beside the road. Then he returned to our group and lay prone with the rest of us. My wet body started to shiver. The desert is hot during the day but cold at night, and being wet didn't help matters. I was eager to get moving again, but not eager to get shot for moving too soon. Fifteen minutes later, a local vehicle stopped on the side of the road next to the rock. We covered it with our sound-suppressed CAR-15s. A man in a white robe stepped out of the truck and walked the 100 yards in our direction.

"Stop," I said in English. "Turn around."

He did.

"Back up to my voice."

As he walked backward toward us, we grabbed, bound, and searched him. Then we walked with the driver to his vehicle and searched it. He drove us twenty minutes to the target somewhere in the middle of the desert. The driver parked the car and walked the rest of the distance with us. There lay the missile. Even though it had crash-landed, it was still in good shape. We set up a loose perimeter while Smudge prepared two C-4 socks. Each large green canvas sock had 2 pounds of C-4 in the bottom. He slipped one sock over the tip of the missile and ran the line sewed into the mouth of the sock to a hook in the sock's toe, cinching it tight. Finally, Smudge did the same on the other end of the missile.

He tapped me on the shoulder, taking my place securing the perimeter while I inserted a blasting cap into each block of C-4. In more ways than I had time to think about, I did not want to screw up. I crimped the two blasting caps into two timed fuses, keeping them straight. After that, I screwed two underwater fuse igniters (M-60s) tightly onto the two fuses. Holding the fuse igniters in one hand, I pulled both lanyards at the same time. *Pop!* "Fire in the hole." I could smell the cordite of the fuses burning. Before the big explosion, there would be a three-minute time delay, give or take a few seconds.

I joined the others, and we patrolled away. Swiftly.

We took cover behind a natural berm that looked like a giant speed bump. *Kaboom!* Sand rained down on us.

We returned to the missile, making sure it was in small enough pieces. Mark gave the OK signal, so we returned to the vehicle.

The driver took us back to the spot on the road with the rock, but Mark told him to drive us farther, to avoid our parking in front of an ambush. After the driver dropped us off, we waited for him and the agent to leave before we exfilled back to the beach. On the beach, DJ called the helo and told the pilot we were on our way. We unbungeed our fins and entered the water. I was happy to be out of the danger area and swimming fast. Everyone swam fast. The swim heated our bodies. What they told us in BUD/S was true: *Mother Ocean is your comfort and safety.*

As the helo neared, we lined up 15 feet apart, snapping infrared chemlights attached to our inflatable life vests. The helo hovered overhead, its main rotor stirring up the ocean. Saltwater cut at my face mask. From the helo dropped a caving ladder, and I hooked one of the rungs with the bend in my elbow. I climbed up. When my feet stepped on the ladder, I used them to drive me upward, rather than pulling with my arms, so I wouldn't expend my arm strength. At the top, I used my arms to pull myself into the chopper.

When we all arrived safely on the helo, a crewman hauled in the ladder, and the helo flew us away. Inside the helo, we slapped each other on the back and breathed easy. The *Kennedy* must've moved in closer to us, because the return trip wasn't as long. We'd completed a classified op that someone thought was extremely important.

A few days later, I stood outside the CVIC again. This time it was only DJ and I. Mark called us in and, once again, we met the Man with No Name.

He shook our hands and wasted no time. "Shall we get to it?"

We nodded.

He explained, "The PLO voiced support for Saddam Hussein's invasion of Kuwait. Now they have set up shop in Iraq. The Iranians are working with the PLO to train terrorists to attack coalition forces. Recently, they planted a roadside IED that hit one of our vehicles. We want you to target the PLO-Iranian compound in Southeastern Iraq for a guided missile strike, then report a BDA [battle damage assessment]."

Mark discussed his plan with us, and then DJ and I went off to prepare our gear. As always, we made sure we had nothing shiny or noisy on us—nothing that a little sand-colored spray paint or tape couldn't fix. After prepping our gear, we took a late-afternoon flight on a Sea King from the *John F. Kennedy*'s flight deck. I fell asleep during the flight and woke up when we landed at the forward operating base. The sky had become dark—time was ticking. A civilian named Tom with a plain face who wore blue jeans and a gray T-shirt handed us the keys to a Humvee. "I just had her washed and waxed."

I looked at the dirty vehicle and smiled. *Perfect.*

With no clouds and a half moon overhead, DJ and I could see in the darkness. So could the enemy, but the clear skies would help the missile find its target. After driving 30 miles through the desert avoiding roads, buildings, populated areas, and telephone poles, we arrived in an area where the ground gently dipped 10 feet, just as we had seen on the satellite map in the CVIC. After creating false tracks past our location, we stopped in the dip and blotted out our real insertion tracks. Next, we covered the vehicle with desert camouflage netting. We lay on the ground next to each other, facing opposite directions. Quietly we watched and listened to find out if anyone would visit us. The first few minutes were maddening. *Is that really a bush? Maybe they're watching us. How many of them are there? Will the Humvee start up again if we need to bug out? Will we be able to get away fast enough?* Thirty minutes later, I calmed down, and we moved forward on foot, using a GPS for navigation.

With only two of us, we had less firepower than a boat crew and exercised additional caution not to be seen. Our ears became sharply tuned to the slightest sounds. We crouched as we walked—slow and silent, avoiding high ground that might cause our silhouettes to stand out.

Three miles later, we reached the base of a hill. The PLO-Iranian compound lay on the other side. I walked point with DJ behind me, and we climbed nearly 600 feet until we neared a slope. Keeping the slope below us and the ridge above, we low-crawled around toward the other side of the hill. A mile ahead on the ground, I saw the wall of a compound form a triangle with guard towers in each corner surrounding three buildings inside. I also saw an enemy soldier sitting about 60 yards away to the right of our hill with binoculars around his neck and an AK-47 assault rifle slung over the back of his right shoulder.

I stopped and signaled DJ with a clenched fist: *Freeze.* DJ stopped.

The sentry remained still.

After pointing two fingers to my eyes, then in the direction of the enemy sentry, I crawled in reverse. DJ backed out, too. We stalked around the back of the hill until we found another slope. This time when we crossed over, we had a clear view of the target with no sentries nearby. Our eyes searched the immediate area around us, then farther out until the compound came into view. The only people visible were the guards in the towers.

While I guarded the perimeter, DJ sent an encrypted transmission burst over his radio to tell the USS *San Jacinto* we were in position. A burst message must've come back, because DJ nodded his head, giving me the green light.

I unpacked the lightweight laser designator (AN/PED-1 LLDR), which wasn't very lightweight, and its tripod while DJ covered our perimeter. After marking our position with a beacon, I painted the middle building in the PLO-Iranian compound, marking it with coded pulses of invisible laser light. The light would sparkle off the target and into the sky for the incoming Tomahawk missile to find.

The cruise missile seemed to fly parallel to the earth. A trail of white smoke followed its flaming tail. The Tomahawk gradually descended until it shot into the center building, and 1,000 pounds of explosives burst in a ball of flame followed by clouds of black smoke. The shock wave and debris ripped apart the two other buildings and walls, causing a secondary detonation in one building—probably housing explosives used in making IEDs. Two of the three guard towers were ripped off. Through my binoculars, I clearly saw a soldier blasted out of his tower and sailing through the air like a stuffed doll. Only remnants remained of the compound wall. I could see no movement coming from the compound. From our hill the sentry ran toward the compound, probably hoping to find survivors among his friends.

We packed up and moved out, taking a different path to our vehicle. It's easy to become complacent on the way home, so it's important to be extra cautious. After removing the camouflage netting, we hopped in and drove away. Again we drove back a different route than we came in.

During the drive back, I noticed what appeared to be an enemy bunker, halfway exposed out of the ground. As I drove around to avoid it, the Humvee bogged down in the sand. When I tried to drive out, the Humvee wheels dug deeper, making the situation worse.

Meanwhile, Iraqi soldiers exited the bunker.

DJ and I aimed our CAR-15s at them.

Fourteen of them walked toward us with their hands in the air. I saw no threat in their faces. They were dirty and stank. Their skin stretched tight over their bones; there was no telling how long they'd been without food. They put their hands to their mouths, the international gesture for food. During the war, some Iraqi soldiers had

actually surrendered to camera crews, they were so willing to surrender and unwilling to fight.

On the ground, rags stuck from the ends of their rifles
to keep the sand out. We stepped out of our vehicle and
told them to dig a hole with their hands. Next we ordered
them to toss in their weapons. As they did, they seemed
more frightened, as if they expected us to execute them.
We motioned for them to cover the hole. Their fear sub-
siding, they complied. Some of them probably had
wives. Kids. Most of them were around my age. Their
lives were totally in my hands. They looked at me like I
was Zeus coming down from Mount Olympus.

Feeling sorry for them, I took out two MREs that I
had broken down as emergency rations for escape and
evasion. For fourteen guys, that wasn't a lot of food, but
they split the two meals up among themselves. One guy
even ate the Chiclets. *Well, you know, that's really candy-
coated chewing gum, but go ahead. Knock yourself out.*
We gave them most of our water. They put their hands
together and bowed with gratitude, thanking us. Wisely,
they didn't try to touch us or get in our personal space.

The faint glow of the sun began to appear on the horizon. Time to move. We made them put their hands on
their heads. I marked the position of our Humvee on the
GPS and walked the point while DJ followed at rear security. If a pilot had flown over and seen us, it would've
looked bizarre with only two Americans patrolling fourteen captured enemy through the middle of the desert.
We looked like the gods of war. *Two Navy SEALs capture fourteen Iraqi soldiers.*

When we reached the base, Tom's response was,
"Why in the hell are you giving us these guys?"

"Well, what did you want us to do with them?"

"Keep them."

"We can't keep them."

Soon our helicopter arrived, and we left our prisoners there, still bowing with their hands together and thanking us. The helo lifted off and took us back to the *John F. Kennedy*.

In BUD/S and up until that point, I had been in the mindset that everyone I went up against was a bad guy. *We* were morally superior to *them*. I used language to make killing more respectable: "*waste*," "*eliminate*," "*remove*," "*dispatch*," "*dispose*" . . . In the military, bombings are "clean surgical strikes" and civilian deaths are "collateral damage." Following orders takes the responsibility of killing off my shoulders and places it on a higher authority. When I bombed the compound, I further diffused personal responsibility by sharing the task: I painted the target, DJ radioed the ship, and someone else pressed the button that launched the missile. It's not uncommon for combat soldiers to dehumanize the enemy—Iraqis become "ragheads" and "camel jockeys." In the culture of war, the line between victim and aggressor can become blurred. All these things helped me do my job, but they also threatened to blind me to the humanity in my enemy.

Of course, SEALs train to match the appropriate level of violence required by the situation, turning it up and down like the dimmer on a light switch. You don't always want the chandeliers on bright. Sometimes you do. That switch is inside me still. I don't want to, but I can turn it on if needed. However, the training didn't prepare me for seeing the humanity in those fourteen men. It's something you have to be in real combat to see. Not simulated combat. Maybe I could've put a bullet in every one of their skulls and bragged about how many confirmed kills I got. Some people have this concept of SEALs just being mindless, wind-me-up killing machines. "Oh, you're an assassin." I don't like that. I don't adhere to it. Most SEALs know that if you can do an op without any loss of life, it's a great op.

Seeing those fourteen men, I realized they were not bad guys. They were just poor sonsofbitches who were half starved to death, underequipped, outgunned, having no clue, and following some madman who'd decided he wanted to invade another country. If they didn't follow the madman, the Republican Guard would execute them. I suspect they lost the will to fight. Maybe they never had the will to fight in the first place.

They were human beings just like me. I discovered my humanity and the humanity in others. It was a turning point for me—it was when I matured. My standards of right and wrong in combat became clearer, defined by what I did and didn't do. I did give the fourteen Iraqi soldiers food and take them to a safer place. I didn't kill them. Whether you're winning or losing, war is hell.

Back on board the *Kennedy,* my eyes had opened wide. Wearing shorts and a T-shirt, sitting on a chair and cleaning my rifle, I thought about how I had seen my enemy up close and knew I could match him and overcome him on a violence-of-action scale. Moreover, I realized it's important to understand that our enemies are human.

* * *

Desert Storm only lasted forty-three days. We were furious that we didn't go to Baghdad and finish it. The *Kennedy* stopped in Egypt, where we unloaded all our gear and checked into a five-star resort in Hurghada. Not being tourist season, and with the recent war, we were the only guests. During dinner, our platoon chief came in and slapped me on the back. "Congratulations, Wasdin, you made First Class." I'd been promoted from E-5 to E-6. Life was pretty good for Howard. We waited two weeks for a flight back to Machrihanish, Scotland, to finish our six-month deployment.

I didn't have flashbacks, nightmares, trouble sleeping, impaired concentration, depression, or self-devaluation about having killed for the first time—seeing the soldier blasted out of the PLO guard tower and landing lifeless on the ground. Those kinds of feelings seem less common among special ops guys. Maybe most of the people susceptible to that stress were already weeded out during BUD/S, and maybe the high levels of stress in our training prepare us for the high levels of stress in war. I began to control my thoughts, emotions, and pain at an early age—it was a matter of survival—which helped me cope with challenges in the Teams. I had endured the trauma of my dad's harshness, Hell Week, and other experiences, and I endured war.

I did have a moral concern about having killed for the first time, though. I was worried whether I'd done the right thing. On TV and video games, it may seem like killing is no big deal. However, I had made the decision to end someone's life. The people I killed will never see their families again. Will never eat or use the restroom again. Never breathe again. I took everything that they had or ever will have. To me, that was a big deal. Something I didn't take lightly. Even now, I still don't take it lightly. During a visit home, I talked to Brother Ron. "I killed in combat for the first time. Did I do the right thing?"

"You lawfully served your country."

"How is this going to affect me as far as eternity goes?"

"It won't have a negative affect on your eternity."

His words comforted me. My youngest sister, Sue Anne, who is a therapist, is convinced that I've got to have something wrong with me. There's no way I'm functioning as normally as I am without repressing something. She just doesn't get the fact that I really am OK with my decisions and mental peace.

There are few secrets among SEALs. We're around each other constantly and know each other inside and out. I would know a guy's daughter's hair color, his wife's shoe size, and everything that was going on. I knew more details about guys than I wanted to know. I also knew who wanted to try out for SEAL Team Six.

Smudge, DJ, four other SEALs from Foxtrot Platoon, and I handed in our applications for joining SEAL Team Six. Smudge, DJ, and I passed the application stage, but the others didn't. One guy was extremely pissed because he'd been a SEAL longer than I had. Our applications were accepted, and when Team Six's master chief visited our command, he interviewed us. The odds were that only one of us would pass the interviews and be accepted to the next stage, but all three of us passed—which meant some other Team would have a higher rate of failure.

We were given a time period to show up for our interview, which was only done once a year. In May, I underwent the main screening in Dam Neck, Virginia, even though Six usually required applicants to have been SEALs for five years. SEALs were lined up for interviews like kids at Disneyland anxiously waiting for a ride on Space Mountain. Guys like us had flown in from Scotland. Others flew in from California, Puerto Rico, the Philippines, and other places. For some, this wasn't the first time they'd interviewed.

Inside the interview room, my interviewers were mostly older enlisted SEALs—actual Team Six operators. They conducted themselves in a professional manner. The interviewers asked me a lot about my perception of things. About the combat I'd been in. "What are your shortcomings? Where do you need work?" It's hard for a young SEAL to come clean with those answers. If you can't recognize these and don't have the will to work on them, how can you get to that next level?

One tried to rattle me a bit. "Do you drink a lot?"

"No."

"But you go out drinking with the guys."

"Yes."

"You're full of it."

"No."

"Do you drink a lot?"

"I don't know how to answer that again. Other than to say I don't drink for effect." I didn't drink for the purpose of getting a buzz or getting drunk. "If my buddies go into town and they're drinking, ninety-nine percent of the time I'm going to be there drinking with them. If we've got something to do, we don't drink. So I don't know how to answer that again. I don't drink for effect. I drink for camaraderie."

He smiled wryly. "OK."

I left the room wondering how I'd done. The screening and interview process was an incredible experience. Later, a senior chief came out and told me, "That was the best interview I've ever seen."

"But I've only been in the Teams two and a half years."

"You've got enough real-world experience. I'm sure that'll play into it."

If I hadn't been a player in Desert Storm, I probably would've had to wait another two and a half years.

Two weeks later, Skipper Norm Carley called Smudge, DJ, and me into his office. He gave us our date to start Green Team, the selection and training to become a SEAL Team Six operator. "Congratulations. I hate to see you men go, but you're going to have a blast at SEAL Team Six."

PART TWO

It's a whole lot better to go up the river with seven studs than a hundred s***heads.

—Colonel Charlie A. Beckwith,

ARMY DELTA FORCE FOUNDER

8.
SEAL TEAM SIX

Green Team was a selection course—some of us would fail. Most of us were in our thirties. I was exactly thirty. The instructors timed our runs and swims. We practiced land warfare, parachuting, and diving—all taken to a whole new level. For example, we probably did around a hundred and fifty parachute jumps within four weeks: free-falling, HAHO, canopy stacking, etc. Our curriculum included free-climbing, unarmed combat, defensive and offensive driving, and Survival, Evasion, Resistance, and Escape (SERE). Although we spent a little time on skills such as how to break into a car and how to start it with a screwdriver, we spent more time on how to maneuver the vehicle and shoot from it. The instructors evaluated us and ranked everything we did, including an overall score and ranking.

The easiest part for me was the O-course, and the hardest part was John Shaw's shooting range practicing close-quarters combat. More than learning how to pick a lock open, we learned how to blow the door off its hinges. We shot thousands of rounds every day. I was told that in one year, SEAL Team Six alone spent more money just on 9 mm ammunition than the entire Marine Corps spent on all its ammunition.

I learned CQC at a whole new level. Even though I was already a SEAL, I hadn't done it like SEAL Team Six does it. During one drill, we had to enter a room, engage the targets, shuffle-shoot, sprint, and shoot a stop target. The instructors constantly reconfigured the rooms: big, small, square, rectangle, enemy, friendly. They constantly reconfigured the furniture inside the rooms, too. We were constantly under scrutiny; the instructors showed us recordings of our performance on video.

Bobby Z., a tall blond-haired kid, and I were always within a couple of seconds of each other. Sometimes we were so close that I felt the blast of his muzzle blow my hair—this was with live ammo. A large gap grew between us and everyone else. After reviewing the video, we saw that Bobby and I didn't slow down while we shuffle-shot side to side. Most people slow down a lot to engage their targets, but we didn't. Bobby kicked my butt on the runs and swims.

While in Green Team, Bobby and I went back and forth in the number one position. I ended up being ranked at number two. Part of the reason for the ranking was that we actually went through a draft. While we were out at John Shaw's shooting school, scouts from Red, Blue, and Gold Team came out to watch us train—getting feedback from the rankings, cadre, and our live performance. They weren't impressed to find out about the guy who came back drunk from a strip club, crashed his car into a bridge, and flew through his windshield.

SEALs constantly work in danger, but Team Six pushed those danger levels higher. In the first years of Six's formation, during CQC training, a Team member stumbled and accidentally squeezed the trigger, shooting Roger Cheuy in the back. Cheuy later died in the hospital due to a staph infection. "Staph" is short for "staphylococcal," and that strain of bacteria produces toxins similar to those in food poisoning. The Team member was not only kicked out of Six but kicked out of the SEALs. In another incident, a freak CQC accident, a bullet went through one of the partitions in the kill house and entered between the joints in Rich Horn's bullet-resistant vest, killing him. In a parachuting mishap, Gary Hershey died, too.

Six months after my Green Team started, four or five men had failed out of thirty. Although we had some injuries, none of them were fatal. Red, Blue, and Gold made their first picks of the draft. Red Team picked me up in the first round. Just like the NFL draft. Similar to the Washington Redskins, Red Team's logo was the American Indian—some activists may find it offensive, but we embraced the bravery and fighting skills of the Indians.

Just because I got drafted in the first round didn't mean I got treated better in the Team. I became an assault member just like everybody else. My boat crew was one of four. I was still the F-ing New Guy (FNG). Never mind I'd been in combat and some of them hadn't. I would have to earn their respect.

Now I belonged to a cover organization with an official commander, address, and secretary to answer the phone. When applying for a credit card, I couldn't very well tell them I worked for SEAL Team Six. Instead, I gave them the information for my cover organization. I showed up to work in civilian clothes, rather than a uniform. Nobody breathed the words "SEAL Team Six" back then.

Even after passing Green Team and gaining acceptance to Team Six, we continued to hone our shooting skills at John Shaw's Mid-South Institute of Self-Defense Shooting in Lake Cormorant, Mississippi. He had a huge range with left-to-right, pop-up, and other targets. His kill house was top of the line. Eight of us from Red Team went there to train. On the first Friday night we were there, the eight of us went out to a strip bar across the river in Tennessee. Our designated driver was a non-SEAL radio geek assigned to the Team as support. His name was Willie, but we called him Wee Wee. He read a lot and hardly ever said more than three words. Wee Wee wouldn't join us inside, so he waited outside in the van and read a book. The Team van was black with blacked-out windows. It had government Virginia plates and upgraded suspension. The seats were customized and carried eight people comfortably. Team Six had vehicles with armor, bullet-resistant windows, run-flat tires, police lights, and a siren behind the grille, and interior pockets for holding weapons, but this was simply a support van to haul personnel and equipment inside the United States. After we'd finished in the bar, Wee Wee drove us away in the van.

At a stoplight, three rednecks in a jacked-up four-wheel-drive truck with dual exhausts stopped next to us. They saw short, skinny Wee Wee wearing Clark Kent glasses as he drove with his windows down partway but couldn't see the eight of us through the blacked-out windows in back. "Hey, Yankee bastard," yelled one of the rednecks. "Go home!" Never mind that our Virginia license plate came from a state that fought with the South during the Civil War—home of the South's general Robert E. Lee.

One of our guys in the back shouted, "F*** you, redneck!"

The light turned green. Wee Wee drove forward until he came to the next red light and stopped. The rednecks stopped beside us again.

"Hey, you little skinny bastard. You're all mouth, aren't you?" They thought Wee Wee had mouthed off to them.

"Hey, hillbilly," one of us shot back. "How do you feel knowing your father and mother were brother and sister?"

Now the rednecks were pissed. "Pull over, you skinny bastard." They spit tobacco out of their windows. "We'll teach you a lesson."

Wee Wee now had beads of perspiration breaking out on his forehead as he pushed his glasses higher on his nose. We were holding our breath to keep from laughing our asses off and letting them know we were in the van. Someone whispered, "Wee Wee, pull over up here."

Wee Wee drove a couple of miles and pulled over on the side of an on-ramp heading to the interstate highway.

The dumb rednecks followed and stopped next to us. They taunted Wee Wee to get out of the van. "What's wrong, Yankee?" they yelled. "Did your mouth write a check your ass can't cash?"

We stacked on the roll-out door like we would for an entrance to assault terrorists. I had my hand on the door handle with half the guys stacked on each side of me. Three of us would exit and peel left, and three would exit and peel right. "Wee Wee, tell them to come over to the roll-out door." Wee Wee convinced the rednecks to come to the other side of the van so they would be out of traffic.

The rednecks walked around to our door. Just as they arrived, I ripped the door open. Like magic, the six of us appeared in a circle around the three rednecks. Their eyes looked like they were about to pop out of their skulls.

One of the rednecks spit out his tobacco. "See. See, John. I told you. I told you one day your mouth was going to get us in trouble."

"Hey, dumb-ass, first of all, none of us are Yankees." I gave them a history lesson. "Second, Virginia wasn't a Yankee state. Third, the commanding general of the South, Robert E. Lee, was from Virginia."

It seemed like the rednecks were calming down when John started running his mouth again.

So we decided to teach them a life lesson, not to prey on the apparent weakness of others. Basically, we stomped a mud hole in their asses. To drive the lesson home, one of us told them, "You guys take your pants off."

They looked at us strangely for a moment, but they didn't want another beating, so they stripped down to their underwear.

We took their keys, locked their truck doors, threw their keys into the bushes, and took their shoes and trousers. "Go down to the next exit, stop at the first 7-Eleven on the right, and you'll find your stuff inside the bathroom."

The next morning, we were sitting at John Shaw's range having coffee before starting our shooting drills when a police officer who is one of Shaw's assistant instructors drove up and got out of his police truck. He walked up to us and spoke. We knew him well because we trained with him often and went out drinking with him, too. He was also a Harley-Davidson rider who fit in with us. "I heard the funniest story at about one thirty this morning."

"What's that?" we asked innocently.

"I get a call from the 7-Eleven that three men walked up in their undershorts. The cashier locked the door and wouldn't let them in. The three men claimed they needed to get inside to get their clothes. When I showed up, half the police force showed up with me. And I'll be damned, there were three men standing there in their underwear. We listened to their amazing story. Get this, a blacked-out van with Virginia plates, kind of looks like that one there"—he pointed to our van—"pulled up beside them. Suddenly, eight buff guys, kind of like you guys, surrounded them like Indians on the warpath and beat the crap out of them for no reason. So we let the three inside the 7-Eleven and searched for twenty minutes, but we didn't find their clothes anywhere."

We had been laughing so hard that night that we'd forgotten to stop at the 7-Eleven. Their shoes and clothes were still in the back of the van.

The policeman continued, "Before I left, one of the men said, 'See, John. I told you your mouth was going to get us in trouble.' Then, still in their underwear, two of them started punching John in front of the gas pumps. We broke them up and asked what was meant by 'big mouth getting us in trouble,' but they shut up." The policeman shook his head. "Can you believe such a crazy story?"

None of us said a thing. After an awkward moment, we stood up and began our morning drills.

Later that afternoon, the police officer said, "If somebody's going to be a dumb-ass, sometimes a good ass-whooping is just what they need. Whoever those guys were in the black van might've saved those three men's lives from someone who isn't as patient with rednecks mouthing off."

We nodded our heads in polite agreement.

In spite of being the FNG, I had my eyes on the next challenge: becoming a sniper. I was an adrenaline junkie for sure. SEAL Team Six wanted us to be in our individual color teams for three years before applying to become a sniper.

During the fall of 1992, I requested to go to sniper school. Our Red Team chief, Denny Chalker, told me, "You're a great operator, but you haven't been in the Team long enough. It's an unwritten rule that we want you here three years before you go to sniper school. Besides, your boat crew leader doesn't want to lose you."

Red Team only had two snipers, though, and we needed four to six. My being a hell of a shot didn't hurt matters. A week later, Denny said, "You know what?

We changed our mind—you can do it. We're going to send you and Casanova to sniper school."

Although we would stay in Red Team, we would also become members of Black Team—the snipers. Casanova and I could've chosen from three schools. The SEALs had started their own little sniper school. The army had the Special Operations Target Interdiction Course at Fort Bragg, North Carolina. The Marine Corps had theirs at Quantico, Virginia. I knew the Marine Corps sniper school would be the biggest kick in the nuts—like a mini BUD/S Training—but their school had the longest tradition, the most prestige, and, more importantly, the best reputation in the world.

So I went to Marine Corps Base Quantico, which covers nearly one hundred square miles near the Potomac River in Virginia. Also located on the base are the FBI and Drug Enforcement Administration academies. Tucked away in the corner of the base next to Carlos Hathcock Highway is the Scout Sniper School, the Marine Corps' most demanding school. Among the few accepted to the school, only around 50 percent pass.

The ten-week course included three phases. On day one of Phase One, Marksman and Basic Fields Craft, we took the Physical Fitness Test (PFT), checked in our gear, and handed in our paperwork. Those who failed the PFT were sent home with no second chance.

After the cadre figured out which students stayed, we took our seats inside a cinder-block building with blacked-out windows and one classroom, called the schoolhouse, and received a general briefing about the course.

The next day, a gunny sergeant stood in front of us in the schoolhouse. He looked to be in his early forties with a marine high-and-tight haircut. He was a member of the President's Hundred, the top one hundred civilian and military marksmen in the yearly President's Match pistol and rifle competition. Our instructors also included combat veterans and laid-back gurus, cadre of the highest caliber.

"A sniper has two missions," the gunny sergeant said. "The first is to support combat operations by delivering precision fire on selected targets from concealed positions. The sniper doesn't just go out there shooting any target—he takes out the targets that will help win the battle: officers, noncommissioned officers, scouts, crew-served weapons personnel, tank commanders, communication personnel, and other snipers. His second mission, which will take up much of the sniper's time, is observation. Gathering information."

Out on the range, Casanova and I worked together, alternating between spotter and shooter. For rifles, we had to use the Marine Corps M-40, a Remington 700 bolt-action .308 caliber (7.62 × 51 mm) heavy-barrel rifle that holds five rounds. Mounted on the rifle was a Unertl 10-power sniper scope. I would shoot first, so I made sure the scope was focused. Then I adjusted the bullet drop compensator on my scope to modify for the effect of gravity on the bullet before it reached its target 300 yards away. If I changed distances, I would have to correct my dope again.

Casanova looked through his M-49 20-power spotting scope, mounted on a tripod. Without the tripod, the scope's strong magnification causes the visual to shake with the slightest hand movements. Casanova used the scope to approximate wind speed, which is usually a sniper's greatest weather challenge.

Wind flags can be used to estimate wind speed by their angle. If a flag is at an 80-degree angle, that number is divided by the constant 4—to get 20 miles per hour. Likewise, if the flag only waves at a 40-degree angle, 40 divided by 4 equals 10 miles per hour.

If no flag is available, the sniper can use his observation skills. A wind that is barely felt but causes smoke to drift is less than 3 miles per hour. Light winds are 3 to 5 miles per hour. Wind that constantly blows leaves around is 5 to 8 miles per hour. Dust and trash are blown at 8 to 12 miles per hour. Trees sway at 12 to 15 miles per hour.

A sniper could also use the spotting scope method. When the sun heats the earth, the air near the surface ripples in waves. The wind causes these waves to move in its direction. To see the waves, the sniper focuses on an object near the target. Rotating the eyepiece a quarter turn counterclockwise, he focuses on the area in front of the target area, which makes the heat waves become visible. Slow wind causes big waves, while fast wind flattens them out. This method of recognizing wind speed takes practice.

Winds blowing directly from left to right, or right to

left, have the most effect on a shot. They are called full value winds. Oblique winds from left to right, or right to left, are designated as half value winds. Front to rear, or rear to front, are no value winds—having the least effect.

Casanova gave me the wind speed: "Five miles per hour, full value, left to right." Three-(hundred)-yard range times 5 miles per hour equals 15; 15 divided by the constant 15 equals 1. I adjusted the horizontal reticle in my scope one click to the left. If I had two windage from the right, I'd adjust two clicks to the right.

I took my first shot at a stationary target—hit. After two more shots at stationary targets and two at moving targets, I became spotter while Casanova shot. Then we threw on our packs, grabbed our equipment, and ran back to the 500-yard line. As in the Teams, it paid to be a winner. Again, we alternated between taking five shots each at three stationary and two moving targets. Then we did the same at 600 yards. It's tough to slow the breathing and heart rate down after running. At 700 yards, we hit three stationary targets again, but this time, the two movers would stop and go. At 800 yards, the two stop-and-go movers became bobbers, waving left to right and right to left. At 900 and 1,000 yards, the five targets remained stationary. Out of thirty-five rounds, twenty-eight had to hit the black. We lost a lot of guys on the range. They just couldn't shoot well enough.

After the range, we returned to the schoolhouse and cleaned our weapons before doing a field sketch exercise. The instructors took us out to an area and said,

"Draw a sketch of the area from the left wood line to the water tower on the right. You've got thirty minutes." We drew as many important details as we could, and drew in perspective: Nearby objects are larger than distant objects; horizontal parallel lines converge and vanish in the distance. On the bottom of the sketch, we wrote down what we saw: patrol, number of 2.5-ton trucks (deuce-and-a-halfs), et cetera. The instructors graded us for neatness, accuracy, and intelligence value. Seventy percent or higher was a passing grade. Later, we would only have fifteen minutes.

A sniper also keeps a log to be used with the sketch, so he has a written record of information regarding key terrain, observation, cover and concealment, obstacles, and avenue of approach (summarized as KOCOA) in addition to his pictorial sketch.

We also played Keep in Memory (KIM) games. The instructor would pull back a tarp on a table and expose ten to twelve small items: spent 9 mm cartridge, pencil flare, Ziploc bag, pen, broken pair of glasses, photograph of someone, acorn, and other items that could fit on the tabletop. In ten to fifteen seconds, we had to memorize everything. Then we went into the classroom, grabbed a piece of paper, and drew everything we had seen. Finally, we had to verbally describe what we saw. Sometimes we used scopes and binoculars to report full-sized items at a distance. If, on a routine basis, I couldn't remember 70 percent or more, I'd be kicked out. A basic skill of a sniper is being able to remember and report what he sees. We also had to "burn through" grass and bushes—find an observation post (OP) while grass and bushes obstructed our vision—using the vegetation to cover us from being spotted by the primary observation post.

In Phase Two, Unknown Distance and Stalking, those of us who remained after Phase One ran ten 100-pound steel targets out to distances between 300 and 800 yards. Because we didn't know the exact distance to the targets, we had to estimate. First-shot hits scored ten points. Second-shot hits scored eight. There were no third shots. Upon completion, Casanova and I rearranged the targets and did it again. We had to maintain a 70 percent average over the three weeks of shooting to stay in the school.

In addition to shooting skills, sniper school also taught us about concealment. We had to make our own ghillie suits. First, we prepared our clothing: BDU tops and bottoms. Next, using high-strength thread that wouldn't rot, such as 12-pound fishing line, we attached netting (example: a military hammock or fishing net) to the backs and elbows of our suits. Shoe Goo is even easier to use than needle and thread. Then we cut strips of burlap about 1″ wide and 9″ long and tied them with overhand knots onto the netting. We pulled lengthwise at the material from the end so the burlap frayed. Using a can of spray paint, we colored the burlap. Casanova and I added natural foliage from knee level or lower, which is where a sniper moves. Leaves taken from above would stand out on a sniper crawling low to the ground. We were careful not to add anything too long that might wave around like a flag. Leaves work best because they last the longest without spoiling. Grass spoils the fastest—in around four hours. Around the rifle buttstock, we wrapped an olive drab cravat and tied it off with a square knot to break up the weapon's outline. Another cravat went around the barrel and scope, similar to wrapping an arm with a bandage. Attaching burlap straps broke up the cravat's solid green color. Similarly, we camouflaged the M-49 scope, binoculars, and other gear.

On weekends, our time off, Casanova and I learned and practiced the art of invisibility. We worked on our ghillie suits. Then we wore the suits outside and lay down in different environments, trying to spot each other. Most spare hours were spent honing our invisibility skills.

Stalking caused the most students to fail. The location of each stalk varied, and we had to change our color schemes and textures to blend in. Optics came in handy during the stalk. The naked eye can scan the widest area. Binoculars can be used to take a closer look, yet maintain a relatively wide field of vision. The sniper scope usually allows a slightly closer inspection than the binoculars, but with a narrower field of vision. The spotting scope magnifies the greatest, allowing the sniper to investigate objects closely; however, the field of view is the narrowest.

The closer a sniper gets to the target, the more slowly he moves. At two miles to a target, the sniper stalks smoothly and quickly from cover to cover for a mile. He becomes stealthier for the next half mile, adjusting to how much cover and concealment the terrain provides. Within the last half mile to the target, the sniper's movement becomes painstakingly careful—crawling low to the ground. The right hand only moves forward one foot in thirty seconds. Then the left hand moves forward just as slowly.

Sometimes previous stalkers leave a trail. The advantage of using their trail is that they already smashed down vegetation, saving precious seconds of easing each bush or blade of grass down.

Within three to four hours, we had to stalk a distance of 800 to 1,200 yards, arriving within 200 yards of the Observer in an OP. If the Observer spotted us with his spotter scope before we got within two hundred yards of our position, we only got forty points out of one hundred—failure.

If the Observer saw a bush move, he'd call one of the Walkers on the radio. "Walker, turn left. Go three yards. Stop. Turn right. One yard. Stop. Sniper at your feet." Any sniper within a one-foot radius of the Walker was busted. Those who were busted usually hadn't made it within 200 yards of him. The sniper stood up with his gun and walked to the bus. Fifty points—failure.

Upon reaching our final firing position, within 200 yards of the Observer, we had to set up our weapon and fire a blank at the Observer. If the sniper couldn't properly ID the Observer, give correct windage or elevation, or shoot from a stable shooting platform, sixty points—failure. If we *could* do all that, but the Observer spotted the muzzle blast, he'd talk the Walker to our position and bust us. Seventy points—a minimum pass.

If the Observer didn't see the shot, the Walker shouted out to the general area where he believed the sniper to be, "Fire the second shot!"

Most people got busted because the Observer saw brush movement from the muzzle blast on the second shot. Eighty points.

The final part of the stalk was to see if the sniper could observe a signal from the Observer. If the blast of the second shot moved the medium being shot through, such as twigs, grass, or whatever, and the sniper couldn't see the Observer's signal—ninety points.

"Target is patting himself on the head," I said.

The Walker radioed the Observer, "Sniper says you're patting yourself on top of the head."

"Yep, good stalk. Stand up. Go to the bus." Perfect stalk—one hundred points. We needed at least two perfect stalks out of ten, in addition to an overall average of 70 percent or better.

Even in fall, at 70 degrees, Quantico was still hot as hell while under the sun wearing a ghillie suit, pulling gear in a drag bag, and painstakingly creeping low on the ground. People dehydrated. After finishing the stalk, we had to go back and beat the bushes to find those who had passed out. We carried them back to the barracks.

Casanova and I stayed in a hotel room off base, while the marines stayed in the barracks across the street from sniper school. We were still on call. If our pagers went off and we had to bug out, we could leave without a lot of people wondering what was going on. Boy, we were prima donnas, having the best of everything—flying first class and renting a car for each pair of men. In our hotel room following a stalk, I had to check Casanova on the places he couldn't check himself for ticks, which might cause Lyme disease. Left untreated,

Lyme disease attacks the central nervous system. Casanova did the same for me. Nothing more intimate than having your buddy use tweezers to pull a tick out from around your anus.

It took me three or four stalks before the lights went on in my brain: *Now I see what they're trying to get me to do. Keep my overhead movement down. No shine, glare, or glitter.* During one of my earlier stalks, I crept through a field of new wheatgrass. A kid came flying past me.

"Man, you're moving too fast," I whispered.

"I saw the Observer in my binoculars. He hasn't had time to set up yet. I'm going to sprint up here and make up some distance before he starts looking for us."

Dumb-ass.

He cut right in front of me—moving way too fast in a low crawl.

Damn.

"All snipers, freeze," a Walker said.

We froze.

The Observer talked the Walker within a foot in front of me.

The kid was five feet ahead of me because he'd moved so fast.

"Sniper at your feet," came the voice over the Walker's radio.

"Yep. Stand up, Wasdin."

You sonofabitch. What could I do? Go whining back to the instructor and say, "It really wasn't me"?

Forty points. That hurt. Especially for the early stalks, every point mattered. I considered the possibility that I might fail because of this. It didn't please me to imagine showing up at Dam Neck, Virginia, saying I failed sniper school.

Although the kid's tactic was theoretically sound, doing it at my expense was unwise. Needless to say, I had a meeting with the kid back at the compound. "If you think that's a good call because you see the instructor is not ready, you make it, but don't you ever come crawling up beside me or in front of me like that again. If you get me busted again, we're going to have a different type of conversation."

He never made the same mistake again, and he graduated sniper school with my class.

Even after a sniper had enough points to pass, if he got busted on the same thing over and over, the instructors would fail him regardless of his score. Some guys failed because they couldn't make their ghillie suit blend in with the environment around them.

Dude, we've had this class for a month now. We've been working on these suits since before we got to this course. Why can't you go out there and look at the terrain and make your suit match it?

Some guys could make their suits match the environment but couldn't stay flat. I saw so many asses in the air. Guys would crawl up next to a tree and think that the tree made them invisible. The instructors called it "tree cancer." Their eyes would follow a tree down—linear, linear, bump at the bottom. *What's that tree got—a cancerous nodule there?* Fail.

There was a lot more to sniping than just making a long-range shot. An Olympic shooter who could make the shot but couldn't make the stalk wouldn't be a sniper. At around stalks seven, eight, and nine, the instructors called out certain people. Even if those students could've made perfect scores on their final stalks, they wouldn't have enough points to pass sniper school. We never saw them again.

I ended up with a total of eight hundred to eight hundred and fifty points out of one thousand—including the points I lost for the kid's impatience.

Phase Three, Advanced Field Skills and Mission Employment, included a final op. Regardless of how well we did on the shooting range, sketches, KIM games, or stalks, we had to pass the final three-day op. The instructors expected a high level of maturity and independence from us. Snipers often work in pairs without direct supervision. They must be capable of making decisions themselves, which includes decisions to adapt in a fluid environment.

Under cover of night, during the final op, Casanova and I arrived at our FFP and made our sniper hide. First, we dug down four to six inches, carefully removed the topsoil and grass, and laid it to the side. Next, we dug a pit approximately 6′ × 6′ wide and 5′ deep. At the bottom of the pit, Casanova and I dug a sump about 2′ long, 1.5′ wide, and 1′ deep, sloped at 45 degrees to drain any rainwater or unwanted grenades. Also, to prevent the rain from caving in our hole, we lined the top rim of the pit with sandbags. Then we cleared away an area near the top of the hole where we could rest our elbows while spotting and sniping. After that, we covered our hole with logs, rain ponchos, rocks, dirt, and the sod we had placed to the side earlier. Finally, we created a rear exit hole, camouflaging it with fallen tree branches.

Inside the exit hole, we placed a claymore mine to welcome any guests.

We kept a log of everything that went on at the target area, a house in the middle of nowhere with vehicles around it. A patrol walked over us but couldn't see us. At one-hour intervals, Casanova and I alternated between spotting and sniping. We ate, slept, and relieved ourselves in the hole. The hard part was keeping one of us awake while the other slept. At night, we had to get out and go take a look at the back of the house. Listening to our radio at the designated time, we received a shoot window—the time frame for taking out the target: "The man in the red hat will appear at oh two hundred on November 8. Take him out." A man with a blue hat showed up. Wrong target.

Before the op, Casanova and I prepared a range card, shaped like a protractor, of the target area. Upon arrival at our FFP, we modified it by adding details such as dominant terrain features and other objects. We divided the card into three sectors: A, B, and C. Using prearranged arm and hand signals, Casanova motioned that our target had arrived in Sector B, 1200 on a clock face, 500 yards away. Then he pointed at the location on the range card.

I acknowledged with a thumbs-up, having already dialed in my dope. My crosshairs rested on the chest of the mannequin with a red hat standing in front of a window. If I missed, I wouldn't graduate sniper school. Casanova would still get his chance to make the shot, but I would fail. I calmly squeezed the trigger. Bull's-eye. After taking the shot, we stealthily exfiltrated to our pickup point, which required land navigation with a map and compass—no GPS.

Back at the schoolhouse, Casanova and I gave a brief about what we saw on the way in, what we saw on the way out, and when we saw it. We used photographs and field sketches in our presentation. The possibility of failing sniper school still loomed over us.

The major told us, "You two gave an excellent brief. Your FFP was outstanding—one of the better ones I've seen. I personally walked on top of it. Your briefing technique was superb." We breathed a sigh of relief. Of course our briefing technique was outstanding—we'd been doing it since BUD/S.

Unfortunately for the other sniper students, we were first, and ours was a tough act to follow. I looked around the room, and the marines were not looking forward to giving their briefs. One young marine was an excellent marksman, but the major reamed him so much that I felt bad for him. He had reenlisted to become a sniper. Both he and his partner were caught sleeping at the same time instead of keeping at least one awake in shifts. The lane graders busted them on their exfil. Their briefing technique showed no delivery skills. If a sniper can't communicate what he saw, his information is useless. In the world of snipers, we call men like the two young marines "great trigger pullers." Lots of people can pull a trigger. He and his partner would not be attending our graduation.

Dressed in our BDUs, we had an informal graduation. One at a time, our names were called to receive the diploma and the patch our class had designed. Until that point, we couldn't have the patch, let alone wear it. Ours was cool: a skull with a hood and sniper crosshairs in the right eye—silver on black. In script on the bottom it read: THE DECISION IS MINE. A sniper decides the time and place for his target's demise. The major awarded me my diploma. It wasn't the diploma I wanted so much. *Just give me my patch.* He gave it to me. Our class also gave certificates of appreciation and copies of our patches to each of our instructors. They really earned them.

After sniper school, I returned home to Red Team, but I would only have a little time to spend with my family. At work, I immediately started learning how to shoot the .300 Win Mag with the Leupold 10-power scope. Going from shooting the marine 7.62 mm sniper rifle to shooting SEAL Team Six's .300 Win Mag was like going from racing a bus to racing a Ferrari.

The KN-250 was our night-vision scope for the same weapon. Night vision amplifies available light from sources like the moon and stars, converting images into green and light green instead of black and white. The result lacks depth and contrast but enables the sniper to see at night.

Then we took a trip to Fort Bragg, North Carolina, and began learning how to shoot the sound-suppressed CAR-15 while strapping ourselves outside helicopters on special chairs, like bar-stool swivel chairs with backs, attached to the helo's skids. Getting up to speed on everything took a lot of time. This extended to communications—learning how to use the LST satellite radio with a special keyboard for sending encrypted burst transmissions.

Casanova, Little Big Man, Sourpuss, and I flew Down Under to train with the Australian Special Air Service. The flight took forever. We flew commercial, business class, from America's east coast to the west coast. Then we flew to Hawaii. From Hawaii, we landed at Sydney Airport on Australia's east coast. From there we flew across the continent to arrive in Perth, on the west coast. It was the longest flight of my life—worst jet lag I ever had.

In Perth, outside the Campbell Barracks, home of the Australian SAS, stood a monument to every Australian SAS soldier killed in the line of duty during training or combat—nearly forty names, many of them killed in training accidents. Inside the barracks, we stored our weapons in their safes, and they gave us a tour. In the evening, we stayed in town at a hotel on the Swan River. Although Sydney was the more popular destination, Perth cost less, had fewer tourists, and was prettier.

The Australian SAS sand-colored berets each bore a patch showing a metallic gold and silver winged dagger overlaid on a black shield. The major responsibilities of the Australian SAS—similar to the British SAS, which heavily influenced the creation of SEAL Team Six and Delta—included counterterrorism and reconnaissance (sea, air, and land). SEALs have a history of working with the Australian SAS that goes back to the Vietnam War.

When we hit the shooting range, the Australians focused on fast-moving targets at distances of 200 yards. We had trained more on longer-range static targets. They had semiautomatic .308 sniper rifles, while we used our bolt action Win Mags. When sets of four targets whipped past us, we manually operated the bolt-action to load each new round in our rifles, only able to take down half of our targets. Meanwhile, the SAS just kept pulling their triggers, the gas operation automatically loading each new round, as they knocked down all their targets. We sucked booty. I realized that in a fast-moving environment like urban warfare, it's a good idea to have someone with a semiautomatic .308 for the 200- to 400-yard range. Our automatic CAR-15s were maxed out at the 200-yard range.

When we went out to 500 and 700 yards, it was the Aussies' turn to suck booty. Their semiautomatics lost accuracy at longer range, while our bolt action rifles retained accuracy. We also had better optics.

I drilled a target at 725 yards. The SAS guy behind me called on the radio, "Did he hit that one?"

"Yes."

I fired again.

"Did he hit that one?"

"Yes."

Again and again and again . . . He shook his head, and that evening we went to a bar where he bought me a Red Back beer, an Australian wheat beer named after the infamous Australian female spider that eats the male while mating—and has been known to bite humans, injecting them with its neurotoxic venom. It's a popular beer among the Australian SAS. "Excellent rifle, mate," he said.

Days later, with ammo locked and loaded in our sound-suppressed CAR-15s, we ventured into the outback for ten days. One night, on a 20,000-acre ranch, we loaded onto the SAS assault Range Rovers. Each vehicle had a special ram over the front grille where a shaped explosive charge could be attached to blow open a door on contact. Then the operators could jump off of the vehicle's rails and assault the building—an impressive assault to watch. The Range Rover could also drop smoke from the rear to cover its escape. While driving, we shot moving targets: kangaroos. The kangaroos would graze on the rancher's land, threatening to destroy the fragile landscape, leaving little for his livestock to eat, and spreading disease. In contrast to cuddly stuffed kangaroos, especially when provoked or cornered, a wild kangaroo can grab a human with its front claws and disembowel him with its powerful rear claws.

Casanova, Little Big Man, Sourpuss, and I used NODs and Insight Technology AN/PEQ series infrared lasers mounted on our CAR-15s. Shooting from a moving vehicle at running targets is tough. I moved my laser with the kangaroos. From the SEAL vehicle, our guns went *pow-pow-pow-pow-pow-pow*.

Four SAS guys rode in their Range Rover. *Pow.*

The SEAL Range Rover sounded like the American Revolution. *Pow-pow-pow-pow-pow-pow.*

The Australians went *Pow.*

TOP LEFT: SAR training. *(Courtesy U.S. Navy)*

TOP RIGHT: "Drownproofing" in BUD/S. *(Courtesy U.S. Navy)*

BOTTOM: Howard, graduating from BUD/S.

TOP: Aiming an MP-5N while maintaining security on the upper deck of a ship for training. *(Courtesy U.S. Navy)*

BOTTOM: Inside an H-3 helicopter before an actual assault on an enemy ship.

TOP: Howard, reenlisting during sniper training.

BOTTOM LEFT: Howard's ghillie suit during sniper training at Quantico, Virginia.

BOTTOM RIGHT: Sniper class patch.

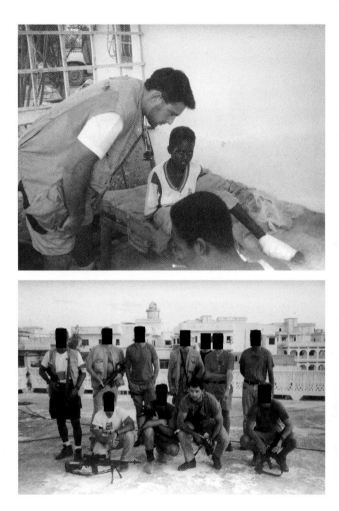

TOP: Helping a child with an amputated leg.

BOTTOM: Pasha team: *(kneeling in front, left to right)* Little Big Man, Casanova, Howard, and Sourpuss.

TOP: Howard, on the roof of Pasha, wielding an AT-4.

BOTTOM: The view from a Pakistani tower—Otto Osman's house and garage are in the distance. *(Osman's house circled in white)*

TOP: The woman on the left carries a baby, while the woman on the right pretends to carry a baby but is really carrying mortar rounds to supply Aidid.

MIDDLE: SEAL Humvee. *(Courtesy U.S. Navy)*

BOTTOM: Confiscated enemy small arms and crew weapons. *(Courtesy Department of Defense)*

TOP: K-4 Circle where Little Big Man was shot.
(Courtesy Department of Defense)

BOTTOM: U.S. peacekeepers under attack in Somalia.
(Courtesy Department of Defense)

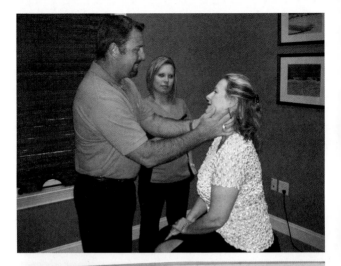

TOP: Howard in his clinic adjusting a patient.

BOTTOM: Howard's wife, Debbie, with Howard and their children, Blake and Eryn.

We fired six times for every one of their shots. *Pow-pow-pow-pow-pow-pow.*

The SAS thought we did a lot of spraying and praying—until we surveyed the damage, and they saw the carcasses surrounding us. For every kangaroo they killed, we killed six. "Wow, you SEALs have some good toys."

The next day, the rancher came out and saw the carnage. "You boys did excellent work. Thank you!" He looked ready to give us an Australian high five.

Back at their headquarters, we sat in a beautiful meeting room. The operators poured us some of their own SAS-regiment-label port wine from their SAS winery. Over drinks, one of the soldiers told us that he'd operated out of the same camp during the First Gulf War as the British SAS unit Bravo Two Zero, which was an eight-man team sent to operate in enemy territory to report enemy positions and destroy targets such as fiber-optic communication lines. During the second day of their operation, a farmer driving a bulldozer spotted them. The SAS let him go instead of detaining or killing him.

Over the next few days, Bravo Two Zero survived several firefights before becoming separated. Iraqi civilian fighters killed Robert Consiglio. Vincent Phillips and Steven Lane died of hypothermia. The Iraqis captured Andy McNab, Ian Pring, Malcolm MacGown, and Mike Coburn (New Zealand SAS), who were later released. Chris Ryan evaded Iraqi troops for eight days, trekking over 200 miles to Syria, the longest escape and evasion by any soldier. During the thirty minutes of telling us the story, the SAS operator became teary-eyed, seeming to know one or more of the operators who died. His main message to us was, "If you're ever compromised, it's better to kill or tie up the person who sees you than to let him go."

The Australian SAS treated us well. They taught us some stuff, and we taught them some stuff. We were all better for it—which is why exchanges are so beneficial. As General George Patton once said, "Thorough preparation makes its own luck."

9.

BORN-AGAIN SNIPER

After General Garrison had thrown the BS flag on all of JSOC's snipers, both SEAL and Delta operators, we saw the light: There's no way we could make that 800-yard shot every time under any condition—one of us was so far off that he hit the windowsill. We repented of our sins by spending a month coming up with what we could actually do every single time regardless of climate, time of day, fatigue (which plays a big part), slant, elevation, country, hemorrhoids, etc. Shooting on rainy days, cold days, crawling out of the sewer—we tried it all. We were born again, "We can make a body shot on land at five hundred yards every single time under every condition." Each day, every sniper would go to the range and shoot his ten rounds—and he better have a killing shot: eight out of ten in the outer five-ring and at least two in the inner four-ring on an FBI-regulation target.

SEAL Team Six held a shoot-off to determine its best sniper. Out of the eighteen snipers there, I came in first.

That didn't go over well with the snipers who'd been around longer than I had. Country, who had been in Team Six a year longer than me, came in second. From Alabama, he was a big, fun-loving good ol' boy with sandy brown hair who often spoke in his native southern drawl about hunting—what he killed, how he prepared it, and how it tasted. Probably started hunting when he was ten years old. Unlike me, he had more shooting experience from childhood. That experience can be a double-edged sword, though. Some snipers have to unlearn bad habits.

SEAL Team Six sent Country and me as a two-man team to the big sniper competition on the Delta compound in North Carolina. Each of the other SEAL Teams also sent their best two. So did Delta, Ranger (a rapid army light infantry unit that can fight against conventional and special operations targets) battalions, FBI Hostage Rescue Team (HRT), Secret Service, the local Cumberland County Sheriff's Department, and others.

Each morning at the Delta range, we started out doing a cold-bore shot from 200 yards on a clay pigeon, a small target made of pitch and pulverized limestone rock in the size and shape of an inverted saucer, taped on a white silhouette target. For Country and me, it was an easy shot. When the bullet struck, the clay pigeon sprayed into dust. Everybody who missed had to buy a case of beer. The FBI and Secret Service snipers bought a case of beer almost every day.

We also did an unknown-distance cold-bore shot—the hardest—using no laser range finder. After the target popped up, we identified it as friend or foe, shooting enemies before they ducked out of sight. In slant range shooting, we shot from high in a building down to a target—requiring a calculation different from other shots.

In another event we had to run to a position, set up in a sniper hide, and shoot. Country ran up the four-story building with my rifle and set it up. I ascended the stairs behind him. Because I didn't have the extra weight of my weapon, when I arrived in position, I could calm down my breathing more quickly—within a few seconds. Clearing my mind to think about nothing had become automatic. I squeezed off the shot at a target across from me in another building—bull's-eye.

Our long-range event ranged from 500 to 750 yards to the target. Only a few teams could really compete at that distance: SEAL Team Six, Delta, some Rangers, and the Department of Energy (DoE) nuclear power plant (they had great training and equipment) sniper pairs.

Country and I became the top sniper team at the competition—until the morning of the last day. We finished some preliminary shots. I spotted one target for Country, and he engaged it. Then I spotted another target.

Country had his crosshairs on the target, and as he squeezed the trigger, the hostage target moved. "Damn!"

"What?" I asked.

"I think I just grazed the Hotel." "*Hotel*" meant hostage.

If we had not shot at all, we would have scored zero points, still having enough points to win the competition. Even though it wasn't a killing shot, we still lost ten points for nicking a hostage. The winning sniper pair included a Ranger who had gone to marine sniper school with me in Quantico. I think Delta came in second. The Savannah River Department of Energy sniping team placed third. Do not mess with DoE nuclear sites.

Even though Country and I lost big points for that mistake, we still finished fourth overall. In the Teams, though, fourth only means third-place loser. Country and I were not pleased. The FBI HRTs and Secret Service finished last—even behind the good ol' boys from the local sheriff's department. Even so, it's better to make mistakes during training and learn from them. For me, the next shots would be for real.

10.

CIA SAFE HOUSE—HUNTING FOR AIDID

Less than half a year after Casanova and I finished sniper school, we received a mission: Capture warlord Mohamed Farrah Aidid and his lieutenants. Educated in Moscow and Rome, Aidid served in the Italian colonial police force before entering the military and becoming a general of the Somalian Army. Aidid's clan (Habar Gidir), Ali Mahdi Muhammad's clan (Abgaal), and other clans overthrew Somalia's dictator. Then the two clans fought each other for control of Somalia. Twenty thousand Somalis were killed or injured, and agricultural production came to a halt. Although the international community sent food, particularly the UN under Operation Restore Hope, Aidid's militia stole much of it—extorting or killing people who wouldn't cooperate—and traded the food with other countries for weapons. Starvation deaths skyrocketed to hundreds of thousands of people, and the suffering rose higher still. Although other Somali leaders tried to reach a peace agreement, Aidid would have none of it.

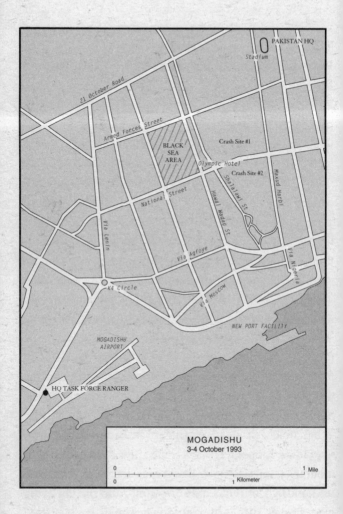

Labels visible on map:

PAKISTAN HQ
Stadium
21 October Road
Armed Forces Street
BLACK SEA AREA
Crash Site #1
Olympic Hotel
Crash Site #2
National Street
Hawai Wadag St.
Shalalawi St.
Maxud Harbi
Via Lenin
Via Agfoye
Via Nigeria
K4 Circle
Via Moscow
NEW PORT FACILITY
MOGADISHU AIRPORT
HQ TASK FORCE RANGER

MOGADISHU
3-4 October 1993

0   1 Mile
0   1 Kilometer

June 5, 1993

A Pakistani force, part of the UN humanitarian team, went to investigate an arms depot at a radio station. There Aidid's people gathered outside in protest. The Pakistani troops went in and completed their inspection. When they came out of the building, the protesters attacked, killing twenty-four Pakistani soldiers. Aidid's people, including women and children, celebrated by dismembering, disemboweling, and skinning the Pakistanis.

Admiral Jonathan Howe, Special Representative for Somalia to the United Nations, was horrified. He put a $25,000 warrant out on Aidid for information leading to his arrest. Howe also pushed hard for JSOC assistance.

August 8, 1993

Aidid's people used a command-detonated mine to kill four American military policemen. Enough was enough. President Bill Clinton gave JSOC the green light. The task force would include four of us from SEAL Team Six, Delta Force, Rangers, Task Force 160, and others. Task Force 160, nicknamed the "Night Stalkers," provided the helicopter support that usually operated at night, flying fast and low (to avoid radar detection). We would conduct Operation Gothic Serpent in three phases: First, deploy to Mogadishu and set up a base; Second, go after Aidid; and Third, if we didn't succeed in apprehending Aidid, go after his lieutenants.

* * *

At the Team compound in Dam Neck, Virginia, Little Big Man, Sourpuss, Casanova, and I joined in getting ready to go to Somalia: training, prepping our gear, growing beards, and letting our hair grow out. Part of prepping our gear meant going to the encryption room and coding our radios for secure voice. It was time-consuming because we had to enter a lot of codes, and they had to be the same for every handheld radio. We decided what the common frequency would be. As a sniper, I had to communicate with Casanova, my partner, and the two of us had to communicate with the other sniper pair, Little Big Man and Sourpuss. Then we all had to be able to communicate with our forward operating base. I made sure my E&E kit was complete and I had bribe/survival cash. Then I test-fired my weapons one last time. Not knowing exactly what we'd be tasked to do, we prepared for everything.

After completing our preparations, we flew down to Fort Bragg, North Carolina, where the Army Special Operations Command and others sit on more than 150,000 acres of hills and scattered evergreens near Fayetteville. There we received more specific information about our mission.

We brought stacked cases of food. "You won't be needing that," an army officer told us. "We'll be bringing plenty of food."

So we left the food at the Delta compound.

Instructors from the Defense Language Institute taught us important phrases in Somali: *stop, get down, walk backward toward my voice, hurry,* etc.

After a few days, we were told the op might be called off, so we flew back to Dam Neck.

Then a Delta officer phoned us. "The op is on, but you won't need long hair and beards."

So we got shaves and haircuts and flew back to Fort Bragg.

August 27, 1993

We boarded one of six C-5A Galaxy cargo planes carrying Task Force Ranger. After eighteen hours in the air, we landed at Mogadishu Airfield within the UN compound south of Mogadishu. Egyptian peacekeepers guarded the outer perimeter. Inside the compound were peacekeeping forces from Italy, New Zealand, Romania, and Russia. West of the landing strip stood an old aircraft hangar where we would stay. Beyond the hangar stood a two-story building with a lopsided roof—the Joint Operations Center (JOC). Antennas poked out of the roof like spines on a porcupine.

An army officer escorted Sourpuss, Little Big Man, Casanova, and me behind the JOC to General Garrison's personal trailer. Inside, Garrison had no visible family photos or knickknacks; at a moment's notice he could leave without a trace. His aide had just awakened him for our arrival. Garrison took one look at the four of us and said, "Hey, how come you all got your hair cut? I wanted it long, so you could go out in town and operate."

"We were told that you wanted us to cut our hair, sir." We suspected that Delta had tried to disqualify us from the op. Go Army, beat Navy.

General Garrison gave the op to us anyway. "The

four of you are going to be the hinge pin of the operation," he said, then filled us in.

After meeting with Garrison, we hooked up with Signals Intelligence (SIGINT), run by a CIA communications officer. Their team would gather information by intercepting signals between people (communications intelligence) and electronic signals emitted from enemy technology such as radios, radars, surface-to-air missile systems, aircraft, ships, etc. (electronic intelligence). SIGINT deciphered encrypted information in addition to conducting traffic analysis: studying who was signaling whom and how much. They could intercept cell phones and radio communications, as well as use directional microphones to pick up conversations from great distances. Most of our SIGINT team spoke two or three languages, and they had aircraft dedicated to their mission.

Next, we went up to the CIA trailer on top of the hill and met the CIA operations officer, a black Vietnam veteran code-named Condor. Senior to him was the deputy chief of station, an Italian American code-named Leopard. They answered to the thickly built, thick-mustached CIA chief of station, Garrett Jones, code-named Crescent. In the Teams, we often refer to the CIA as "Christians in Action," and the CIA sometimes uses the same nickname when referring to themselves. In Somalia, the Christians in Action had their work cut out for them—it's hard to steal a government's secrets where there is no government.

Before our arrival, Washington hadn't allowed the CIA to operate in town, considering it too dangerous. With us on the scene, the spooks could penetrate into downtown Mogadishu. The CIA gave us an excellent briefing about Mogadishu, including some culture and history. They also code-named us in order of rank: Sierra One, Sourpuss; Sierra Two, Little Big Man; Sierra Three, me; and Sierra Four, Casanova. Our safe house would be called Pasha, the title of a high-ranking person in the Ottoman Empire. Ahmed would serve as our interpreter. Behind his round-framed glasses, his eyes seldom looked directly at me when he talked—Ahmed always seemed nervous. Our main Somali operative was Mohammed. Constantly risking his life, he was always serious.

After meeting with the CIA up on the hill, we returned to the hangar and requisitioned four AT-4s, tear gas (CS) grenades, flashbangs, and fragmentation grenades. Also, we requested an SST-181 beacon so aircraft flying overhead could get a fix on our area if they needed to. We had to prepare to defend the safe house in case the enemy attacked—and prepare our escape in case they overran us.

That night, we stayed in the hangar with the rest of the American military, about 160 men in all. Each soldier had a $4' \times 8'$ place to call his own. On my cot, four wooden poles stood up, one in each corner, to drape a net on to keep the mosquitoes out. Hawks swooped down and caught rats the size of small dogs, flying them back up to the rafters for dinner. Sections of the tin walls had space between them, allowing Mother Nature in. The hangar doors were stuck open. Beyond the doors, helicopters sat quietly on the tarmac, filling the air with the smell of fuel. The elevation inland rose, and I could see lights and fires in Mogadishu. Behind us an American flag hung from the rafters. I could taste the salt in the air from the ocean behind our hangar. Despite the luxurious accommodations, our four-man team wouldn't be staying long. Aidid sent three mortar rounds near the hangar to wish us good night. Someone wisely turned out the hangar lights.

August 28, 1993

Saturday, we encrypted our PRC-112 handheld survival radios before gearing up. Outside, the tarmac simmered under our feet as we walked to our helicopter. I put on my Oakley sunglasses. The best sunglasses tone down the sun's glare and protect my eyes from debris, helping my sense of peace. They also make eye contact impossible. Sunglasses can disguise identity, be intimidating to others, project detachment, and hide emotions. Like a good friend, a good pair of sunglasses is hard to forget.

Some Delta boys were on board the chopper ready to take off on a training flight.

The Task Force 160 helicopter pilots, among the best in the world, told Delta, "Hey, sorry, we got a real-world op. You know, you need to let these guys on."

Delta unassed the helicopter. They were not happy. "Heaven forbid; we wouldn't want to stand in the way of a *real-world op*."

We boarded the chopper. "Tell you about it when we get back." The four of us, two sitting in the doorway on each side with our legs dangling out, buckled our gunner's belts, and the helicopter lifted off. The Delta operators became smaller and smaller as we gained altitude.

The chopper flew us inland so we could look for routes and alternate routes to drive to and from our safe house. Sunshine and war had blasted much of the color out of Mogadishu. The only structures held sacred by both sides in the civil war had been the Islamic mosques—among the few buildings standing unmolested. Many of the other major buildings had been destroyed. People lived in mud huts with tin roofs in a maze of dirt roads. Hills of broken concrete, twisted metal, and trash rose from the landscape, with charred car frames scattered about. Militiamen wielding AK-47s rode in the back of a speeding pickup truck. Fires steadily burned from piles of rubbish, metal drums, and tires. It looked like flames from hell.

Turning back toward the ocean, we scouted out possible landing zones near our safe house—just in case we had to call in a helo to get out in a hurry. During our flyover, we also checked the seashore for possible locations where we could be extracted by boat. Light brown and white sand bordered the emerald sea. It would've been the perfect setting for a vacation resort.

After coming back down to earth from our reconnaissance, we drove a Humvee from the compound through a secret hole in the back fence and up the hill to a trailer where the CIA gave us a human intelligence (HUMINT) brief. Technological gizmos and doodads are useful in the spy game, but they mean little without brave human beings to infiltrate the enemy's territory and ask the right questions—human beings who can see and hear what technology can't, who can extract meaning from the surrounding context.

Using a diagram of Pasha, Little Big Man made

plans for getting to the safe house and setting up. He delegated the patrol order to me and the course of action for battle stations to Casanova. Little Big Man also worked out the communications drills. Sourpuss loved the training aspect of SEAL Team Six, swimming and running, but when it came to actually operating, he fell behind us in talent and desire. Although he should've played a more central role in leading and planning, he limited his role to setting up who would stand watch on Pasha's roof at what times. The four of us also began constructing a large mosaic map of the city.

Before we headed out, Crescent gave a brief. Even though my Teammates and I had just met the CIA, SIGINT, and our interpreter, we would be working with them in a district in northern Mogadishu called Lido, close to the heart of where the enemy gunslingers lived. At Pasha, we would add more strangers to our team: guards, a chef, and assets—locals providing us with intelligence. "If you aren't comfortable with anyone on your team, they're gone," Crescent said. "This is your show. If your cover is compromised, General Garrison will get you out of there within fifteen minutes. Good luck."

August 29, 1993

Under the black cloak of Sunday morning, we flew on a Black Hawk helicopter three miles northwest across town to the Mogadiscio Stadium—Somalia's national stadium for soccer and other events, seating thirty-five thousand people. The trip only took five minutes. Because it housed the Pakistani UN troops' compound, we called the bullet-riddled stadium the Pakistani Stadium. From there, we loaded onto three indigenous trucks. Only needing two trucks, we used a third as a decoy and also in the event that one broke down. Looking at the vehicles, it seemed a miracle they even ran. The Somalis used things until they were no longer mechanically viable. Then they used them some more. Someone did a pretty good job of keeping those pieces of crap running.

We drove out of the stadium and into the city. Mogadishu smelled like urine and human excrement mixed with that tangible smell of starvation, disease, and hopelessness. The odor hung in the air like a dark cloud. It made my heart feel heavy. The Somalis dumped raw sewage in the streets. It didn't help that they used trash and animal dung to fuel the fires that constantly burned in rusted metal barrels. Elementary-school-age boys carried AK-47 rifles. We'd heard that cholera ran rampant because of a nasty water supply. Mogadishu seemed like the end of the world in *I Am Legend*—our mission was to stop the mobs of evil Darkseekers and save the good Somali humans. *No problem, we're SEALs. This is what we do.*

After driving half a mile, we arrived at Pasha. Somali guards armed with AK-47s opened the iron gates for us. Earlier, we had sent one of our assets to give them a radio in preparation for our arrival. Altogether we had four guards protecting Pasha at one time. Four others would rotate with them in shifts. All of them looked alert. Their skinny arms weren't much thicker than the width of three fingers, making the AK-47s appear huge in comparison. They wore T-shirts and *macawis,* a colorful kiltlike garment. We sped inside, and the guards closed the gate behind us.

Pasha stood two stories tall and was surrounded by an enormous concrete wall, the house of a wealthy doctor who left with his family when Somalia became too volatile for them. Somalia's widespread poverty fueled robbery, so when the concrete was originally poured for the wall around the property, the builders stuck bottles in the holes of the blocks while the concrete was still wet. When the concrete dried, the builders broke the bottle tops off. Anyone trying to climb over the wall would have to climb over broken glass. Although effective, it looked butt-ugly. One evening, a shot was fired two houses down. Later, we found out that it came from a homeowner warding off a robber. The robbers liked to frequent our area, where the more affluent lived.

Inside, the running water was fed to the faucets by gravity, rather than pressure. Opening a valve allowed the water to come down from a large holding tank on the roof—the weakest shower I'd ever taken. We couldn't drink it, unless we ran the water through our Katadyn pump for filtering out dangerous microbes. Sometimes we boiled the water. For the most part, we brought in cases of bottled water. By Somali standards, we were well-off.

I'm sure that when the doctor left, he took all the nice furniture. We had a basic table to sit around at mealtime. I had a cotlike bed made out of 2×4s and a thin mattress. Compared to living in a shack and sleeping in the dirt like most people in the city did, we lived like kings.

As we quickly unpacked our gear, one of the skinny guards, probably no more than 110 pounds, bent over to pick up one of my bags that weighed at least as much as he did. I tried to take it, but he insisted I let him carry it. He put my bag on his shoulder and hiked upstairs.

Our Somali chef arrived on the same day as we did. He cooked halal food, permissible by Islamic law—no pork, no alcohol, etc. Somali food is a mix of cuisines—Somalian, Ethiopian, Yemeni, Persian, Turkish, Indian, and Italian—influenced by Somalia's long trade history. For breakfast, we ate pancakes, thin and breadlike, called *canjeero.* Some days we ate Italian-style porridge (*boorash*) with butter and sugar.

At lunch, the chef made dishes from brown long-grain basmati rice. He spiced up the aroma and taste with cloves, cinnamon, cumin, and sage. We also ate pasta (*baasto*) served with stew and banana instead of pasta sauce.

The chef cooked azuki beans on low heat for more than half the day, then served them with butter and sugar, a dish called *cambuulo,* for dinner. He made amazing goat meatballs—amazing everything. Even the camel tasted excellent.

My favorite drink was red (*rooibos*) tea, which is naturally sweet and nutty. We never ate our MREs at Pasha. Had we known the food would be so good, we could've left the heavy, space-consuming packages of MREs at the army compound.

Even though the guards were obviously undernourished, they wouldn't try to take our leftover food. We had to offer them food and coax them to take it. Except for the items containing pork, which they wouldn't eat because they were Muslim, we gave them our MREs; they would only eat a small amount themselves and take the rest home for their families. Also, we gave them our empty water bottles, which they used as water storage containers. Often they'd shake our hands and touch their heart as a sign of appreciation and respect. Our interpreter told us that the guards were happy the Americans had arrived. They appreciated that we'd left our families and were risking our lives to help them. Maybe the media wanted to represent America as bullies, but they missed the rest of the story. I think most of the Somalis wanted us to help them end the civil war.

The SEALs' cost of the chef's meals came out of the money SEAL Team Six had given us for escape and evasion. I rolled mine up in hundred-dollar bills stuffed in the butt of my CAR-15. If I ever had to E&E on my own, I planned to find a Somali fisherman and hire him to take me down the coast to Mombasa, Kenya, where the United States had people I could reach out to and be well taken care of.

Condor briefed us on the actions of the assets, who would visit Pasha every day. For example, if an asset was supposed to come to Pasha from the southeast, but he came from the southwest, we knew he'd been made or was under duress, so we would shoot the person following him. Our asset might do something simple like pause for a second at a corner—then the person behind him would eat a bullet. If he paused twice, both people behind him would eat a bullet. Our procedures were covert enough that an enemy wouldn't know a signal was being given, and although we kept the procedures simple enough for our assets to remember, we spent hours reviewing the procedures with them. A SEAL on the roof always covered each asset's entrance and exit to keep him safe—and to keep impostors out. Usually, when an asset arrived in the dark, he wore an infrared chemlight or a firefly (an infrared strobe light).

The most common motivator for the assets was money—especially in such a poverty-stricken area. Some people had more noble reasons for helping us, but the most common reason was money. We didn't even have to pay them very much.

On the same day, four SIGINT guys arrived separately from us, using a different infiltration method and route, then set up shop. Their room looked like the NASA control room for launching a rocket into outer space: monitors, control knobs, switches. They also set up their antennas and other gear on the roof. We looked like CNN.

Little Big Man gathered everyone together and briefed us on the E&E plan. As always, he carried his Randall knife in a sheath on his belt. "Little man, big knife." I rebriefed the battle plan. Casanova split us up into patrol pairs: I'd be with him, and Little Big Man would partner with Sourpuss.

When our mosaic map of the city was complete, it covered the entire wall of the biggest room in the house. If an asset told us about a threat, we would stick a pin in the location and plan grid coordinates in case we needed to call in an attack on it.

In a separate brief, an asset came in and gave us possible locations of Mohamed Farrah Aidid, the Somali warlord. We stuck more pins in the map: Olympic Hotel, an officer's barracks, etc. Then we sent the eight-digit coordinates to Crescent, back at the CIA trailer up on the hill.

That same day, twenty mortar rounds hit the airfield, tactical operations center, and CIA headquarters. A round hit so close to the CIA trailer that it blew out the windows. Aidid's men had figured out that assets had been going to the trailer. The mortar round had just missed us by a day.

We doubled our watch at Pasha and explained the "grab-and-go" to everyone: grabbing the SIGINT encryption devices, loading them in a rucksack, destroying the other SIGINT gear with a thermite grenade, meeting up at a rendezvous point, then moving out to the extraction area.

That first night, Casanova and I kept watch from the roof. A horrible smell like the remains of a dead carcass filled the air. "What the hell is that?"

August 30, 1993

On Monday, I looked around the neighborhood for the source of the stench, but it had disappeared. Nothing. While I fixed tea downstairs, an asset arrived with some information. I brought him some tea.

He politely refused.

"No, it's OK," I said.

He only took half a cup, as though I had given him something of great value. These Somalis conducted themselves so as never to take away too much.

SIGINT told us they'd picked up a conversation between a fire controller and his firing positions. The mortarmen would fire from concealed positions while the fire controller watched where the rounds exploded in relation to the target. If the mortar round hit the target, the fire controller could assess how much damage had been done. The fire controller advised, "Don't chew your khat until the adjustments and battle damage assessments are made." Khat, a flowering plant native to Somalia, contains a stimulant in the leaves that causes excitement, loss of appetite, and euphoria. A user would stick a wad of leaves in his mouth and chew on it like chewing tobacco. Most of Aidid's mortarmen were enticed to do their job for khat. They became dependent on Aidid's people to continue feeding their addiction, similar to how a pimp strings out his prostitutes on drugs to control them. Because the drug suppressed appetite, Aidid didn't need to feed them much. They were obviously not well disciplined. Although nothing happened this time, later SIGINT would vector in military strikes and succeed in destroying some of the mortar positions.

That evening, the smell came back. "What the hell *is* that?" I came down off the roof and covertly went next door. On the front porch, I saw a teenaged boy sleeping on a futon. At a distance of around 10 yards, it was obvious I'd found the source of the stench. Later, I found out the fourteen-year-old Somali boy had stepped on a land mine in his school playground. His right foot was blown completely off. Part of his left foot was missing. Gangrene had set in. Aidid's people had planted explosives in the schoolyard to kill or maim children, preventing them from growing up to be effective fighters—turning them into liabilities. The infection in the boy's leg stank so badly that his family couldn't sleep at night with him in the house. So they made him sleep on the porch. During the day, they brought him back inside. I asked the CIA for permission to help the crippled boy next door. They denied my request, not wanting to compromise the safe house.

We noticed a lot of movement between 2200 and 0400 from the street in front of Pasha and surrounding buildings. Based on a tip that Aidid's people hung out there, at 0300, Delta Force fast-roped down on the Lig Ligato house. They captured nine people, but they were only UN employees and their Somali guards. Delta had launched on a dry hole.

August 31, 1993

On Tuesday, an asset sighted Aidid in a vehicle. Crescent wanted the asset to deploy a mobile transmitter in the vehicle, but Condor, not wanting to sacrifice his asset, denied it as being too risky.

Aidid was slippery. Rather than stay home, he lived with relatives, staying in the same place only one or two nights. Sometimes he traveled in a motorcade. Sometimes he only used one vehicle. He would dress as a woman. Although he was popular within his own clan, people outside Aidid's clan didn't like him.

Casanova and I dressed up like locals and ran a vehicular route reconnaissance in a Jeep Cherokee that had been beaten more than once with an ugly stick. Secretly, our vehicle was armored. I wore a turban, a flowery Somali shirt, and BDU trousers under my *macawi*. With my beard starting to grow out and dark skin, I could pass for Arab. For weapons we each had a sound-suppressed CAR-15 down between the seats, partly concealed by our skirts. I carried a magazine of ammo in my CAR-15 and an extra in the cargo pocket of my BDU trousers. We also carried our SIG 226 9mms in a breakaway butt pack turned around to the front under our shirts—making it look like we had pooch bellies. To get to my pistol, I could just lift my shirt, reach into the upper right corner, and pull down and away, separating the Velcro and readying my SIG. Besides the magazine of ammo in the pistol, an extra magazine sat in the top of the breakaway butt pack.

Clipped inside my pocket was a Microtech UDT tactical automatic knife, a switchblade—extremely sharp. In the cargo pocket on my right thigh, I carried a blowout kit.

By SEAL standards, we were lightly armed. It was a calculated risk. If a bear showed up in the woods, we couldn't fight him off. However, traveling light allowed us to blend in better to collect intelligence. It was a trade-off. If we were compromised, we'd have to run and gun.

While Casanova drove, I took pictures with a 35mm camera. We noted a location for a possible helicopter landing zone where Delta and their indigenous people could insert. Then we figured out routes where they could be inserted by truck.

We figured out something else, too. Previously, even though our people walking on foot, riding in Humvee motorcades, hovering in helos, and flying over in planes gathered information, we continued to wonder how Aidid's people kept transporting mortar rounds to their crews. I took a picture of two women in colorful robes walking side by side, each carrying a baby in her arms. As I rotated the lens to zoom in, I could clearly see the first baby's head, but the second woman was actually carrying two mortar rounds. The ruse had almost fooled me.

During our vehicle recon, we completed a concept of ops for inserting and extracting people from Pasha. For example, when the time came for turnover, we could drive to an abandoned camel slaughterhouse on the seashore, signal out to sea for a boat of replacement SEALs, and give them our vehicles while we took their boat out to rendezvous with a ship. The replacement SEALs could travel lighter than we had because we'd already stocked Pasha with the heavy SIGINT equipment and other supplies.

The slaughterhouse, huge as a city block, had been owned by the Russians, who abandoned it when the civil war began. They had used the camel meat and bones, but threw everything else out into the ocean. The water along one of the most beautiful beaches in the world became infested with sharks: hammerheads, great whites, and all kinds of bad-ass sharks. I've never been afraid to swim anywhere, but I did not want to swim in that water. Neither did the locals, which kept the location private for our needs. As a bonus, the beach was close to Pasha. The slaughterhouse could be seen easily from the water, covering and concealing a large area of the coast. Ideal for the guys to bring Zodiacs— black inflatable rubber boats with outboard motors—or RHIBs in to the shore.

We returned to Pasha, and that evening, the boy next door groaned like he was dying. I knew what it was like to be a child in pain. *Screw this.* Casanova, a SIGINT medic named Rick, and I did a hard entry on the boy's house, blacked out with balaclavas and carrying MP-5 machine guns. We didn't take any chances. Kicked in the door. Flexicuffed the boy's mom, dad, and aunt. Put them on the floor next to the wall. Of course, they feared we would kill them. We brought the boy inside, so the parents could see what we were about to do. Rick broke out his supplies. We scrubbed the dead tissue out of the wounds with betadine, a cleaner and disinfectant. It hurt the kid so bad that we had to put our hands over his mouth to keep his screams from waking the neighborhood. He passed out from the pain and shock. We gave him intravenous antibiotics, bandaged his wounds, and injected each butt cheek to stop the infection. Then we vanished.

September 1, 1993

Wednesday, while conducting observation from the rooftop, we saw an elderly man leading a donkey pulling a wooden cart mounted on an old vehicle axle. On top of the cart were stacks of bricks. During his return trip, he had the same load of bricks. *What?* We asked an asset to follow him. The asset found out the old man hid mortars in the stack of bricks. We reported it. Our superiors issued compromise authority—giving us permission to off the old man.

A sniper must be mentally strong, firmly anchored in a religion or philosophy that allows him to refrain from killing when unnecessary, and to kill when necessary. During the Beltway sniper attacks in 2002, John Allen Muhammad killed ten innocent people and critically injured three. Shooting can make a person feel powerful. Obviously, a good sniper must not give in to such impulses. On the other hand, if a sniper allows himself to be overcome by Stockholm syndrome, he cannot perform his job. (In 1973, robbers held bank employees hostage in Stockholm, Sweden. During their six-day ordeal, the hostages became emotionally attached to the robbers, even defending them after being released.) Through his scope, the sniper becomes intimately familiar with his target, often over a period of time, learning his lifestyle and habits. The target probably has done nothing to directly hurt the sniper. Yet, when the time comes, the sniper must be able to complete the mission.

On the roof of Pasha, a walkaround wall concealed Casanova and me. I aimed my Win Mag in the old man's direction, 500 yards away.

Casanova viewed him in the spotter scope. "Stand by, stand by. Three, two, one, execute, execute."

Target in my sights, I squeezed the trigger on the first "execute." Right between the eyes—I nailed the donkey.

Expecting to see the old man die, when the donkey dropped instead, Casanova couldn't hold back a little throat chuckle—not very sniperlike.

The old man ran away.

Casanova's throat chuckle sounded like he was gagging.

Old men were a dime a dozen, but the donkey would be hard to replace. No one ever came to get the dead donkey, still hitched to the wooden cart. They just left it there in the middle of the road.

Later, one of our assets informed us that the old man didn't want to carry the mortars, but Aidid's people threatened to kill his family if he didn't. I felt pretty good about not shooting the old fart.

The same day, SIGINT guys intercepted communication about a planned mortar attack on the hangar at the army compound. SIGINT knew the mortar crews' communication frequencies. Notifying the base gave the personnel there some time to find cover before seven or eight mortar rounds landed. No friendlies were injured. Just a few minutes' warning is huge.

SIGINT routinely jammed communication between Aidid's fire controllers and the mortarmen. SIGINT vectored in military strikes to destroy the mortar positions. Also, we made khat readily available to the mortar addicts. "You don't need to become Aidid's mortar men to get your fix. Here, go chew this." They smiled like jack-o'-lanterns, their teeth stained black and orange. I know it's a terrible thing to give an addict drugs, but it saved others from being blown to bits by mortar attacks. It probably saved the addicts from dying in one of our military counterstrikes, too. Aidid's people started finding it more difficult to coordinate mortar attacks.

That night, we spotted a man with an AK-47 on the balcony of one of the houses out back and a couple of streets over. I flicked the safety off my sound-suppressed CAR-15 and held the red dot of my sight on his head—an easy shot. Over each of our CAR-15s, we had mounted Advanced Combat Optical Gunsights (ACOGs), a 1.5-power close-range point-and-shoot scope made by Trijicon. At night, it dilated ten times more than my pupil, giving me extra light. Its red dot appears in the scope, unlike a laser that actually appears on the target itself. The ACOG worked just as well in the night as it did in the day. I waited for the man to level his AK-47 in our direction. He never did. After consulting with our guards, we found out the man with the AK-47 was one of our young guards at his own house trying to mimic the SEALs' tactics of defending from the roof. Of course, the idiot never told us of his plans, and he probably couldn't conceive our capability to see him with night vision. We told him, "That was good thinking, but if you're going to be on the rooftop with a weapon at night in this neighborhood, let us know. Because that was almost your ass."

September 2, 1993

Thursday morning, we held a meeting to discuss future plans and personnel. Pasha was doing well, so we needed to keep the machine running after we completed our stay and it came time for someone to relieve us.

Later in the day, we received the break we needed. Aidid was wealthy, and his college-age daughter had friends in Europe, Libya, Kenya, and other places. Someone slipped her a cell phone, and SIGINT tapped it. Although Aidid moved around a lot, his daughter made a mistake, mentioning on the phone where he was staying. An asset helped pinpoint the house. Our navy spy plane, a P-3 Orion, picked up Aidid's convoy, but the convoy stopped, and we lost him in the maze of buildings.

In the evening, Casanova and I lay on Pasha's roof, protecting the perimeter. During our time at Pasha, we had been playing a game of trying to trap rats, using peanut butter from our MREs as bait. We tied string to a stick and propped a box on it. Through our night-vision goggles, we saw the rat go in. Casanova pulled the string, but the rat escaped before the box fell down on top of it. Our technique evolved into a science. I took apart some ballpoint pens and used the springs to make a one-way door into a box. Inside the box sat the peanut butter. Soon the rat sniffed around the trap. It slipped inside the door. The springs slammed the door shut behind the rodent.

"Yes," I whispered.

Casanova smiled.

"What are we going to do?" I asked.

"Kill it."

"How?"

"What do you mean *how*?"

While we discussed how to dispatch the rat, it escaped.

The next time, we made the box smaller, so the rodent wouldn't have wiggle room to escape. The rat crawled inside. Trapped. I stomped my boot down on top. Dead rat—but I had sacrificed the trap. One trap, one kill.

I felt proud to have the only confirmed rat kill. Now I was screwing around with another trap trying to get my second rat.

"Hey, come here," Casanova whispered.

"What?" I slid over next to him.

He pointed to a house across the street where we had just placed two guards the day before. Three men were attempting to break in. They picked the wrong house in the wrong neighborhood. If they'd tried it before our guards were in there, we would've said, *Screw it. None of our business*. Now our guards were inside, and it *was* our business.

Casanova took the man on the left side, and I took the one on the right. Lining up the red dot on my first target, I squeezed the trigger. His legs buckled before he sank. Casanova's ate the dirt, too. Although the man in the middle had a moment longer to live, both Casanova and I hit him at the same time. If the three would-be intruders were only burglars, they paid a heavy price for thievery.

Later, SIGINT heard chatter from the bar around the corner that Aidid's people might gather. Maybe they were planning to do a hit on us. Pasha went to full alert. We staged AT-4 antitank rockets and took up perimeter positions. It turned out Aidid's people were only having a recruiting rally.

An asset sighted Aidid but couldn't pinpoint his building. This was our logistical nightmare. Even though our assets had spotted Aidid, they couldn't relay to us his exact building.

A SIGINT aircraft, having flown in from Europe and now dedicated to us, arrived in the evening to help track and pinpoint Aidid. This tremendously increased our surveillance abilities. We could use transmitters and beacons more effectively. It also made us able to intercept communications better than from the rooftop of our building.

In the big house next to Pasha on the right was the Italian ambassador's residence, where the ambassador threw a big party with many Italian officers in attendance. Italy had occupied Somalia from 1927 to 1941. In 1949, the UN gave Italy trusteeship of parts of Somalia. Then, in 1960, Somalia became independent. Now the Italians were real bastards, playing both sides of the fence. Whenever the Black Hawks spun up for an operation, the Italians flashed their lights to let the locals know the Americans were coming. Their soldiers employed electric shock on a Somali prisoner's testicles, used the muzzle of a flare gun to rape a woman, and took pictures of their deeds.

The UN accused the Italians of paying bribes to Aidid and demanded that Italy's General Bruno Loi be replaced. The Italian government told the UN to stop harassing Aidid.

One of Italy's main players was Giancarlo Marocchino, who left Italy, following allegations of tax evasion and married a Somali woman in one of Aidid's clans. When the UN confiscated weapons from the militia, the Italian military gave them to Giancarlo, who is suspected to have sold them to Aidid.

Italy dumped trillions of lire into Somalia for "aid." With help from people like Aidid, even before he became an infamous warlord, most of the money went into the pockets of Italy's government officials and their cronies. The Italians constructed a highway that connected Bosasso and Mogadishu—from which Giancarlo Marocchino, in the trucking business, is reputed to have received kickbacks. Marocchino also cultivated a close relationship with news correspondents by wining and dining them during their stay in Mogadishu.

Also living in our neighborhood and playing both sides of the fence was a Russian military veteran with some intelligence background, now a mercenary operating out of a building two houses down from Pasha. He would work for either side as long as they paid. We suspected he helped both sides with finding safe houses and recruiting. He and the Italians seemed to be working together. The Sicilian family that taught me how to cook loved America; in contrast, the behavior of the Italians in Somalia came as a huge punch in my gut.

We received a report that Aidid might have acquired portable infrared homing surface-to-air missiles—Stinger missiles—which can be used by someone on the ground to shoot down aircraft.

Casanova, the SIGINT medic, and I did another hard entry on the house of the boy with wounded legs. The family wasn't as scared the second time, but they weren't relaxed, either—a hard entry is a hard entry. We cuffed them again, then held security as we tended to the boy. He looked a lot better and didn't need to scream or pass out as we cleaned him up.

September 3, 1993

The following morning, we prepared for a trip to the army compound. Our Somali guards did an advance, making a recon of the route before we headed out. During the actual trip, the guards used a decoy that split from us to a different route. Anyone trying to follow would've had to split their forces to follow both vehicles or flip a coin and hope they followed the correct vehicle. Although I received formal training for such tactics, our guards figured this out on their own. Their experiences fighting in the civil war taught them to adapt out of necessity. They were highly intelligent.

The inside of the army compound was fortified with sniper hides, guard towers, and fighting positions. We picked up some infrared chemlights and fireflies in preparation for upgrading Pasha's perimeter security. While there, we also held a meeting with Delta, telling them about the mortar attack details and suspected firing points. They climbed up onto the roof of the hangar and did a recon by fire: Snipers shot into suspected areas of mortars and hoped our SIGINT would pick up communication of near hits, verifying locations. When General Garrison found out, he whacked our pee-pees. He didn't like the recon-by-fire action.

That night, back at Pasha, in order to help our guards have a better understanding of what we were doing and how we were doing it, Casanova attached an infrared chemlight to himself and walked around the perimeter of the house. To the naked eye, the chemlight was invisible. I let the other guards look through our KN-250 night-vision scopes, so they could see the glowing light on Casanova. The guards gasped, their faces looking like they'd just seen their first UFO land. They lowered the scopes and looked with their naked eyes. Then they looked through the scopes at Casanova again. Their speech became rapid and their bodies animated, as if they were now riding on the UFO that had just landed. Casanova and I chuckled at their reaction.

Later in the evening, we went with Stingray, working under Condor, to do a dog and pony show with the chemlights and other gear for the chief of police, one of our major assets and responsible for recruiting a number of others, giving him a taste of how we operated. As a result, the chief of police felt more secure about putting his people at risk working for us. Fifty thousand dollars made him financially secure. Maybe he only used a thousand dollars of that to pay his twenty or thirty assets and pocketed the rest of the money.

Casanova and I hit the house of the wounded teenager again. Mom and Dad obediently took their positions on the floor next to the wall before we put them there. The aunt went down on a knee and held up a tray of tea for us.

I took a drink and offered the family some.

They refused.

We had brought our interpreter with us this time to direct the family as to the boy's care. The family had gone to great lengths to get the tea, and it was all they had. It was the only way they knew to say thank you. They'd been using a witch doctor, but he obviously hadn't been much help in curing the boy.

By now, the stink of the boy's wounds had almost gone. Some of his fever remained. Still, we did another surgical scrub. We gave the family some amoxicillin, an antibiotic for infections. "Give this to the boy three times a day for the next ten days."

I noticed his gums were bleeding. The inside of his mouth was a bloody mess.

"He's got scurvy," our medic said. Scurvy is caused by vitamin C deficiency. Sailors of old used to get this disease before Scottish surgeon James Lind, of the British Royal Navy, figured out that sailors who ate citrus fruits had fewer problems with scurvy. With limes readily available from British Caribbean colonies, the Royal Navy supplied men with lime juice. This is how British sailors got the nickname "limey."

September 4, 1993

Casanova and I went out for a drive to recon alternate E&E routes, find out about mortar attack locations, and get a better feel for the area. Later, an asset told us that two mines had been placed on a road and were to be detonated on American vehicles—the same road I'd traveled the day before to meet with Delta at the army compound. They must've found out about our trip and just missed us.

In our neighborhood, little girls walked a mile a day just to get drinking water and carry it back home. A four-year-old washed her two-year-old sister in the front courtyard by pouring water over the top of her. Most Americans don't realize how blessed we are—we need to be more thankful.

By this time, we had become celebrities, controlling a two- to three-block area. When Casanova saw schoolkids, he'd flex and kiss his huge biceps. They imitated him. A small group of kids would gather, and we'd hand out parts of our MREs: candy, chocolate cookies, Tootsie Rolls, and Charms chewing gum. Yes, we gave up our cover, but Condor thought this was good for winning the hearts and minds of the locals. I agreed.

I took a bag of oranges to the crippled boy next door, but he couldn't eat because the citric acid stung his bleeding gums. Casanova held his body down while I put him in a headlock and squirted the liquid into his mouth. After two or three more visits, the oranges didn't sting. Eventually the scurvy would go away. To help the boy, Condor told the CIA that the boy was related to one of our assets even though he wasn't. We had an asset take him some crutches, and I requested a wheelchair.

Later, the boy next door stayed on the porch to spot us when we made our rounds up on the roof of Pasha. He gave us a wave and a smile. It was my most successful op in Somalia, and I had to disobey direct orders to get it done. Better to ask forgiveness than permission.

Aidid ran his own hearts-and-minds campaign. He made public announcements against Americans and started recruiting in our area: anyone from children to the elderly.

Our assets informed us of a trail to be used to supply Aidid with Stinger missiles: Afghanistan to Sudan to Ethiopia to Somalia. The missiles were leftovers from those that the United States gave Afghanistan to fight the Russians. Years later, the United States offered to buy the Stingers back: $100,000 for each one returned with no questions asked.

Aidid received help from al Qaeda and the PLO. Al Qaeda had snuck in advisers from Sudan. Not too many people knew about al Qaeda then, but they supplied Aidid with weapons and trained his militia in urban warfare tactics like setting up burning barricades and fighting street to street. If Aidid didn't have the Stingers yet, they'd be arriving soon. In the meantime, al Qaeda taught Aidid's militia to change the detonators on their

RPGs from impact detonators to timed detonators. Rather than having to make a direct hit on a helicopter, the RPG could detonate near the tail rotor, the helo's Achilles' heel. Firing an RPG from a rooftop invited death by back blast or the helicopter guns. So al Qaeda taught Aidid's men to dig a deep hole in the street—a militiaman could lie down while the back of the RPG tube blasted harmlessly into the hole. They also camouflaged themselves, so the helos couldn't spot them. Although I didn't know it at the time, the al Qaeda advisers in Somalia probably included Osama Bin Laden's military chief, Mohammed Atef. Similarly, the PLO helped Aidid with advice and supplies. Now Aidid wanted to hit high-profile American targets.

Our SIGINT intercepted communication about a plot to launch a mortar attack on the American Embassy. Furthermore, assets informed us that the Italians continued to allow Aidid's armed militia to cross UN military checkpoints responsible for safeguarding the city. His militia merely had to find out where the Italians had their checkpoints in order to move freely—right into the backyard of the United States and everyone else.

Two of Aidid's bodyguards wanted to give up their master's location for the $25,000 reward. Leopard wanted to meet them at Pasha. To get to Pasha, Leopard planned to travel through the Italian checkpoint near an old pasta factory—Checkpoint Pasta.

However, Leopard didn't know that the Italians had secretly turned Checkpoint Pasta over to the Nigerians. Minutes after the turnover, Aidid's militia ambushed and killed the seven Nigerians.

That evening, I heard a firefight close to Pasha, and

the closest mortar yet. Obviously, the bad guys had started to figure out what was going on and where. Our days at Pasha were numbered.

September 5, 1993

Sunday morning, before 0800, Leopard and four bodyguards rode two Isuzu Troopers out of the UN compound. When the vehicles reached Checkpoint Pasta, a crowd swarmed around them. A couple of hundred yards ahead, burning tires and concrete blocked the road. Leopard's driver floored the accelerator, crashing through the ambush. Forty-nine bullets struck their vehicle. One shot passed through a space in Leopard's flak jacket, striking him in the neck. The driver raced them out of the ambush and helped Leopard to a hospital in the UN compound. After twenty-five pints of blood and one hundred stitches, General Garrison flew Leopard to a hospital in Germany. Leopard survived.

Later that day, I heard .50 caliber shots, the kind that can penetrate bricks, fired in the northwest 300 to 500 yards from our location.

With shooting nearby and a recent ambush, we knew our ticket was about to get punched. On full alert now, we took up battle stations. I called in an AC-130 Spectre to fly overhead in case we needed help. Capable of spending long periods of time in the air, the air force plane carried two 20mm M-61 Vulcan cannons, one 40mm L/60 Bofors cannon, and one 105mm M-102 howitzer. Sophisticated sensors and radar helped it detect enemy on the ground. You could let loose a rabbit on a soccer field, and the AC-130 Spectre would make rabbit stew. I had trained in Florida at Hurlburt Field on the plane's capabilities and how to call for its fire to rain down on the enemy. It aroused me to know we were getting ready to light up some of Aidid's people. Instead, fortune smiled on them as they chose to fight another day.

That same day, we found out that one of our primary assets had been made, so we had to fly him out of the country.

At 2000, an asset told us that Aidid was at his aunt's house. Condor called in a helo to fly Stingray and the asset to the army base and brief General Garrison. All of us in Pasha were ecstatic. Everything we had done at Pasha—running the assets, SIGINT, everything—had led to this moment. We had good intel and the cloak of darkness to protect our assault team. The asset even had a diagram for the house—ideal for special operators doing room entries. Aidid was ours.

The request was denied. I still don't know why. Condor and Stingray were outraged. "We will not get another chance this good!"

The rest of us couldn't believe it either. "Whiskey Tango Foxtrot?!" In the military phonetic alphabet, "Whiskey Tango Foxtrot" is *WTF*—"What the f***?"

I was angry that we had worked so hard for such an important mission only to be ignored. It seemed that military politics were to blame. I also felt embarrassed at how my own military had treated the CIA. "Condor, I'm really sorry. I don't know what the hell . . . I don't know why we didn't do this . . ."

Condor wasn't mad at us SEALs, but he was mad at General Garrison. "If Garrison isn't going to do it, why did he even send us out here?! Why do all this work, spend all this money, put ourselves at risk, put our assets at risk . . ."

"If we aren't going to pull the trigger," I finished his sentence. "We had Aidid."

"You're damn right we had him!"

At the time, I was mad at Garrison, too. Delta launched on the dry hole at the Lig Ligato house, but they couldn't launch when we really had Aidid. It wasn't going to do any good to punch anything or yell at anybody. When I become ultrafurious, I become ultraquiet. After Condor and I shared our misery, I went mute. The others let me have my space. We all mourned the loss of that mission.

September 6, 1993

At 0400, on the roof of Pasha, Casanova and I heard a tank make a wide circle. We didn't even know Aidid had a tank. We readied our AT-4s.

Hours later, Casanova and I told Little Big Man and Sourpuss.

"There can't be a tank here," Sourpuss argued. "We'd have seen a tank by now."

"We know what we heard," I said.

"I'm not impressed," Sourpuss said. "You might impress the CIA with your nonsense, but I'm not impressed."

"Whatever."

That same morning, one of our assets was shot stepping out of his vehicle.

Before long, a second asset, our maid's brother, was killed—shot in the head. He was one of the good guys. He wasn't in it for the money as much as he was in it to help his clan end the civil war. She couldn't hide the sadness in her eyes.

As if things weren't bad enough for us, a third asset was beaten almost to death. By the Italians.

A report came in that Aidid possessed antiaircraft guns. Aidid continued to grow stronger and more sophisticated thanks to help from al Qaeda, the PLO, and the Italians turning a blind eye. The locals recognized the growth, too, and were encouraged to join Aidid.

Delta had intelligence that Aidid was in the old Russian compound. So Delta went after him and took seventeen prisoners—but no Aidid. Only two of the seventeen were considered to be of interest. They were detained, interrogated, and then freed. Delta had given Aidid's people another exhibition of how they operate: fly in, fast-rope down, and use a Humvee blocking force of Rangers to protect the operators as they take down the house. This would come back to bite us in the ass.

September 7, 1993

One of our primary assets, Abe, called in four hours late. We feared him dead.

Finally, he showed. "I do tonight's mission."

"Sorry, you've already been scratched."

"Scratched?"

"Mission canceled. No mission for you tonight."

* * *

In the evening, Casanova and I escorted Condor to deliver $50,000 to an asset. The high-level assets were wealthy and influential and had a number of people working under them. Condor went to the high-level assets rather than making them come to him: checking the number of new recruits, collecting their pictures, finding out how they would divvy up the money with their own assets, briefing them about procedures. The whole meeting took about an hour and a half. While Casanova and I stood guard outside, we heard a firefight approximately 200 yards north.

Little Big Man and Sourpuss saw the tracers from the firefight in our direction. "Do you guys need assistance?" they radioed us.

"No, we weren't involved." If we fired a green flare, Little Big Man and Sourpuss would call in a helo extract, then fight their way to our position to assist until the helo arrived.

Later that night, back at Pasha, I got my second confirmed rat kill.

September 8, 1993

The Rangers reported that they spotted an old Russian tank a couple miles out of town and destroyed it. I reminded Sourpuss about the tank Casanova and I had heard several nights earlier, "See? It's called a tank. You know—they make a certain sound while moving."

Sourpuss walked away.

That day, Abe became our main asset. We gave him an infrared strobe light and a beacon with a magnet attached. He seemed confident he could get close to Aidid, so we put Delta on alert.

"Aidid is moving," Abe called. As the night grew old, Abe couldn't pinpoint Aidid's position.

Although no communication traffic reached SIGINT, several large explosions came from the direction of the airport. Aidid's mortar crews had figured out how to communicate their fire and control without being intercepted by us. *Damn, they are resilient.*

September 9, 1993

General Garrison received permission to go to Phase Three—going after Aidid's lieutenants. Delta flew over Mogadishu as a show of force with the entire package: ten to twelve Little Birds and twenty to thirty Black Hawks. Delta snipers rode in the light Little Bird helicopters, which could carry guns, rockets, and missiles. In the medium-sized Black Hawk helicopters, also armed with guns, rockets, and missiles, the Delta entry teams and Rangers had fast ropes ready in the doorway to make an assault at any moment. The idea was to show Aidid that ours was bigger than his—making him less attractive to the local population and, hopefully, hurting his ability to recruit.

On the same day, near the pasta factory, two kilometers away from the Pakistani Stadium, the Army's 362nd Engineers worked to clear a Mogadishu roadway. A Pakistani armored platoon protected them while the Quick Reaction Force (QRF) stood by in case they needed emergency reinforcements. The QRF was made up of men from the conventional army's 10th Mountain Division, 101st Aviation Regiment, and 25th Aviation Regiment, their base located at the abandoned university and old American Embassy.

The engineers bulldozed an obstacle from the road when a crowd of Somalis gathered. One Somali fired a shot, then sped away in a white truck. The engineers cleared a second obstacle. Then the third: burning tires, scrap metal, and a trailer. Someone on a second-story balcony fired at them. Engineers and Pakistanis returned fire. The enemy fire increased, coming at them from multiple directions. The crowd moved obstacles to block the soldiers in. The engineers called in the QRF helos. In three minutes, armed OH-58 Kiowa and AH-1 Cobra helicopters arrived. Hundreds of armed Somalis moved in from the north and south. Enemy RPGs came in from multiple directions.

The Cobra opened up on the enemy with 20 mm cannons and 2.75-inch rockets. More QRF helos were called in for help while the engineers tried to escape, heading for the Pakistani Stadium. Aidid's militia fired a 106 mm recoilless rifle, blasting the lead Pakistani tank into flames. A bulldozer stopped dead, so the engineers abandoned it. As thirty Somalis tried to take the abandoned bulldozer, two TOW missiles destroyed them and the bulldozer. The engineers, two wounded, and the Pakistanis, three wounded, fought on until they reached the stadium. One Pakistani died. It had been the largest battle in Somalia to that point.

Our intelligence sources told us that Aidid had commanded the ambush from the nearby cigarette factory. More than one hundred Somalis died, and hundreds more were wounded, but Aidid had succeeded in keeping the road closed, restricting the UN forces' movement. In addition, the media assisted Aidid by reporting the many "innocent" Somali deaths. *I hate our liberal media. Must be easy to sit back and point fingers when you're not involved.* President Clinton also helped Aidid, halting combat operations in Mogadishu until an investigation could be completed. *Political popularity trumps American lives.*

Aidid launched artillery over Pasha. Machine-gun fire and firefights reached closer to us. We remained on full alert and high pucker factor. Aidid's militia also launched mortars on the Nigerian checkpoint at the Port of Mogadishu—turned over by the Italians.

Condor's assets infiltrated a rally held in a vehicle repair garage where Aidid tried to pump up his troops. If Aidid was actually there at the rally, we wanted to know. He wasn't.

September 10, 1993

At 0500 the next day, Aidid's militia fired more artillery at the Port of Mogadishu checkpoint. That same day, an asset told us that Aidid's people knew about Pasha. They described our guns and vehicles, and they knew Condor from before we set up Pasha.

Aidid ambushed CNN's Somali crew. Their interpreter and four guards were killed. Aidid's militia had mistaken the CNN's crew for us.

We also found out that an Italian journalist had arranged to do an interview with Aidid. One of our assets put a beacon on the journalist's car, so we could track him. The journalist must've suspected something was wrong, because he went to the house of one of the good guys instead, probably hoping we'd launch an attack there. Fortunately, we had an asset on the ground verifying the location.

Even so, the CIA was screwed. So were we. We had good intel that Aidid's people were going to ambush us. Instead of two SEALs on watch and two resting, we went to three SEALs on watch and one resting.

September 11, 1993

I finally got to bed at 0700 the next morning—no ambush. Sourpuss woke me up at 1100 to tell me that our assets were reporting that Aidid's militia was closing in on us.

Another asset told us that the bad guys had targeted our head guard, Abdi, because they knew he was working for the CIA. One of the guards in his employ was his own son. The head guard took responsibility for paying the guards; moreover, he had responsibility for their lives. He held an important status in his clan. The head guard put his family and clan at risk to help the CIA. Part of his motivation was money, but the greater motivation seemed to be a better future for his family. Now he was made. Later we would find out who ratted him out: the Italians.

Condor called General Garrison. "We've been compromised, and we need to get the f*** out of here."

At 1500, leaving nonessential equipment such as MREs, everyone in Pasha packed up, and we drove to the Pakistani Stadium. Helicopters extracted us at 1935, taking us back to the hangar on the military compound.

In retrospect, on the first day at Pasha, we should've flexicuffed the Italians and taken them out of the area, and we should've assassinated the Russian mercenary. Then we would've had a better chance of running our safe house and capturing Aidid. Of course, it would've helped if our own military had let us capture Aidid when we had him at his aunt's house.

Although we had lost Pasha, we still had targets to act on.

11.

CAPTURING AIDID'S EVIL GENIUS

September 12, 1993

Casanova and I walked into the hangar, beard and hair still growing out. I didn't get a haircut the whole time I was in Mogadishu. In the hangar, everyone seemed happy to see us. They knew we'd been living for nearly fifteen days in booger-eater territory, and they'd heard rumors about some of the work we'd done. Several Rangers approached us. "Wish you guys would've been with us when we were ambushed." Others wanted to ask, "What've you guys been doing?"

We lived with Delta Force, the Combat Control Team (CCT), and pararescuemen (PJs). CCTs were the air force's special operations pathfinders who could parachute into an area and provide reconnaissance, air traffic control, fire support, and command, control, and communications on the ground—particularly helpful to us in calling down death from above. SIGINT drafted many of their people from the CCTs. The air force's PJs, also special operations, focused on rescuing pilots downed in enemy territory and administering medical treatment. Both Delta and SEAL Team Six had begun augmenting their forces with CCTs and PJs. On a SEAL Team Six boat crew of eight men assaulting a building, the addition of a PJ, who could take care of patching up bullet wounds, freed up a SEAL hospital corpsman to kick more doors. Likewise, the addition of a CCT carrying a radio on his back and calling for air support freed up a SEAL radioman to carry other mission-essential gear on his back and help with the door-kicking. Although the air force CCTs and PJs were not as specialized in skills like door-kicking, they were experts in their fields—to a higher level than SEAL or Delta operators. Integrating them into SEAL Team Six and Delta was one of the best moves JSOC ever made. Although not held to as high a tactical standard (standards such as physical fitness remained the same) as SEALs, particularly for close-quarters combat training, they received Team Six's Green Team training. During my Green Team, although a CCT and a PJ were among the four or five who failed, a CCT and a PJ passed. The CCTs and PJs also rotated over to Delta Force for their training. Then, after some time at home with their air force units, they rotated back and forth between Six and Delta again. In the hangar, the four of us SEALs mostly hung out with CCTs and PJs because we knew them from training together in Dam Neck, Virginia. Like most of Delta, they had high-and-tight haircuts to blend in with the Rangers, but the pale skin on their scalps gave them away.

One of our CCTs was Jeff, a pretty boy who was a

woman magnet like Casanova; they even hung around together sometimes. Another CCT was Dan Schilling, a thirty-year-old laid-back Southern Californian. Dan left the Army Reserves to become a CCT. In the middle of the hangar, when we played cards on the fold-up planning table, Dan often gave me a cigar—he liked to smoke Royal Jamaica Maduros.

Tim Wilkinson quit his electrical engineering job for the adventure of becoming a PJ. Scotty served as the PJs' team leader.

Near the air force planning table in the middle of the hangar, the CCTs and PJs set a blowup doll named Gina the Love Goddess on a chair with a sign around her neck advertising services and prices. She was a birthday gift from Dan Schilling's wife and Jeff's girlfriend for one of the air force guys who never got mail and didn't have a girlfriend. After a congressional visit, Gina disappeared. *No sense of humor!*

The Rangers outnumbered everyone, but they remained cautious about crossing the imaginary line, like a wall that reached the ceiling, into our area. Maybe we had a mystique that they respected—or a body odor. Whatever the reason, they gave us our space. A lot of the Delta guys seemed to have the attitude, *If you aren't Delta, we don't want anything to do with you.* We probably had some of the same attitude, but there were only four of us. If we'd had all of Red Team, we might have been more arrogant. Being the only four SEALs in Africa, we had to hang out with somebody.

Around the hangar, we wore shorts, T-shirts, and Teva flip-flops. When we wore military uniforms, we didn't wear names or rank insignia. Military rank held less meaning for us than it did for Rangers and the conventional military. In the Teams, we often followed leaders because of reputations they earned or a certain skill set they possessed. Unlike the conventional military, our enlisted men usually called officers by their first names or nicknames. We didn't subscribe to the robot-like military mentality of top-down leadership, either. Just because a person outranks someone else in the Teams doesn't mean he'll be leading anything—other than on paper. We adapted our weapons and tactics to changing environments and situations.

At 2100, we received mortar fire, now becoming such a regular occurrence that guys in the hangar cheered. Some had a mortar pool going. A person could buy a time slot for a dollar. Whoever chose a slot closest to the actual time the mortar hit won the pool.

No one had leads on Aidid.

September 13, 1993

The next day, true to form, although he was the senior SEAL, Sourpuss didn't initiate much of anything and didn't exert control. He was content to sit around and write his wife letters. Little Big Man checked into using QRF helicopters as sniper platforms. We were also encouraged to go out on patrol with the Rangers when we didn't have anything else going on.

A Pakistani convoy came in to resupply. Under

General Garrison's orders, Casanova and I rode with Steve (a Delta sniper working a lot with military intelligence), Commander Assad, and Assad's Pakistani troops. We drove across town to the northwest, near Pakistani Stadium, where the Pakistanis ran a tight compound. Their troops exhibited excellent military bearing and a by-the-book attitude. They kept the area tidy. Nothing like the sloppy Italians who were constantly trying to undermine us.

During the night, Aidid's militia fired on one of our helicopters, and they used the abandoned Somali National University as their sniper hide. Casanova and I climbed six stories to the top of a tower. From there, we could see the house of Osman Ali Atto—Aidid's financier and evil genius. Atto allegedly used income from drug trafficking (mostly khat), arms trafficking, looting, and kidnapping to buy more weapons and support for Aidid's militia. Next to Atto's house stood his vehicle repair garage, an enormous open-top concrete building where his mechanics worked on cars, bulldozers, and technicals—pickup trucks with .50 caliber machine guns on tripods bolted onto the truck bed. This was the same garage where Aidid had held the rally to pump up his militia while we were in Pasha. *If we capture Atto, we cut off the financial support for Aidid's militia. He who controls the purse strings controls the war.*

Nothing significant happened at Atto's house except that the porch light flickered on and off three times. Probably some kind of signal, but we didn't see any movement in the house. It was only a matter of time before we captured Atto.

September 14, 1993

We continued to observe Atto's garage. People constantly came and went. Three mechanics worked on vehicles. Casanova and I spotted someone who looked like Atto, flashing a big white smile, having a meeting.

We took a picture, then transmitted the data via secure link back to the intel guys so they could make sure the man in the garage really was Atto. We lost him when he left the garage and drove away.

The same day, a Ranger thought he spotted Aidid in a convoy. Delta hit a building to find out they had captured General Ahmed Jilao instead, even though Jilao was much taller, heavier, and lighter-skinned than Aidid—and was a close ally of the United Nations. Aidid had become like Elvis—people saw him where he wasn't.

At night, the Pakistani compound received fire from the area of nearby trees and buildings. Commander Assad said, "We keep receiving fire from there on a regular basis. Can you help us?"

"We can spot them with our infrared scopes and fire tracers at them, and your machine gunners can open fire on that area." (The tracers are phosphorous covered rounds that burn with a glow.)

Allah was with those militiamen—they didn't fire again that evening.

September 16, 1993

Two days later, three women entered Atto's house, and two left. One man also entered. Another meeting was held, including one person who appeared to be Atto, grinning with those pearly whites. He seemed in charge, directing people what to do.

Casanova came down from the tower in the Pakistani compound and moved closer to the retaining wall facing Atto's compound. Casanova noticed that people were entering a house near the garage, rather than directly entering Atto's house. We called the QRF to launch a mortar strike, but the three mortars landed nowhere near it.

Later, we exfiltrated back to the hangar at the army compound. There we debriefed with a Delta captain.

During the brief, I said, "We don't mind patrolling with the Rangers, but we'd rather drive ourselves. We know what we'll do when we come under fire, but we don't know what they'll do."

The captain approved.

"Also, we'd like to do night sniper flights with the QRF: eyes over Mogadishu."

"OK."

Casanova and I took a trip to the CIA trailer and shared intelligence about Osman Atto with them.

The first time Casanova and I rode in a QRF helo, we found out their rules of engagement allowed them to keep a magazine in their weapon but no round in the chamber until an enemy fired at them. We always kept a round in our chamber, so all we had to do was flick off the safety switch and shoot. In a war zone, the QRF's rules of engagement were ludicrous.

One day, Casanova and I boarded a Humvee with the QRF. I said, "Lock and load."

The soldiers gave me a strange look. "What the?" Gradually, the lightbulbs came on. Each man made sure his weapon was still on safe and loaded a round in the chamber. Casanova and I would take responsibility for any repercussions from the army brass.

The next time some Rangers, Casanova, and I drove up in our Humvees at the QRF compound, the QRF soldiers who had ridden with Casanova and me before hurried to ride with us again because they knew what our first command would be. "Lock and load."

Later, as more soldiers had an opportunity to ride with us, they'd be standing in line waiting to see which of the Humvees Casanova and I drove up in. We laughed at the sight of them fighting to see who would ride in our vehicle.

At 2400, we boarded a helo with the QRF, both of us sitting on one side of the aircraft. "Lock and load."

The two QRF snipers sitting on the other side of the bird locked and loaded.

Our flight crew used to wait until being fired upon to return fire, but they had taken small-arms fire and two RPGs the night before. "Shoot anyone you feel threatened by." If anyone aimed at us or took an aggressive stance, or positioned themselves to take a shot at us, then we could fire at them.

Although the daytime temperatures averaged 89°F, nights cooled off to around 59 degrees. During our flight over Mogadishu, campfires burned in the upper stories of abandoned buildings. I could imagine refugees gathered around them to keep warm.

Two Somalis on the ground pointed their weapons up at us. Casanova aimed his CAR-15 at one of them. He squeezed the trigger—capping the Somali. The buddy took off running between some buildings, and our pilot couldn't get us near him.

That same night, a Delta operator with a CAR-15 shot a Somali three times in the chest—one of Aidid's lieutenants.

Unfortunately, Delta also had their second accidental discharge (AD). An operator from one of the best fighting units on the planet accidentally fired his weapon in the hangar. He could've killed someone. I remember seeing the look on the operator's face afterward—he knew what was coming. Garrison and others were irate. Even though the operator had trained most of his career to put his gun in a fight, now he had to pack up his gun and leave. His military record would suffer, too. Whether Delta Force or SEAL Team Six, an AD meant a quick trip back to the States. Although we could endure physical pain and suffering, being ostracized from the group was often the heaviest punishment—as I would personally find out later.

September 17, 1993

The next day, Casanova and I climbed up to the top of the Pakistani tower and relieved Little Big Man and Sourpuss. They had observed Atto for three hours at his garage.

A CIA asset had to go inside the garage and verify that the person was indeed Atto before we launched the full package—at least a hundred men, including a Humvee blocking force, Little Birds with Delta snipers, and Black Hawks with Rangers and Delta operators. To signal us, our asset would walk to the middle of the garage area, remove his red and yellow cap with his right hand, and walk around. Casanova and I would then call in the full package—an enormous responsibility for two enlisted men.

We found out that Atto would have a meeting in his garage the next day at 0730. Our HUMINT was amazing, telling us exactly when and where a meeting would be taking place for Atto. Unfortunately, we couldn't acquire that kind of intel for Aidid as we had before.

Delta launched on the radio station to capture Aidid but hit another dry hole.

That evening, Casanova stayed in the tower while I snuck over to the edge of the Pakistani compound and looked over the wall at the adjacent Save the Children house. There was just too much activity going on in the dark of early morning and night. Later, HUMINT sources told us that one of the Somali drivers secretly used the trunks of the cars to transport weapons and ammunition, including mortar rounds. Flying the Save the Children flag on their vehicle, they could drive through almost any roadblock unchecked. I don't think that the people at the Save the Children compound knew the drivers were using their vehicles in this way, but it answered a lot of questions for us about equipment and ammo transportation.

September 18, 1993

Casanova and I began surveillance on Atto's garage from the Pakistani tower at 0600. At 0745 the CIA asset, mustache on his long face, wearing a red and yellow cap, a blue T-shirt, and a *macawi* made out of blue and white plaid material, appeared at the garage. He would earn $5,000 if he succeeded in fingering Atto.

After twenty-five minutes he still hadn't given the pre-determined signal. Then Atto arrived, sporting his Cheshire cat grin. His bodyguards and an old man arrived with him. We radioed it in, but we were required to have the asset's confirmation before launching the package.

Instead of giving us the signal nonchalantly, the asset acted like he'd seen too many B-movies or we were stupid. He took his hand straight out to the side, reached in an arc to the top of his hat, pulled his hat straight up, reversed the arc, and lowered it to his side. If I'd been one of Atto's guards, I would've shot the idiot in the head right then. I fully expected him to be executed before our eyes, but no one had noticed his exaggerated act.

Casanova and I launched the full package. The QRF went on standby. Little Birds and Black Hawks filled the sky. Soon Delta Force operators fast-roped down inside the garage, Rangers fast-roped around the garage, and Little Birds flew around with snipers giving the assault force protection. Atto's people scattered like rats. Militia appeared in the neighborhood, shooting up at the helicopters. News reporters showed up, and sniper Dan Busch threw flashbangs to scare them away from walking into a kill zone. It would later be erroneously reported that hand grenades were thrown at the crew. *Ungrateful idiots. A hand grenade thrown at that range would've killed them all.* Dan personally told me later that the Bat Phone rang from the Pentagon, and he had to explain to the higher-ups that he wasn't throwing fragmentation grenades.

Having crawled over the ledge of a retaining wall and out to the lip of our six-story tower, I lay prone—four rounds loaded in my Win Mag with a fifth in the chamber. Casanova covered the left half of Atto's garage area. I took the right. Through my Leupold 10-power scope, I saw a militiaman 500 yards away firing through an open window at the helos. I shot him in the chest. He fell backward into the building—permanently.

Another militiaman carrying an AK-47 came out a fire escape door on the side of a building 300 yards away from me and aimed his rifle at the Delta operators assaulting the garage. I shot him through his left side, and the round exited his right. He slumped down onto the stairs never knowing what hit him.

About 800 yards away, a guy popped up with an RPG launcher on his shoulder, preparing to fire at the helicopters. It was too time-consuming to keep adjusting my scope for the distance to each target. I dialed in at 1,000 yards—I could mentally calculate the distances under that—but I forgot to physically make the adjustment on the mil dots. Putting the crosshairs on Mr. RPG's upper sternum, I squeezed the trigger. The bullet hit him right underneath his nose. People picture that when a guy gets shot, he flies backward, but the opposite is often true. The bullet penetrates at such a high velocity that it actually pulls the man forward as it goes through, causing him to fall on his face. This militiaman pulled the trigger of the RPG as he fell forward, firing it straight down into the street below. *Boom!*

Hovering overhead in the Little Birds, Delta snipers

saw me make the shot. Minutes later, one of the choppers buzzed our tower. "Hell, yeah!" the snipers yelled, giving me the thumbs-up. I was glad Casanova and I had been lying prone, because the windblast of the snipers' chopper came close to blowing us off our six-story tower.

Delta took fifteen prisoners, but the Rangers in the Humvees hadn't arrived in time to secure the area by cordoning off vehicle and foot traffic. Atto had exchanged shirts with one of his lieutenants and walked out the back of his garage—slipping away.

September 19, 1993

In the dark hours of morning, I woke up to the QRF pulling a raid on houses 500 yards north of our position. The QRF took small-arms fire and RPGs. Aidid's militia chose the wrong convoy to fire on that morning. From the tower, with my night vision, I had an excellent view of the enemy. I picked up the radio mike and vectored helo fire to the source of Aidid's militia. The QRF helo showered down .50 caliber and 40 mm rounds, and QRF ground forces assaulted so heavily that the sky vibrated and the earth shook. The few enemy who survived couldn't get out of there fast enough, running for their lives past Casanova's and my position.

We had used the tower effectively, but Aidid's people put two and two together. A Somali woman stopped and looked up at us. Then she gave Casanova and me the throat-cutting sign. We decided our sniper hide in the Pakistani tower had been compromised and received permission to close it for a few days.

We left the Pakistani compound at 1700 and arrived in the hangar at around 1730. Half a dozen Delta snipers met us at the front door, high-fiving me. "Wasdin, you rock!" One of them looked at the other Delta snipers. "If I ever have someone shooting at me, I want Wasdin making those thousand-yard headshots!"

Later, Casanova and I lasered the actual distance of the head shot: 846 yards, making it the longest killing shot of my career. It also improved our relations with Delta. I never told them I was aiming for the guy's chest.

September 20, 1993

At 0230, Casanova and I took a QRF flight until 0545. During the flight, we spotted a man erecting a mobile transmitter. We thought we'd found the location of Aidid's Radio Mogadishu, where he transmitted operation orders, how to fire mortars, and propaganda. *The UN and Americans want to take over Somalia, burn the Koran, and take your firstborn children.* Even when Aidid's militia got its butt kicked, Radio Mogadishu broadcasted cries of victory, keeping his own people motivated and encouraging other Somalis to join his winning team. Casanova and I couldn't shoot a man for raising a transmitter, but we marked the location as the possible location of Aidid's station.

The QRF aircrew asked if we could fly with them all week. They'd been shot at enough that they wanted SEAL snipers.

Later that day at the compound, Condor contacted us. One of his assets reported that Atto would be at his

house for a meeting. The four of us were the only operators who had frequently seen Atto and could ID him.
Condor wanted a SEAL to go along with him and some
Delta operators. We selected Casanova, but the mission
was scrubbed. Our QRF flight got canceled, too. Although we'd loaded up the Humvees for an assault on
Atto's house, that was also canceled. *Jock up, stand
down, jock up—and every time might be the last.* The
stand-downs bothered me, but not to the point of weak-
ening my motivation to jock up again. Whatever the
challenges, I knew I had to pick myself up and keep
trying. I grew up with a knot in the pit of my stomach, a
perpetual state of worry over when my father would
come after me. At BUD/S, Instructor Stoneclam told us,
"I can make anybody tough, but it takes someone special for me to make mentally tough." Although SEALs
are known for their small numbers and efficiency, the
military as a whole is huge and cumbersome—requiring
us to be patient. My Teammates and I shared a similar
mindset. We had learned how to control feelings of
frustration. I knew I could overcome the challenges of a
fluid environment. Nothing ever goes exactly as
planned. Even with the best plan, when the bullets start
flying, that plan is going to change.

September 21, 1993

Our asset Abe reported sighting Osman Atto in Lido
near our old safe house, Pasha. In dealing with human
intel, we always had to figure out what was real and
what was made up for personal gain. I don't think any

of our assets out-and-out lied to us, but they would exaggerate, probably to get more money. Abe didn't seem to be doing this just for the money. Soft-spoken, he wouldn't become anxious like the others. He talked calmly and matter-of-factly. We liked working with "honest Abe."

In the movie *Black Hawk Down,* someone marks the roof of Atto's vehicle with what looks like olive green military rubber-based adhesive duct tape (riggers' tape). That would've stuck out like a turd in a punch bowl. What really happened was like something out of a James Bond movie. The CIA's Office of Technical Services in Langley mounted a homing beacon inside an ivory-handled cane as a gift for Aidid, but the mission was scrubbed. Condor resurrected the cane and gave it to Abe, who passed it to a contact who met regularly with Atto. The contact would give it to Atto as a gift. While the contact with the cane rode in a car to northern Mogadishu, a helicopter in the air followed the beacon. When the car stopped for gas, Atto materialized. An asset called Condor to let him know that Atto was in the car. Condor radioed Delta.

Delta launched. The assault helo landed almost on top of the target vehicle, and a sniper fired into the engine block, stopping it—the first helicopter takedown on a moving vehicle. Atto threw open the car door and fled. The bodyguard fired his AK-47 at the assault team, but a sniper shot the bodyguard in the leg, disabling him. Assaulters jumped out of the helo, rushed the building, and captured Atto.

Other Delta guys formed a perimeter around the

building. The Somalis burned tires to signal others for help. A few probed Delta's perimeter. A crowd formed. AK-47 and RPG rounds were shot at the helos. Delta snipers in one helo and the guns on another helo fired at the enemy, taking ten to twenty of them down, and pushing back the mob.

Inside, Delta took Atto to the top of the building, where a helo landed and picked them up.

Later, back at the compound, Delta asked us, "We're not sure if it's Atto or not. Could you guys come over and verify his identification?"

"Hell, yeah." Casanova and I walked over to the other end of the runway near the CIA building where they were holding Atto captive in a CONEX box. In *Black Hawk Down,* he was a large man who wore nice clothes, coolly smoked a cigar, and ridiculed his captors. In reality, although he dressed in semiformal shirt and *macawi,* he sniveled. Short, skinny as a broom handle, and shaking like a leaf, Atto looked at Casanova and me like we were the Grim Reaper coming to dispose of him. I almost felt sorry for Atto. Part of me wanted to give him a hug and say, "It'll be OK," and part of me wanted to shoot him in the face.

"Yeah, this is him," Casanova said.

"I don't know," I joked. "Every time we saw him before, he was smiling a big white smile."

Casanova looked at the interpreter. "Tell him if he doesn't smile we're going to beat the crap out of him."

Before the interpreter could translate, Atto flashed a fake smile.

We hadn't realized Atto spoke English. Casanova and I high-fived each other. "That's him!"

Delta whisked him away to a prison on an island off the coast of Somalia. A note found on Atto advised him to meet with reporters to set up a negotiation session with the United Nations Operation in Somalia (UNOSOM). We assume the note was from Aidid—the big fish we still wanted to catch.

12.

EYES OVER MOGADISHU MISSION

In order to capture Aidid, we'd have to overcome the military game of Red Light, Green Light. We'd be told that there wasn't good intel to act on. Suddenly, we'd get the green light to act on something. Then someone above would cancel our mission before we lifted off the ground.

A senior sniper from Blue Team at SEAL Team Six called on the secure line from Dam Neck and asked about mission and tasking in preparation for replacing two of us on October 15. We told him about what we were doing, what to expect, what equipment to bring, and what not to bring.

September 22, 1993

While we sat on our cots in the hangar, the JSOC sergeant major came over and shot the bull with us. He sagely recommended that we mingle more with Delta operators, particularly the assaulters from Charlie Squadron. In some ways SEALs were quite similar to

Delta. For instance, we both excelled at door-banging and shooting. In other ways, though, we were quite different—for instance, takedowns of ships vs. planes. The busy tempo of ops, often done separately, added to the difficulty of getting together with Delta. Plus, in the highly competitive environment of special operations units, especially at the tier-one level, some Delta operators seemed jealous of us. We were tightest with the Delta snipers because we had the most in common with them, and we hung out with the Air Force CCTs and PJs that we knew from before.

The upper echelon canceled our rides on the QRF flights "to work out kinks." I can only guess that the conventional army leaders of the QRF couldn't get along with the unconventional leaders of Delta. Commander Eric Olson, the Team Six officer who would one day become JSOC's first navy commander, met with us in the hangar. He had come to relieve SEAL Commander Tewey, who would go to another assignment at UNOSOM.

"I just came by to say hi and see what you guys have been up to," Commander Olson said.

We told him what we knew.

September 23, 1993

Maybe it was due to Commander Olson's influence or maybe not, but we were able to reestablish QRF flights, now officially tasked as the Eyes over Mogadishu Mission. From 0300 to 0715 Casanova and I flew with the

QRF. During that time, we received a call about a machine gun nest. In the five minutes it took us to reach the area, the gunner had evacuated. After returning to base, I caught a few hours of sleep.

I woke up at 1200 and boarded a helo with the PJs, Scotty and Tim, to do a "goat lab." We flew south of the hangar and landed in a field with some goats we'd purchased from a farmer. I stood in the field with my back to a goat while the Delta surgeon, Major Rob Marsh, shot it. Then he'd say, "Go."

I turned around and had to figure out what was wrong with the animal. Stop arterial bleeding, restore breathing with a trachea tube, patch up a gunshot injury, fix a sucking chest wound . . . He'd screw with us—shoot the gun up in the air a couple of times. I turned around and checked the goat for a gunshot wound but there wasn't one. Turned it over and found a knife puncture wound on the right side of its lung. So I sealed the lung and put the good lung on top. Another time, Major Marsh had his foot on the goat's hindquarters. When he lifted it, blood spurted like a geyser from a femoral artery. Very similar to the arterial bleeding of a human. So I stopped the bleeding. Of course, if we failed, the goat died.

Animal rights activists would be upset, but it was some of the best medical training I ever had. After we finished with the goats, we gave them back to the locals and they ate them. A small price to pay, especially in comparison to the millions of cows and chickens the world kills, for training so realistically in how to save a human life.

September 24, 1993

The next day we were briefed on raiding a teahouse frequented by Colonel Abdi Hassan Awale (a.k.a. Abdi Qeybdid), Aidid's interior minister. All four of us would handle prisoners, and, if needed, Casanova and I would assist Delta with the assault.

While waiting for our next mission, four Delta snipers, Casanova, and I hopped on two Little Birds and went on an African safari out on the plains—training. Armed with our CAR-15s, we sat on the skids of the helos and hunted wild pigs, gazelles, and impalas. I was the only one who shot a wild pig. We landed and picked up the pig with the other kills. For snipers, it was great training for shooting moving targets while flying. We returned to the hangar, where I cut out the tusk for my son, Blake. I didn't think a tusk made a proper gift for my daughter, and there were no gift shops in Mogadishu, so I would have to find Rachel something later. I gutted the pig, skinned and cleaned it, and put it on a spit. Then we had a big barbecue for everyone—a welcome change from the MREs and cafeteria food.

All work and no play makes Jack a dull boy. It was time to blow off some steam. Volleyball, special ops style, is a contact sport. The officers challenged the enlisted men to a game. Before the match, we ambushed the officers. I helped snatch Delta Force's Charlie Squadron commander, Colonel William G. Boykin. We put a ROGUE WARRIOR II tank top on him and flexicuffed his hands and feet to a stretcher. Delta shared my distaste for the Dick Marcinko *Rogue Warrior* nonsense. Then we took pictures of Colonel Boykin.

When Boykin was twenty-nine years old, he attempted to pass selection for Delta Force. Lieutenant Colonel "Bucky" Burruss didn't think Boykin would make it with his bad knee. In addition, a Fort Bragg psychologist tried to reject Boykin for Delta because he was too religious. Boykin surprised a lot of people by passing selection to become a Delta Force operator. He served in the 1980 Iranian hostage rescue attempt, Grenada, Panama, and the hunt for Colombian drug lord Pablo Escobar.

In the regular military, enlisted men don't snatch commanding officers and flexicuff them to stretchers, but the special ops culture is different. For SEALs, the tradition of enlisted men training alongside officers goes back to our World War II frogmen ancestors. After we finished taking pictures of Colonel Boykin, he said, "I just wish you guys would've kicked the crap out of me instead of making me wear that tank top."

September 25, 1993

Even though we and the QRF pilots liked our Eyes over Mogadishu Mission, the upper echelon canceled our evening QRF flights, again. Military politics bounced this back and forth—some nights we were allowed to participate and some nights we weren't—probably because someone above didn't like sharing his piece of pie with Delta and the SEALs.

That night, Aidid's militia used an RPG to shoot

down one of the QRF helicopters. The pilot and copilot were injured, and three others died. Aidid supporters had mutilated the dead soldiers' bodies while the pilot and copilot evaded capture. The Pakistanis and United Arab Emirates (UAE) forces secured the area within minutes, protecting the surviving pilot and copilot as well. Our PJs, with us in support, were ready to rescue the survivors within fifteen minutes, but it was the opinion of all of us in the hangar that the QRF leadership was too ineffectual to do their job properly and too proud to let us help. It took QRF's Search and Rescue two hours to arrive. Totally unacceptable. Not only did the QRF leave their pilot and copilot vulnerable, they also endangered the Pakistanis and UAE forces protecting them on the ground. Where was the *quick* in the Quick Reaction Force? *If Casanova and I had been on that flight, we probably could've saved them.*

Some in the military thought that this RPG shooting down a Black Hawk was a fluke. The RPG was made for ground-to-ground fighting, not ground-to-air. Aiming one at the air meant the back blast would bounce off the street and probably kill the shooter. Also, the white rocket trail marked the shooter's position for helicopter gunfire to take him out. The Black Hawk seemed too fast and too well armored to be shot down by such a weapon. The military would be proved wrong.

September 26, 1993

Next morning we stood by for a raid on the teahouse. If it didn't go down, we'd shift to another mission. No sense spending all our time preparing for a dry hole.

One of Aidid's lieutenants turned himself in to UN-OSOM and said he was no longer an Aidid supporter. Now he'd be working for us.

In the evening, a .50 caliber antiaircraft weapon was being set up at the pasta factory, and the next day it was dismantled. Aidid's people had seen how we operated on more than one occasion—and now they were preparing to shoot us out of the sky. They were smarter than we gave them credit for.

September 27, 1993

Qeybdid and two other lieutenants were in the NBC building. We jocked up with the helo and ground forces, but we had to cancel the mission because Aidid was supposedly sighted elsewhere, and they wanted us to stand by to chase Elvis.

The CIA, SIGINT, and military counterintelligence took eleven guys into custody who were believed to be the controllers and launchers of the enemy mortar teams.

September 28, 1993

We went to the memorial service in the 10th Mountain Division hangar for the three men who died in the QRF helo crash. Condor attended. After the service, he told me, "We've got a lot of targets, but all the military red tape and smoke prevents us from touching them." He was clearly disgusted.

The QRF had difficulties working with Delta. Delta had difficulties working with the CIA. Beyond those difficulties were the problems within the United Nations, particularly Italy. The Clinton administration's lack of support compounded the mess. The three QRF bodies were loaded onto the plane to fly home.

Later that day, although I didn't want to, we got together with Delta on the runway for a group picture. I unhappily stood at the back of the group. *Why are we doing this? So someone can get a copy and target each of us individually?* I was told to do it, so I did. Looking back, I'm glad. It's the only picture I have of my buddy Dan Busch, a sniper in Delta Force's Charlie Squadron, standing next to me. It's my only picture of others, too. Sometimes I look at this picture, which I keep in my personal office, and honor their memory.

September 29, 1993

Wednesday, we received a brief that no hard intel was available, running contrary to what Condor had told me the day before. I flew out to the USS *Rentz* (FFG-46), a frigate carrying guided missiles, sailing off the coast, where I studied for my upcoming exam for promotion to E-7. When I returned to the hangar, I found out we had a mission in five minutes, but it was canceled.

The lieutenant colonel who had responsibility for Delta Force's Charlie Squadron on the ground informed me of a plan to upgrade the compound to include air conditioners, tents, and trailers. There wouldn't be any personnel rotation. We would leave when the mission was complete. I was slated for a signature flight with Sourpuss at 2200, but our bird broke before we could take off.

September 30, 1993

The following day, outside, under the U.S. flag, instead of flying Delta's flag, for the first time they flew SEAL Team Six's flag, a black American Indian head on a red background. Little Big Man on his own initiative had carried it from the Red Team ready room with his other equipment to Mogadishu. When SEALs go somewhere, we surreptitiously let people know where we've been. While I was with SEAL Team Two, as we departed a Norwegian submarine, we covertly covered their dinner table with our flag. It would be nice to take a picture with the four of us and our Red Team flag draped across Aidid. Or if we caught General Garrison asleep we could tuck him into bed using our flag: *Garrison likes Delta, but he feels safer wrapped up in a SEAL Team Six security blanket.* Then we'd post the pictures in our ready room alongside the other photos. That would be big bragging rights for us. *Buy us beer for the rest of the year, suckers. While you stayed home going to driving school, look what we did.*

Around noon, we received a report that Qeybdid had been sighted. We prepared to go, but the reconnaissance bird lost him, and we didn't launch. Finding one man in the maze of Mogadishu was like finding a mole inside an elephant's butt. We should've taken him when we had the chance before, but instead, we chased Elvis sightings.

Contrary to what the lieutenant colonel had told us the previous day, Commander Olson told us we would be rotating out two at a time.

That afternoon, a hammerhead shark attacked a soldier getting some R&R in waist-deep water at the beach. The soldier lost one leg up to the hip, the other leg up to the knee, and lots of blood. I lined up with others to give blood. He took twenty-seven units of blood. Unfortunately, someone put a breathing tube in his esophagus instead of his trachea. He wasn't expected to make it through the night. Although he survived, he was brain dead—remaining in a coma. I don't know who was more to blame, the shark or the person who put his breathing tube in wrong.

October 2, 1993

In the afternoon, we geared up to hit Aidid at Sheik Aden Adere's house. We stood on alert for three and a half hours. Aidid had been at the same house for four hours. Again, the CIA seemed to have a sure thing, but the hit didn't go down. The Agency was furious.

October 3, 1993

When I woke up, the CIA told me they wanted to set up a couple of repeaters in the Lido district of Mogadishu. An asset could use his handheld radio to transmit to the repeater, which could relay the transmission back to the army compound. Likewise, the base could transmit to the asset via the repeater. This would allow for stronger radio transmission at longer distances.

I wore desert cammies with body armor underneath, including the hard armor inserts. Over my cammy top, I put on a bandolier with ten magazines, thirty rounds in each, for a total of three hundred rounds. The bandolier gave me freer movement as a sniper, especially when in the prone position or standing up against something like a wall, than the bulkier web gear. Also, I wore my trusty Adidas GSG9 boots over my military olive drab wool socks. Cotton socks stay soggy wet in the desert, but wool pulls the moisture away from the skin. The evaporation process also helps cool the feet during the day. In the evening, when the desert becomes cold, wool keeps the feet warm. As a sniper, I didn't wear knee pads or the Pro-Tec helmet of assaulters (because of various types of head trauma during the Battle of Mogadishu, JSOC would later change to an Israeli ballistic helmet). For communication, we wore bone phones with the durable waterproof Motorola MX-300 radios, capable of encryption, on our belts. The earpiece went behind the ear, so it wouldn't obstruct our hearing. Two mike pads pressed against the trachea. The mike didn't come out in front of the face, so while aiming, we easily settled a cheek to the butt of the rifle without interference. Of course, I carried water in the Camelbak. As usual, I carried my Swiss Army knife, which I used almost daily.

We rode Huey helicopters out to the Pakistani Stadium, then rode indigenous vehicles to two houses. After inserting the repeaters, we drove back to the camel factory on the beach, where the helos picked us up. I had no idea this was about to be the longest day of my life—and nearly my last.

PART THREE

Do the right thing even if it means dying like a dog when no one's there to see you do it.

—Vice Admiral James Stockdale,
NAVY PILOT

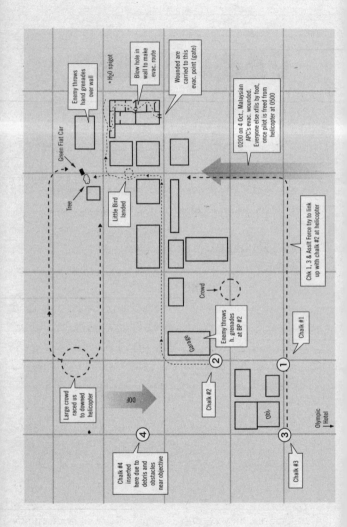

13.
BATTLE OF MOGADISHU

As we pulled back into the compound, everyone was jocking up for something big. Helicopters spun up, Humvees pulled into position, and everyone topped off their magazines. Although the sun shone brightly through clear blue skies, I knew the troops weren't heading out on a picnic. "What's going on?"

Commander Olson approached us before we stepped out of our "cutvee"—a cut Humvee without a top, doors, or windows, officially called the M-998 cargo/troop carrier. It had no special armor. Tech reps from the States had arrived less than a week earlier and put a Kevlar ballistic blanket underneath the vehicle to protect against land mines or other fragmentation. I sat in the driver's seat with Casanova riding shotgun. Behind me was Little Big Man, Sourpuss beside him. To the rear of them we had two benches running parallel to the vehicle where two army guys sat—I think they were Rangers, but they could've been Delta operators. In addition, a Ranger manned the .50 caliber machine gun.

Commander Olson briefed us in just a few minutes. "You'll be part of a blocking force. Delta will rope in and assault the building. You guys will grab the prisoners. Then get out of there." Usually such a brief would last an hour to an hour and a half. Delta, the Rangers, and others got that briefing, but we missed it. Although the mission was important enough for us to be briefed on, it had popped up suddenly while we were out in town setting up repeaters for the CIA. Commander Olson slapped me on the shoulder. "Shouldn't take long. Good luck. See you when you get back."

Each of four light AH-6J Little Birds carried four snipers, two on either side of a helo. The Little Birds also carried rockets underneath—where we would be going wasn't going to be good. The two AH-6Js, armed with 7.62 mm miniguns and 2.75-inch rockets, would guard the front of the target building from the air while two hovered to the rear. Delta's C Squadron would fast-rope from two MH-6 Little Birds and assault the building.

Eight Black Hawks would follow, two carrying Delta assaulters and their ground command. Four of the Black Hawks would insert the Rangers. One would hover above with a Combat Search and Rescue team. The eighth Black Hawk contained the two mission commanders, one coordinating the pilots and one directing the men on the ground.

Three OH-58D Kiowa helos, distinctive for the black ball mounted above the rotor, would also fly in the airspace above the target. The black ball was a sight with a platform that contained a TeleVision System, a Thermal Imaging System, and a Laser Range Finder/Designator to provide audio and video of the ground to General

Garrison at the Joint Operations Center. High above everyone circled a P-3 Orion.

I drove into position at about the third vehicle in the convoy. Behind our Humvees idled three 5-ton trucks, and five more Humvees brought up the rear. Rangers made up most of our convoy. In all, nineteen aircraft, twelve vehicles, and 160 men.

Aidid's men had already seen how we did this six times before, and now we'd be operating under broad daylight on his home turf. Many of his militia would be pumped up on khat at this time of day, not coming down off their high until late in the evening. Risks that pay off are bold moves. Those that don't pay off are stupid. Part of my job included taking risks.

At 1532, the helicopters took off first, following the coast. When we received word that the birds were headed inland, our convoy headed out. I wasn't afraid—yet. *This is going to be a routine op.*

On the way, the lead Humvee took a wrong turn. Nobody followed. They would have to catch up to us later. We sped northeast on Via Gesira. Before reaching the K4 traffic circle, we encountered sporadic fire. Little Big Man yelled, "Aw hell, I'm hit!"

Are we driving into an ambush? Does Little Big Man have a sucking chest wound? The needle on my fear meter was still close to zero. Little Big Man was shot, not me. All the same, I worried for Little Big Man's life, and my alert level went up.

I pulled off the road underneath an overhang, slammed on the brakes, jumped out, and checked Little Big Man. He lay on the floor with part of his Randall knife blade beside him. I expected to see blood come from somewhere but only found a huge raspberry on his leg. An AK-47 round had hit that Randall knife he loved so much and carried everywhere. The blade lay on the floor. It saved his leg—worth all the kidding he had ever endured about that big-ass knife.

The convoy continued moving during the minute we were parked on the side of the road. I returned to the driver's seat, then sped forward, catching up to our former position. The convoy passed the K4 circle and went north on Via Lenin, then east on National Street. Finally, we turned left on a dirt road parallel to and south of Hawlwadig Road.

At 1542, we arrived near the white five-story Olympic Hotel. I didn't know that a mile west of the target, militia gathered at the Bakara Market, distributing smuggled weapons and ammo. To the east, a mile away, was where foreign insurgents had recently arrived. We were already being sandwiched and didn't know it.

Our intel guys had probably already jammed all the cell phones in the target area. In a sandstorm kicked up by the helos, Delta operators roped down to the target building, a white building with two stories in front, three stories in back, an L-shaped structure on top, and trees in the courtyard—one of Aidid's militia headquarters. Delta stacked up near the door, lining up behind each other in preparation to enter and snatch their target. Four groups of Rangers, twelve in each, fast-roped down and sealed the four corners of the city block around the target building. They made up the blocking force. No one gets in, and no one gets out.

I left the cutvee and took up a firing position in an

alley parallel to the hotel. To the rear of the hotel, an enemy sniper moved behind a wall. Five stories above and to the left, another sniper moved on a veranda.

Shifting my position to get a better look, I realized we couldn't get a clear shot from where we were. I told a Delta sniper, "We're going to have to move on them."

We bumped up, moving forward to within less than 100 yards. As we settled into our new position, the enemy had already begun firing into the target building where Delta assaulted. This felt like a setup to me. They were too well prepared. It seemed like too much of a coincidence that those snipers had set up so perfectly. *Probably a United Nations leak*.

The ground sniper sticking his rifle over the wall, approximately 100 to 150 yards away, aimed his scope at the Rangers in my convoy. The sniper had a good shooting position, only exposing his head. With a squeeze of my trigger, I overexposed his head.

Through an alleyway, I saw the veranda of the nearby five-story building. Less than 200 yards away on the fifth floor, two men fired AK-47s into the back of the target house where the Delta assaulters were. From where I was, I couldn't get a clear shot.

I looked over at the Delta operator. "We need to move on these two or it's going to get real bad."

We slipped through the alley and took positions behind a pillar to our right. Still didn't have a good shot.

The two men on the fifth floor continued to pop out, spray at Delta's assault force, then pop back inside.

The Delta operator and I moved forward again. Finding a good spot, I lay in the prone position while my partner protected the perimeter around me. I set the red dot of my sight on the spot where the bad guy had appeared on the right. In sniper talk, it's called an ambush—aiming at a point and waiting for the target to appear there. The same technique could be used for a running target—aiming at a spot ahead of the runner's path. When the man with the AK-47 appeared on the right, I squeezed the trigger, hitting his upper torso. He popped back into the building and didn't pop out again. With a concrete divider hiding his demise, the second man with an AK-47 didn't learn from the first one's mistake. The second man popped out to spray with his AK-47 but also took one of my rounds to his upper torso and disappeared. If I hadn't taken out those two, they would've had more opportunities to kill someone by shooting through the target building's windows—an assaulter's worst nightmare. While the assaulter takes down the building and controls everything inside, suddenly bullets come through the windows at him from the outside.

At least thirty minutes had passed since we'd arrived. Every minute we stayed in the target area increased the level of danger. Over the radio came the command to return to the convoy. On my way through the alley, heading back to the cutvee, a ricochet hit me in the back of the left knee, knocking me to the dirt. For a moment, I couldn't move. On a fear scale of 1 to 10, 10 being out of my mind with fear, the needle jumped up between the 2 and the 3. The pain surprised me, because I had reached a point in my life when I really thought I was more than human. I was better trained. People around me got shot or injured, but not me. Even other SEALs got shot or injured because they were not me. *That's why you fell off that caving ladder—because you're not Howard Wasdin. That's why you couldn't pass me on the O-course—because you're not Howard Wasdin.* Even after getting shot that first time in the Battle of Mogadishu, I clung to my arrogance. I was stunned with disbelief more than anything else.

Dan Schilling, the CCT, appeared. Casanova arrived and calmly shot one booger-eater. Then another. A medic had just started treating me when Dan grabbed my bandolier and pulled me out of the enemy's kill zone. The medic stuffed my leg full of Kerlix gauze and wrapped it up. Then I was on my feet again.

The bad guys burned tires—a signal to their comrades to join the fight and a black smoke screen to obscure our vision. Militiamen with AK-47s popped up from behind smoke, side streets, and buildings—everywhere. As soon as I shot someone down, a replacement popped up. Unarmed women walked out as spotters, then pointed out our positions to the enemy. RPGs went off.

Aidid's men yelled into megaphones. I didn't understand that their words meant "Come out and defend your homes," but I understood they meant us harm.

One of the 5-ton trucks in our convoy smoldered from being hit by an RPG. Someone in our convoy finished off the truck with a thermite grenade so it wouldn't fall into enemy hands. The vehicle flamed brightly.

Delta loaded two dozen flexicuffed prisoners into two of the remaining 5-ton trucks. Included among the prisoners was Aidid's top political adviser, Foreign

Minister Omar Salad. Although Delta missed snatching Qeybdid, they'd captured a lieutenant of similar rank, Mohamed Assan Awale. They found a bonus, too, a clan chieftain named Abdi Yusef Herse. After returning to the compound, Delta would sort out the big fish from the others and release the little ones.

At thirty-seven minutes, word came over the radio, "Super Six One down." An RPG had shot down a Black Hawk with a cartoon of Elvis Presley on its side, captioned VELVET ELVIS. Its pilot, Chief Warrant Officer Cliff Wolcott, had performed Elvis impersonations and was one of the pilots who'd taken us on safari. Now our mission shifted from a prisoner snatch to a rescue.

We loaded up in the convoy to move out again. Aiming a Squad Automatic Rifle down an alley lay a Ranger who didn't look more than twelve years old.

I sat in the driver's seat calling to him, "Load up, let's go!"

The kid remained frozen.

I hopped out of the cutvee, ran over to the corner of the building, and kicked him.

He looked up at me with dazed eyes.

"Load your ass into the vehicle!"

He picked himself up and climbed into his Humvee.

Sometimes the young Rangers got so focused on the one thing they were supposed to do that they lost sight of the big picture. Their vision didn't widen in response to changes in the environment, and their ears missed verbal commands. Experiencing sensory overload of the sympathetic nervous system, they couldn't catch everything that was going on.

Fortunately, my father's harshness to me as a child

had prepared me for difficulties like this. Adding to that preparation were Hell Week, SEAL Team Two, SEAL Team Six, Marine Corps Scout Sniper School—intense training for years. The more you train in peace, the less you bleed in war. Desert Storm helped prepare me. I had developed a tolerance for sensory overload. Some of these Rangers had only been out of high school a couple of years, but every one of them fought bravely.

I loaded into the cutvee with Casanova, Little Big Man, and the others. Sourpuss wasn't with us. My mind was so focused on the combat that I didn't hear Little Big Man tell us that Sourpuss was tasked to three Humvees evacuating a Ranger casualty back to the compound. Little Big Man and Casanova stayed together with me in the cutvee, riding in the main convoy.

I drove out of the target area north on the sandswept paved Hawlwadig Road. With my left hand on the wheel, my right fired the CAR-15. AK-47 rounds came at us left and right. As bullets passed over my head, they created pressure waves faster than the speed of sound, waves that crashed into each other like two hands clapping. I heard the rounds coming—the clap—then the sound of them passing by.

White trails of smoke stretched out, resulting in exploding RPGs that shook the air, filling it with a bitter smell. The smell of burning tires and burning refuse rose above the normal stench of Mogadishu, stinking like hell.

Our .50 caliber machine gun rattled off, shaking our Humvee and pounding our ears. Still, it felt good to have the .50 cal, and I was too busy using my eyes to scan for booger-eaters in my field of fire to be bothered by the horrendous noise. SEAL veterans had often talked about how reassuring it felt when their machine gun fired in battle. We're trained to use surprise, speed, and violence of action to win battles. In our convoy, we weren't surprising the enemy and couldn't move faster than the Humvee in front of us. The .50 helped us with the violence of action. Its barrel glowed from the steady stream of bullets pouring out, chewing through concrete, metal, flesh—it literally knocked out walls. *Yeah, the .50 is kicking ass.* Unfortunately, the enemy had .50s, too, bolted to the beds of their pickup trucks courtesy of Osman Atto's garage. The trucks ducked in and out of alleys shooting at us.

A helicopter gun blasted at the enemy, demolishing the side of a building. Somalis ran in all directions. Some screamed. Some froze. Dead people and a dead donkey lay on the ground.

Aidid's people are way better equipped than we thought, they fight better than we thought, and there are a lot more of them armed than we thought. Now I was afraid we were going to get our asses kicked. On my fear scale, the needle jumped past 3 and hit 5. Anyone who says he wasn't scared in combat is either an idiot or a liar. Everyone becomes scared. It's a healthy fear. I'd never want to go into combat with someone who wasn't a little afraid. What makes a warrior is being able to control and focus that fear. He develops this ability to control fear by believing he *can* control fear. This belief is gained by having overcome fear in previous experiences, seeing Teammates overcome such fears, knowing that he is an elite warrior, and channeling that anxious energy to boost his performance.

In our convoy, we had wounded men in *every* vehicle. We still wanted to rescue Velvet Elvis and his crew in the downed Super Six One. Nearing a road where a couple of Rangers lay wounded, I thought, *What the hell is wrong with these Somalis? We're here to stop the civil war, so people can get food, and they're killing us. This is how we're repaid?* I couldn't believe it. I pulled our cutvee off the road and stopped. The first Ranger I picked up was shot in the leg. We loaded him in the back of our cutvee. Then we loaded the other one, who'd been shot in the web of his hand—not such a debilitating injury. As I returned to the driver's seat, I looked back. The Ranger with the wounded leg was helping resupply us with ammo while the other Ranger sat there in a daze with his head down staring at his wounded hand.

The Ranger resupplying us with ammo was hit again, this time in the shoulder, but he kept feeding us ammo in the front. Then a round tore into his arm. He *still* kept feeding us ammo.

Meanwhile, the Ranger who'd been shot once through the web of his hand remained out of it, the needle on his fear meter stuck on 10. He was the only Ranger I saw back down from the fight. Then again, it's not every day a person gets shot. His reaction of shock is understandable—he was just a young kid in a horrific battle. Considering some of their youth and lack of experience, all of the Rangers fought bravely.

Stepping hard on the accelerator, I caught up with the rest of the convoy. It turned right on a dirt road. When the first Humvee slowed down at the intersection, each vehicle behind was forced to slow down, creating an accordion effect. Then we turned right again, toward the south—but we had just come from the south.

I was getting pissed at our ground convoy leader, Lieutenant Colonel Danny McKnight, but I didn't know he was just doing what the birds in the sky told him. The Orion spy plane could see what was happening but couldn't speak directly to McKnight. So it relayed information to the commander at JOC. Next, the JOC commander called the command helicopter. Finally, the command helicopter radioed McKnight. By the time McKnight received directions to turn, he'd already passed the road.

All I knew was that I was getting shot at again, holes being poked into the holes of our cutvee. Our men in the back were getting hit. *Holy crap.* I wanted to stomp the accelerator to get out of the kill zone, but I could only go as fast as the Humvee in front of me. I shot militia coming at us from the side streets. Trying to drive and shoot militia ducking in and out of side streets, I'd be surprised if I had as much as a 30 percent kill rate.

People in buildings on the second floor shot down at us. I took some time to get into my ACOG scope, lining up the red dot on my first target and squeezing the trigger. One enemy down. Then another.

The bad guys had thrown up burning roadblocks and dug trenches to slow us down. While the convoy tried to drive through and around the roadblocks, the enemy ambushed us. Ahead and to the side of us, five women walked shoulder to shoulder holding their colorful robes out to both sides, advancing toward the convoy. When a Humvee reached the ladies' position, they pulled their dresses in and the men behind opened fire with their AK-47s on full auto. Later, they tried the same tactic on our cutvee. For the first time in the firefight, I flicked my selector switch to full auto. With one hand on the wheel, and the other holding my CAR-15, I fired thirty rounds, cutting down the women—and the four armed militia hiding behind them. Better to be judged by twelve than carried by six.

Then over the radio I heard that an RPG had taken down a Black Hawk piloted by Mike Durant. The word came down from the command helo to rescue Velvet Elvis first, then move on to Mike at the second crash site.

We stopped on the street, set up a perimeter, provided first aid, replenished ammo, and figured out what to do next. A medic bandaged the Ranger's shoulder and arm and other guys' wounds in our cutvee. Some Rangers looked like zombies, shock in their eyes.

A Delta operator came over. "I took a hit. Can you take a look at my shoulder?" A shot had clipped the hard armor plate in his back, but it didn't take him out of the fight.

The .50 cal machine gunner in another Humvee wore an armored vest, good for resisting small-caliber rounds. He had also inserted a specially designed 10″ × 12′ ceramic plate in the front for protection against heavier rounds like the AK-47. However, he hadn't worn a plate on his back. Probably, like many other soldiers, he considered the extra plate in back too hot and too heavy. Besides, most shots are from the front anyway. He rolled the dice—and lost. Over the radio, we offered to let our .50 gunner replace him. The Humvee of the dead

.50 gunner pulled up next to our vehicle. Inside, tears streamed down a Ranger's face as he held on to his buddy, one arm under his head. "You dumb sonofabitch. I told you. I told you to wear your back plate. I told you."

They pulled the dead gunner out, and our gunner replaced him. Without a qualified .50 gunner like our Ranger, their Humvee would've lost the ability to use its hardest-hitting weapon. Our gunner would end up saving their Humvee.

Casanova and I had used up the ten thirty-round magazines in our bandoliers, plus five more magazines that the Ranger with the wounded shoulder and arm re-supplied us with. Because both of us carried the CAR-15s, which used the same 5.56 mm ammo as the Rangers in our Humvee, they could resupply us with their ammo stockpile in back. Little Big Man realized he'd brought the wrong weapon to the gunfight—a SEAL modified M-14. Nobody had extra 7.62 ammo for Little Big Man's depleted M-14 rifle.

The convoy moved forward, and we turned left, heading east, then left to the north. I didn't know that McKnight was hit, with shrapnel in his arm and neck. We stopped. McKnight radioed the command helo for directions, but miscommunication would send us on the wrong path again. The convoy continued north to Armed Forces Road and made a left.

I also didn't realize that Dan Schilling had taken over for McKnight while he was wounded. Dan succeeded in bypassing the convoluted communication loop and communicated straight to one of the helos. When Dan told them to vector us to the crash site, he assumed the helo knew we were headed to Velvet Elvis at the first crash site, but the helo assumed we were headed for the nearest one—Mike at the second crash site.

We turned left on Hawlwadig, heading near the Olympic Hotel and the target building. The convoy had gone around in a complete circle! We had showed our hand to Aidid's people during previous assaults, then launched the current assault during daylight, and now I was getting shot at again—I was beyond pissed! SEAL cadre had taught us, "If you live through one ambush, go home, get in your rocking chair, and thank God the rest of your life." I remembered Commander Olson slapping me on the shoulder before we left the compound: "Shouldn't take long." *Yeah, right. These are the same booger-eaters who were shooting at us a while ago. What the hell is McKnight doing? Hey, dumb-ass, we just did this. It didn't work out too well the first time.*

While there was confusion on the radio about whether we were heading to the first crash site or the second, I heard that a crowd was closing in on Mike Durant with no ground forces in the area to help, and I remembered what happened to the Pakistanis when a crowd descended on them—they were hacked to pieces.

The first time Aidid's men ambushed our convoy, they killed some of our guys and wounded more, but we had pulled out a can of whoop-ass on them. Corpses lay everywhere. Now the enemy ambushed us a second time—dumb bastards. They paid a hell of a price. In particular, our helicopter guns and rockets sent bodies and body parts flying.

During the fight, I called for more helicopter fire to get the enemy off our backs.

A pilot answered, "We're Winchestered." They had used up all their ammunition, including the 20 percent they were supposed to keep in reserve to defend themselves during the return to base. I was counting on that extra 20 percent. Even though they were out of ammo, the pilots buzzed over the bad guys almost low enough to hit them with the skids. The enemy turned away from us and directed their gunfire at the helos. While the booger-eaters aimed at the sky, we shot them. The pilots didn't just do that once. They did it at least six times that I remember. Our Task Force 160 pilots were badass, offering themselves up as live targets, saving our lives.

As I drove, I ran out of ammo in my CAR-15. I let it hang from the battle sling harnessed to me and drew the SIG SAUER 9mm pistol from the holster on my right hip. Our convoy slowed down, and a booger-eater emerged in a doorway, aiming his AK-47 right at me. I brought my SIG SAUER across. Double tap. I'd made that double head shot over a thousand times in training. Under the present combat conditions, I rushed the shot. Miss. Adrenaline pumping at full blast, the world seemed to decelerate around me. The booger-eater pulled the trigger in slow motion. The bullet hit my right shinbone, practically blowing off my lower right leg. His bolt went back. The empty casing ejected. *This guy ain't playing around.* I took an extra half second and got on my front sight. Like John Shaw says, "Smooth is fast." Double tap. Both rounds hit him in the face. If I'd have taken that extra half second the first time, I could've capped his ass and saved my leg.

Our cutvee slowed down. *What the hell is wrong with our cutvee?* I tried to stomp on the accelerator and couldn't. Looking down on the floorboard, I saw a big toe pointing behind me. I didn't even realize it was my leg twisted inward. Surely I'd be in a lot more pain if it was my leg. I tried to step on the accelerator again. My right foot flopped. *Sonofabitch. That's my leg.* Reaching with my left foot, I jabbed the accelerator. *Wow, this is some really serious crap. I better get on top of my game.* Even though this was my second time getting shot during the battle, I still embraced my own superhuman strength. My fear meter rose to 6, but it hadn't reached 10. I felt numbness more than pain because my nerve receptors had overloaded. Although surprised for the second time during combat, I still felt superior as a SEAL Team Six sniper—Howard Wasdin.

I was furious with McKnight and called him on the radio. "Get us the hell out of here!"

Finally out of the danger zone, the convoy stopped to help the people who were leaking to stop leaking, feed our weapons more ammo, and plan our next move. Casanova helped me crawl over the center console and into the passenger seat, so he could drive. The battle sling of my CAR-15 got hung up on the center console. Little Big Man wrestled with it, trying to get it clear. Whatever love he had for the M-14 and its longer range seemed to have faded. Little Big Man wanted my CAR-15.

My shattered bone had jagged edges that could slice into an artery and cause me to bleed to death. Casanova propped my wounded leg up on the hood of the

Humvee and placed my left leg next to it as a brace. The elevation would also slow the blood flow. "I'm going to get you home," Casanova said.

The convoy moved out, and Casanova stepped on the gas. Our cutvee ran on three flat tires. The convoy made a U-turn and turned right at the Olympic Hotel, heading toward the first crash site, Velvet Elvis. It was like the movie *Groundhog Day,* repeating the same actions over and over again.

Five or ten minutes later, an enemy round shot through my left ankle. Unlike the fracture in my right shin, where my central nervous system shut off the pain, this one hurt like a bitch. My fear level rose from 6 to 7. My emotions toward the enemy rocketed off the anger scale. They had taken away my superhero powers. Suddenly, I realized I was in trouble.

True to form, our convoy missed Velvet Elvis at the first crash site—again. Then we stopped. Guys stepped out of their vehicles and set up a perimeter. McKnight got out of his vehicle with someone, and it looked like they laid a map on the hood of their Humvee, plotting our location. It was surreal. *While we're getting shot, why not walk into the 7-Eleven and ask for directions?*

Our convoy had failed twice to navigate its way to one of the downed pilots. We had used up most of our ammunition. Wounded and dead bodies filled our vehicles. Half of the men were severely wounded, including most of the leaders. If we didn't return to base and regroup, we might not have anyone left to launch a rescue.

Our cutvee had more holes in it than a sponge. The side mirrors dangled from their L-brackets. As the convoy moved forward again, our cutvee hit a land mine. The ballistic blankets covering the floor saved us from fragmentation. (I would later be made an honorary member of the Kevlar Survivor's Club.) Casanova pulled off the road, where our cutvee died. The booger-eaters descended on us. *We're about to be overrun.*

I remembered the old 1960 movie *The Alamo,* starring John Wayne as Davy Crockett. It was one of my favorite movies, and Davy Crockett was my favorite person in the Alamo. *This must be how Davy Crockett felt before they killed him: outgunned, undermanned, without protection. Seeing his people get wiped out while the enemy continued to advance. This is it. Howard Wasdin checks out in Mogadishu, Somalia, on the afternoon of October 3, 1993. My one regret is I haven't told the people I love that I love them enough. During my time on earth, it's what I should've done more of.* The first two people who came to mind were my children, Blake and Rachel. I probably only told them I loved them about six times a year. Part of the problem was that, with frequent training deployments and real-world ops, I just wasn't around for a large part of their lives. Even though I was married, now I didn't think of my wife, Laura. My relationship with the SEAL Team had been more important than my marriage. I wanted to tell Blake and Rachel how much I loved them.

My fear meter peaked at 8. It never reached 10. When you hit a 10, you can't function anymore. You succumb to the mercy of events going on around you. I wasn't dead yet. Firing back with my SIG, I tried to keep six or seven of the booger-eaters from surrounding us. Physically, I couldn't shoot effectively enough to kill anyone at that point. I had used up two of Casanova's pistol magazines and was down to my last. Over the radio, I heard that the QRF were on their way to rescue us— four hours into the gunfight. Quick Reaction Force— *what is their definition of "quick"?*

Our vehicle still disabled on the side of the road, I looked up to see the QRF drive past our road. *Sonofa-bitch. We had a chance to get rescued and there they go. They are going to leave us here to die.* Then the QRF stopped and backed up with a deuce-and-a-half. *Thank God, at least they can see us.* When they reached the road beside us, the booger-eaters took flight. The QRF stopped.

Casanova and Little Big Man helped transfer the wounded over to their vehicles.

A Ranger struggled to coil up a fast rope that had been dropped from a helicopter during the insertion— just doing what he'd done on training ops many times. In sensory overload, soldiers rely heavily on muscle memory, fighting the way they trained.

Unable to walk, I stared at the Ranger in disbelief. "This is not a training operation!" I yelled. "Put the rope down, get your ass in the deuce-and-a-half, and let's get out of here!"

The Ranger continued trying to recover the rope, not conscious of the situation around him and not listening to verbal commands.

I pointed my SIG SAUER at him. "I won't kill you, but you will walk with a limp if you don't get your ass in that truck!"

The Ranger looked confused for a moment before dropping the fast rope. He hurried into a vehicle.

Finally, my guys loaded me into the deuce-and-a-half. "Be careful with him," Casanova said. "His right leg is barely hanging on."

We rode back to the compound unmolested by Aidid's forces. Arriving inside the gates, we met chaos: forty to fifty American bodies laid out all over the runway with medical personnel trying to get them through triage—figuring out the nonsurvivable from the survivable, the critical from the less critical—and attending to them accordingly. A Ranger opened a Humvee tailgate—blood flowed out like water.

Casanova and Dan Schilling carried me to the triage area.

Still in daylight, the medics stripped off all my clothes and treated me. They left me lying naked on that runway covered with bodies. Exposed.

Once again, death had just missed me. Like it missed when the enemy shot down the QRF helo, killing three men. Like it missed when Aidid's militia massed to attack us at Pasha. Like it missed when mortars bombed the CIA compound I had visited the day before. Like all the other misses. I thought maybe Casanova and I could've made a difference if we'd been riding in the QRF helicopter flight when the three men died. It hadn't occurred to me that maybe I could've been killed. It hadn't occurred to me that God was looking out for us. Now forty-eight years old and not as cocky, I wonder, *Would I have been able to get the enemy before he got me? Maybe people would've been coming to my memorial ceremony.*

Before the Battle of Mogadishu, the Clinton administration's support for our troops had sagged like a sack of turds. They had rejected or removed M-2 Bradley infantry fighting vehicles, M-1 Abrams tanks, and AC-130 Spectre gunships. The Clinton camp was more interested in maintaining political points than keeping some of America's finest troops alive.

During the Battle of Mogadishu, eighteen Americans were killed and eighty-four wounded. Also, one Malaysian died and seven were injured. Two Pakistanis and one Spaniard were wounded, too. In spite of only about 180 soldiers fighting against nearly 3,000 of Aidid's militia and civilian fighters, we captured Omar Salad, Mohamed Hassan Awale, Abdi Yusef Herse, and others. Thousands of Aidid's clan members were killed, with thousands more wounded. They'd depleted much of their ammunition. A number of the chieftains evacuated in fear of America's inevitable counterattack. Some were ready to turn in Aidid to save themselves. Four fresh SEAL Team Six snipers from Blue Team were on their way to relieve us. Delta's Alpha Squadron was gearing up to relieve Charlie Squadron. A new batch of Rangers was coming, too. We had broken Aidid's back, and we wanted to finish the job.

In spite of the gains, President Clinton saw our sacrifices as losses. Even though we could've finished the job of taking down Aidid and getting food to the people, Clinton turned tail and ran. He ordered all actions against Aidid stopped. Four months later, Clinton released Osman Atto, Omar Salad, Mohamed Hassan Awale, Abdi Yusef Herse, and the other prisoners. *Whiskey Tango Foxtrot.*

We had spent so much time working with local Somalis to build their trust, to convince them that we would be with them in the long run. Many of these Somalis risked their lives to help us. Some endangered their families. Our former Somali guards at Pasha joined in the Battle of Mogadishu, loyal to the end. Only one of them survived. Other Somalis died on our side trying to stop Aidid. We left our Somali friends dangling in the breeze. I felt like our sacrifices had been in vain. *Why did they send us if they weren't willing to finish the job?* We shouldn't have become involved in Somalia's civil war—this was their problem, not ours—but once we committed, we should've finished what we started: a lesson we are required to keep relearning over and over again.

Somalia lost the assistance of the international community to bring peace and food to the country. Chaos and starvation spiked sharply. Aidid tried to downplay his losses, but he would never rule over a united Somalia. He died in 1996 during an internal battle against his evil genius, Osman Atto.

14.
FROM THE ASHES

The sun had disappeared when medical personnel whisked me away to the Swedish field hospital. The thought sank in that I might lose my leg. I was scared. At the hospital, a nurse gave me a shot of morphine. It didn't take effect. Turned out I was in the one percent of people whose receptor for morphine doesn't make the pain go away. The nurse gave me another shot. My leg still hurt like hell. They debrided my wounds—removing damaged, infected, and dead tissue to help me heal. Then they prepared me for transportation to Germany.

The medical personnel loaded us onto a plane. Inside the impressive aircraft, it looked like a hospital with wings: beds, IV units, machines. A nurse walked by me.

I reached out and grabbed her leg. "I'm hurting so bad. Can you please just give me something?"

She looked at my medical chart. "You've had two shots of morphine. You can't be feeling pain." Then she walked away to see another patient.

A little while later, a doctor came by and saw me.

This was bone pain—the worst kind of pain. With a cut, the body compensates by constricting arteries to decrease blood flow to the area in order to prevent bleeding to death. With a bone injury, the body can't compensate. My pale body shook, and sweat poured out of me as I clenched my teeth, trying to will the pain not to consume me. *Calm your pulse down. Slow your breathing. Block the pain; will it away. I could do it as a kid; why isn't it working yet? I could do it as a kid; why can't I do it now?* It was the same principle I used when I was getting my ass beat as a child: remove myself from the pain and not become physically involved. Self-preservation mode. I couldn't stop the physical symptoms of paleness, shaking, and sweat, so I tried to control how my mind coped with the pain.

"This man is in pain," the doctor said.

"No kidding. I've been trying to tell you all."

He gave me a shot of Demerol. "How's that?"

I felt almost instant relief. "Thank you so much."

The doctor spoke with the nurse. Then she came over and apologized. "I'm sorry. I'm so sorry. I didn't know." She was almost in tears.

Will I lose my leg? We landed at the Ramstein Air Base in Germany. Air force personnel loaded us onto a bus. The air force guys were cheerful and helpful. "We heard you guys kicked ass. We're going to take good care of you." They pumped up our spirits.

Upon my arrival at the army's Landstuhl Regional Medical Center, the largest American hospital outside of the United States, the doctors took me straight to surgery.

In the operating room, they prepped me. A nurse tried to give me a general anesthetic.

"I don't want to go to sleep," I said.

"We need to put you to sleep for the surgery," she reasoned with me.

"I don't want to go to sleep. I know you're going to take my leg off."

She and a male nurse tried to hold me down, but I fought them off.

The situation was pretty intense when the surgeon came in. "What's going on?"

"The patient is resisting," the nurse explained. "He won't let us administer the general anesthetic."

The surgeon looked at me. "What's the problem?"

"I'm just afraid you're going to take my leg if you put me to sleep. I don't want to go to sleep. Please."

The surgeon told the nurse, "Give him an epidural."

She gave me the shot in my lower back. Used for women giving childbirth, it deadened everything in me from the waist down.

The surgeon took my arm and looked into my eyes. "I may be the best orthopedic surgeon in the air force. I'll save your leg."

He may have been BS-ing me, but he seemed sincere, and I felt reassured.

The doctor performed surgery on me as I watched. When I realized they weren't going to take my leg off, I fell asleep.

Later, I awoke to pain on my right thigh. The epidural had started to wear off. The surgeon had an instrument he used to scrape grafts of skin off my thigh. He put the grafts through a machine that looked like a cheese grater, which he used to punch holes in the skin to make it bigger. Then he stapled the skin onto the site where they'd performed the surgery. Gradually, I started to feel some pain. When they did the next skin graft, I flinched.

If it had been the Vietnam era, the doctors would've amputated. Due to advances in modern medicine and a great surgeon, I was able to keep my leg.

After the surgery, they carted me to my room. The nurse hooked up an electrical pump to my bed. "If you're in pain, just hit this button, here. You can't overdo it, but when you're in pain, just give yourself a dose."

"Cool." I hit the button a couple of times and went to sleep.

Waking up, I had no concept of time. A voice cried out, "Damn, it hurts! Damn, it hurts!"

A nurse's voice said, "Just hold on. We're trying to find a pump."

I looked over. He was the brave Ranger who'd been shot in the leg once, shoulder twice, and arm once—and still fed me ammo during the Battle of Mogadishu.

Some time had passed, and the nurse still hadn't brought his pump. The hospital was not quite prepared for the mass casualties they now had on their hands.

The Ranger continued to cry out.

I called him by name.

He looked over at me. "Hooah, Ser'nt." The Rangers abbreviated "Sergeant" to Ser'nt, and as a navy petty officer first class, my rank was equivalent to an army staff sergeant.

A mop leaned against the wall near my bed. I reached over, grabbed it, and extended the handle to him. "Grab this."

He took hold of the mop handle.

"Let's pull our beds together," I said.

We pulled until the wheels under our beds rolled. With our beds together, I took the needle of my catheter out and stuck it in the Ranger's catheter, then hit the button a couple of times. Having expended most of my strength, I couldn't push the beds back apart. Both of us became sleepy.

When the nurse returned, she went ballistic. "What happened to your beds? What's going on? Why are you giving him that medicine? If he was allergic to that, you could've killed him!" She took the needle out of his catheter and put it back in mine.

A full bird colonel must've heard all the commotion. He came in.

The nurse chattered about what happened.

The colonel looked at me. "Well, soldier, do you think you run the hospital?"

I explained, "We were just in an intense firefight. He was hurtin'. I made him quit hurtin'. Shoot me if you want to."

The edges of the colonel's lips rose in a slight smile. He took the nurse to the end of the room. "These guys are trained to take care of each other. Just let it go this time."

The nurse had her back to me as the colonel turned and gave me a wink. Then he walked out of the room.

* * *

The next day I noticed my scalp itching terribly. I scratched it. Black stuff accumulated under my finger-nails. During the battle, a Ranger I had carried back to the Humvee had bled on me. The black stuff on my scalp was his dried blood.

Uncle Earl, from my wife's family, happened to be in Germany visiting one of his companies. He heard where I was and came to visit.

When he saw me, he just stared for a moment. Then he walked out and went high-order detonation on the staff. "Wasdin is lying in his own urine!" I hadn't real-ized it at the time, but after my epidural, I lost bladder control. "His body is filthy!"

The hospital staff tried to calm him.

He wouldn't calm down. "I want him cleaned up right now! I want some fresh clothes on him, and I want some fresh linen on that bed! Wash the blood out of his hair! Get in there and brush his teeth! You better take care of him immediately, or I'm calling somebody in Washington right now, and I'm going to rain down hell on this hospital!"

Maybe the hospital staff had been too busy due to the sudden flood of us coming in to perform the regu-lar patient care. Whatever the reason, within minutes, an attendant washed my hair. I felt like I was in heaven. The assistant gave me a toothbrush, and I brushed my teeth. Also, the assistant took the linen off my bed and, even though the mattress had a plastic cover on it, flipped it over. They gave me a fresh gown. I felt so much better.

Uncle Earl brought in a wheelchair. "Anything I can do for you?"

"Yes, get me out of this hospital gown."

He helped me into the wheelchair and rolled me to the gift shop, where he bought me a pair of sweatpants, a sweatshirt, a ball cap, and a teddy bear. Uncle Earl asked the cashier, "Could you cut these sweatpants off at the knee for us?"

She looked at him, puzzled, for a moment, then looked at me. "Sure," she said sweetly. The cashier pulled out a pair of scissors and cut the sweatpants. She handed them to Earl.

"Thank you." Earl wheeled me into the gift shop restroom and put the sweatpants on over my external fixator. The surgeon had drilled holes into the uninjured part of my bone near the fracture. Then he screwed pins into the bone. Outside my leg, a metal rod attached to the pins to hold them in place. The pins and rod made up the external fixator. Then Earl put the sweatshirt and cap on me.

He wheeled me out of the restroom and over to the cafeteria and picked up some *Hefeweizen* beers, traditional German unfiltered wheat beers that have less bitterness and more carbonation than the filtered variety. "What do you want to do?" he asked.

"Can you roll me out in the courtyard for some sunshine?"

He pushed me out there, and we had our drinks. Cleaned up with fresh clothes and drinking beer in the sunshine, I thought, *This is pretty good.* I drank half my beer and fell asleep. Later, I would give the teddy bear to my three-year-old sweetheart, Rachel.

* * *

The next day, a Delta guy from across the hall who had an injured shoulder came and visited me. We talked about the battle. He said, "I didn't have a good appreciation for you guys since you weren't actually part of our team, but you guys kicked ass. We had no idea SEALs could throw down like that! You especially. I saw you two or three times during that firefight. Wish I had more to do with you before the firefight."

"It's cool," I said.

"Hey, Brad is down the hall. Want to go see him?"

"Sure."

He wheeled me over to see Brad, one of the Delta snipers. I saw Brad's amputated leg—sheared off when an RPG hit his helo. He shook my hand. "Want a dip?" he said as if everything were normal. He extended his hand and held out a fiberboard can of moist dipping tobacco—Copenhagen.

"Hell, yeah." I pinched some and put it in my mouth.

The three of us sat talking and spitting.

"Hey, they were able to save your leg," Brad said.

"I was told that if it had been a quarter of an inch more, they would've had to amputate." *Brad is taking this way better than I am, and his leg is cut off. Here I am feeling sorry for myself. Angry at the world and God. Here he is with no leg and a positive attitude.*

Seeing Brad was good therapy for me. Brad was a sniper on Black Hawk Super Six Two. Along with him were Delta snipers Gary Gordon and Randy Shughart. They flew over the second downed helo and saw the pilot, Mike Durant, moving. Somali crowds closed in. With no friendlies on the ground to help, Mike was all alone. The three snipers and their door gunners fired at the mob.

Brad, Gordon, and Shughart looked at each other. They nodded.

Gordon told the pilot, "Insert the three of us to assist Super Six Four."

The pilot radioed headquarters, "Three operators request permission to secure Super Six Four. Over."

"Negative. There are too many unfriendlies down there. Can't risk another bird."

When one door gunner got shot, Brad took over the minigun. Everyone needed the big gun in the fight to keep the enemy from shooting them down.

The crowd on the ground grew, moving closer to Mike's crashed helo.

"Two of us are going in," Gordon said. "Put us down."

The pilot radioed again, "Two operators request to secure crash site until rescue arrives."

"Negative."

Gordon insisted.

The pilot lowered the helo to the crash site. Brad stayed on the minigun in the Black Hawk and covered Gordon and Shughart as they fast-roped down.

On the ground the two snipers calmly moved Mike and other crew members to a more secure location with good fields of fire. Then Gordon and Shughart took up defensive positions on opposite sides of the helo, coolly shooting the enemy in the upper torso one by one— Gordon with his CAR-15 and Shughart with his M-14.

Suddenly, Gordon said matter-of-factly, like he'd bumped his knee into a table, "Damn, I'm hit." Then he stopped shooting.

Shughart retrieved Gordon's CAR-15 and gave it to Mike. Shughart resumed fighting. When Shughart's rifle ran out of ammo, he returned to the downed helo and made a radio call. He walked around the front of the helicopter and charged at the crowd, firing point blank with his pistol, pushing them back until he ran out of ammo. The mob fought back, killing Shughart.

Enemy corpses lay scattered on the ground surrounding the fallen snipers. Shughart and Gordon were *bad* in the best sense of the word. The crowd got their revenge by dragging the dead soldiers' bodies through the streets and cutting them up. They captured Mike and held him hostage, hoping to use him for a prisoner exchange. He was released later.

The military's highest award, the Medal of Honor, would go to the two Delta snipers: Gary Gordon and Randy Shughart.

One day, General Henry Hugh Shelton, commander in chief of U.S. Special Operations Command, visited my hospital room. He presented me with my Purple Heart and gave me his commander's coin. His sincerity, caring, and encouragement lifted my spirits.

"Is the hospital taking good care of you?" he asked.

"Yes, sir."

General Shelton asked how well the Rangers fought during the Battle of Mogadishu.

"They fought bravely, sir." I thought for a moment. "We're not going to leave this unfinished, are we?"

"No, we're going to get the tanks and go in and do the job right."

Although I'm sure he meant it, the White House never allowed that to happen.

I stayed in Landstuhl Regional Medical Center for a week before they flew me and others to Andrews Air Force Base, Maryland. As they wheeled me off the plane on a gurney, Laura and the kids met me. Eight-year-old Blake ran to my side and put his arms around my chest. Laura was pregnant. She held three-year-old Rachel, who was too young to understand much about what was going on.

After staying overnight in Maryland, I was taken to the Team compound in Dam Neck. I told them I wanted to rehab down at Fort Stewart Army Hospital in Georgia, the same place Blake was born, thirty minutes away from my home. The Team gave me a special lightweight wheelchair made of composite metal that I heard cost thousands of dollars. My two children, my wife, and I lived with her parents in Odum, Georgia, during my rehabilitation.

When I heard that Delta would be having a memorial service, I wanted to go. The military flew down a C-12, a small passenger plane, to pick me up at Hunter Army Airfield in Savannah. I flew up to the memorial ceremony at the Delta compound in Fort Bragg. Greeting me at the airport in SUVs were Tim Wilkinson and Scotty, the PJs, and Dan Schilling, the CCT. It felt good to see old friends from that hangar in Somalia. Even though they were air force, we had fought in Mogadishu together, which made me closer to them than to my SEAL Team Six Teammates who hadn't been with me in combat. The air force would award Tim the military's second-highest honor, the Air Force Cross (equal to the Navy Cross for Navy, Marine Corps, and Coast Guard; Distinguished Service Cross for Army). Scotty would receive the Silver Star, the military's third-highest honor. Dan received its next-highest honor, the Bronze Star.

They wheeled me past a wall where the names of the fallen Delta Force guys were written. I saw six pairs of desert combat boots, six M-16 rifles with bayonets stuck downward in the base of the display, six bayonets on the rifle butts, and a picture for each of the six men: Dan Busch, Earl Fillmore, Randy Shughart, Gary Gordon, Tim "Griz" Martin, and Matt Rierson.

I remembered Griz, who had a big birthmark on his face. A prankster who came up with new and exotic ways to blow stuff up.

During the memorial service in the auditorium, the chaplain led everyone in prayer for the fallen men. Wives wept. Dan Busch's parents looked devastated. Dan was only twenty-five years old—incredibly young to be a Delta sniper—from Portage, Wisconsin. Squared away. A devout Christian. I never heard him say a cuss word—rare in the special operations community. I remember one day after lunch, we oiled up with suntan lotion and basked in the sun on top of a CONEX box outside of the hangar at Mogadishu. Of the little free time we had, I spent much of it with Dan Busch.

A sergeant read the Last Roll Call. Each man in the unit answered, "Here." Except for the fallen men. The honor guard fired three volleys. A bugler played taps.

In our profession we knew it was a possibility when

we took the job. Still, looking at their parents, wives, and kids really hit me hard. *These guys are really gone. Dan is gone. How come I get to live and they don't? Dan Busch was a much better person and Christian than I was. Why is he dead, and I'm still here?* I felt guilty that I had survived.

After the memorial, when Scotty, Tim, and I were hanging out, a Delta guy asked who I was. They didn't recognize me in my beard. I had been too weak to shave.

Scotty and Tim told him who I was.

"Aw, hell." The Delta operator went to the other Delta guys and said, "Hey, Wasdin is here!"

They swarmed me, took me to Delta's Charlie Squadron ready room, and gave me beers in both hands. We hung out, and they laughed when I told them about giving my medication to the Ranger at Landstuhl. Afterward Delta had a party, but I had a fever and didn't have enough power in my engine to join them. I went back to my hotel room early.

Only Defense Secretary Les Aspin attended the memorial service. For the most part, the Clinton administration seemed to hope the Battle of Mogadishu would just conveniently disappear and America would forget.

After flying out the next morning to Georgia, I showed up at the hospital for my regular visit. I had diarrhea. My fever had worsened—my whole body ached like it was on fire. I felt disoriented. I was literally dying. A medical team descended on me and rushed me into the back, gave me a shot in each butt cheek, and put an IV in each arm. They removed the bandages from my leg and started working on it. The doctor, who had gone home, returned in his civilian clothes. "Where have you been?" he asked. "We've been trying to contact your house, but you weren't there. The blood test results from your previous visit showed that you have a staph infection." The deadly staph infection had crawled deep inside me via the pins in my leg. This partly explains why I didn't feel up to attending the party with Delta after the memorial.

On the hospital bed, I floated up and looked down at myself lying there. *I'm dying. This staph infection sucks a lot worse than combat.*

The next day, the doctor was visibly upset with me. "If you're going to stay under my care, you've got to give us a way to stay in contact with you. If not, you need to go back to Virginia and let those navy doctors take care of you." He was scared. The doctor had done me a favor by letting me rehab in his army hospital—and I repaid him by almost dying on him.

"Yes, sir."

They kept me in the hospital a couple of days until I recovered.

Sitting at home in my wheelchair, I committed one of the Team's gravest sins—feeling sorry for myself. I slipped deep into depression. After waking in the morning, I had to perform my pin care, cleaning the skin around the four big pins sticking out of my leg. If I didn't, the infection would crawl down the pins and into my bone—causing another staph infection like the one that almost killed me. Then I'd bandage everything back up. The whole process took fifteen to twenty minutes. Twice a day. Doing the pin care by myself was tough. I asked my wife and brother-in-law to help, but they didn't have the stomach. It looked terrible—there's nothing normal about four pins screwed into a bone. My skin graft looked nasty, the meat visible.

The walls were closing in on me. I wasn't accustomed to being trapped indoors, and my depression was bearing down on me. I had to get out of the house, so I decided to do something simple and routine, but even something as mundane as grocery shopping turned out to be a bigger blow to my weakened self-esteem. One day, while slowly wheeling myself down the aisle in a Winn-Dixie supermarket in Jesup, Georgia, I started to realize how good it felt to be out of the house, contributing to the family by shopping. Some return to a normal life.

An overweight woman with a chicken hairdo—short in the back and spiky on top, the Kate Gosselin haircut that is common in Wayne County—stared at my leg. Her face twisted like she'd eaten a lemon. I had cut the right leg of my sweatpants off above the knee to accommodate my external fixator. Although the skin-grafted area was bandaged, the pins were visible. "Why don't you stay at home?" she said. "Don't you realize how gross that is?"

I got my leg shot off serving her country. Our country. *Maybe this is how ordinary Americans see me. Are they fine with us going off to die for them but don't want to see us wounded?* I was feeling too sorry for myself to realize that she didn't know who I was or how I was wounded. At the time, when my spirit lay in the dirt, her words kicked me in the teeth. I desperately needed to bounce back, but I couldn't. Those words punted me deeper into depression.

At home, I wheeled around the house in my chair, eating and killing time watching TV. I couldn't take a shower or a bath because I couldn't get my screws wet. I had to wash my hair in the sink and take a washcloth bath.

Every other day I did rehabilitation at the hospital in Fort Stewart. They gave me hot whirlpool treatments for my left foot, to shake loose the dead flesh. It hurt like getting shot again. They gave me crutches. They put me on bars to help me walk. The pain was so intense that I couldn't stop tears from coming out of my eyes—I'd been still for too long before the rehabilitation. Then I had to have another surgery. Later I would have three more.

My internal clock hadn't adjusted from Africa to Germany, then back to the United States. With time on my hands, it became easy to take a two- or three-hour nap, which kept me awake at night.

Pain and depression didn't help matters either. Bone pain. As long as those screws stayed in my leg, I'd have pain. It's understandable how people can become addicted to pain pills, but I despised the pills—they just made me numb. To some small degree, I wanted to feel pain, guilty that I had survived while a lot of good guys, special ones like Dan Busch, lay dead. I thought maybe I was strange for feeling this way. *Suck it up, take the pain.*

Out of the SEAL Team Six loop and with no Team guys around, I suffered the withdrawal symptoms of being cut off from the camaraderie. I was in culture shock, too. People around town could talk to me about their lives, but I couldn't talk to them about mine. I couldn't joke with them about my Hell Week death leap to kill a rack of trays that I thought was a deer. Or laugh with them about the hospital in Germany where I gave the Ranger buddy my painkiller injections. People around town didn't understand. I learned to shut up about those experiences. Now it occurred to me how different I had become from most people. Away from my Teammates, I felt forgotten, too. With no real-world missions, I had gone cold turkey from adrenaline. Now I couldn't even walk. In the SEAL culture, where it pays to be a winner, I was the biggest loser. I was angry at the world in general and at God in particular. *Why did this have to happen to me?*

In retrospect, I see that God was letting me know I was only human, and that being a SEAL was just a job. *Howard, you were too hardheaded to listen to Me after you were shot once. You didn't listen to Me after the second shot. Here, big boy, let Me give you your third bullet hole. Now, do I have your attention? You are not Superman. You are God's gift to special operations only for as long as I allow it to be. You are where you are because of Me. Not because of you. This is My way of getting your attention. Now that I've got it, let Me mold you further. You are not the finished product.* He humbled me and brought me back down to earth. Made me become a father to my children. At the time, no one could've convinced me of all that, but looking back, getting shot in the leg was the best thing that ever happened to me.

* * *

One day, a buddy of mine called me. On his ranch, he had a special hybrid of deer that he bred with American whitetail deer.

"Come over and let's hunt a little."

"Yes. Yes! Let me get out of this house! Anything!"

He picked me up in his pickup truck, took me out to the field, and set me down in my wheelchair on the ground. He pushed me nearly 30 yards through light underbrush, then stopped. He pointed to a spot about 150 yards away. "Over there is where the deer usually come out."

My personal hunting rifle was a 7 mm Magnum with a nice scope. I was so happy—waiting there for nearly an hour and a half.

A huge buck came out. Sitting in my wheelchair, I brought my rifle to my shoulder, pulled the trigger, and the deer went down. Perfect shot. After laying my rifle on the ground, I wheeled my chair over to the animal. Pushing my wheelchair along a dirt road took me a while.

I parked my chair next to the deer. The beautiful buck looked up at me. It snorted, then laid its head back down. It made a last gasp, as if all the air had been sucked out of its lungs. Hearing it die, I thought, *I'd have been just as happy to come out and watch you, instead of taking your life. I've seen enough things die.*

I took the buck and had the head mounted. In South Georgia, hunting is big. The boys head out before the crack of dawn and sit in their tree stands waiting for their prey during the season. I was still willing to kill someone to save myself or save another person—willing to kill in the line of duty—but I never hunted again.

The rehab people treated me like a celebrity. At that time, I was the only combat-wounded veteran in their hospital. Every time I went in, five or ten people would show up to talk to me.

After six or seven weeks, my niece brought me a device that slipped over the pins in my legs, creating a rubber seal, so I could shower. I stood on one leg in the shower and lathered up my hair. It felt like the best gift I'd ever received.

In early December, two months after the longest day in my life, my hometown of Screven, Georgia, threw me a hero's welcome as part of the Christmas parade, with yellow ribbons everywhere. A big sign in the restaurant covered the front window: WELCOME BACK HOWARD, THE HOMETOWN HERO. Nearly all nine hundred of the townspeople must've signed it. People from Wayne County came out to line the streets, see me, and wish me well. They had no idea about the physical pain, the mental anguish, the loss, or the dark hole of depression that tormented me—before they honored me that way. They had no idea how much their welcome meant to me, appreciating me as part of the community. I didn't feel like such a loser.

Mike Durant, the pilot of Super Six Four, the second Black Hawk to crash in Mogadishu, had broken his leg and back. Aidid's propaganda minister, Abdullahi "Firimbi" Hassan, held him prisoner for eleven days until Mike and a captured Nigerian soldier were driven by their captors to a checkpoint at the UN compound. One of Durant's captors pulled out UN credentials hanging on a chain around his neck and showed them to the guard. They waved him in. The checkpoint guard didn't even realize Mike sat in the car. Nobody knew until he was already on the runway. His captors turned him over to the Red Cross. The United Nations showed enough unity with the enemy, but I didn't feel like they showed enough unity with us. I never felt they could be trusted for operational security. You can only trust the people you train and fight with. I had trained with foreign counterterrorism units, and I trusted them. The UN checkpoint guard's coziness with Durant's captor, and the fact that his captor carried UN credentials, confirmed my distrust for the UN.

Mike Durant and I had just gotten to where we could walk unassisted. Our first meeting since Somalia was at Fairchild Air Force Base in Spokane, Washington, to learn advanced Survival, Evasion, Resistance, and Escape. Although SERE schools like the one at the Naval Air Station in Brunswick, Maine, simulated being hunted, imprisoned, and tortured, this school took place in a classroom with ten to twelve students mainly learning the psychological aspects of captivity. With our experience in Mogadishu, Mike and I quickly became guest speakers for that particular class. The instructors called us to the front of the room, where we talked about our experiences and fielded questions from students *and* instructors.

The Navy flew Casanova, Little Big Man, Sourpuss, Captain Olson, and me to the Pentagon to award us the Silver Star. In Mogadishu, Captain Olson left headquarters to participate in rescuing men still pinned down. At our award ceremony, video cameras rolled and still cameras flashed. My citation read:

The President of the United States takes pleasure in presenting the Silver Star medal to Hull Maintenance Technician First Class Howard E. Wasdin, United States Navy, for service set forth in the following citation: For conspicuous gallantry and intrepidity in action against a hostile force during operation UNOSOM II in Mogadishu, Somalia on 3 & 4 October 1993. Petty Officer Wasdin was the member of a security team in support of an assault force that conducted an air assault raid into an enemy compound and successfully apprehended two key militia officials and twenty-two others. Upon receiving enemy small arms fire from numerous alleys, Petty Officer Wasdin took up a firing position and returned fire. As he assaulted down the alley with members of his unit, he was wounded in the calf. Upon receiving combat field condition medical attention, he resumed his duties and continued to suppress enemy fire. As his convoy exfiltrated the area with detainees, his element came under withering enemy fire. Petty Officer Wasdin, along with the security team, stopped to suppress enemy fire which had pinned down the Ranger blocking force. Although twice wounded, he continued to pull se-

curity and engage a superior enemy force from his vehicle. Later, while attempting to suppress enemy fire, during an attempted link-up for evacuation of the helicopter crash site, Petty Officer Wasdin was wounded a third time. His gallant efforts inspired his team members as well as the entire force. By his superb initiative, courageous action, and complete dedication to duty, Petty Officer Wasdin reflected great credit upon himself and upheld the highest tradition of the United States Naval Force.

It was signed for the president by John Dalton, the new secretary of the navy. Casanova and I walked into the secretary of defense's office and shook his hand. Upon exiting, Casanova said, "That man's got the softest hands I've ever felt." Later, I also received a whack on the pee-pee for disobeying a direct order and helping the teenaged Somali boy who'd stepped on a land mine—my most successful op in Somalia.

Casanova and I sat chewing Copenhagen dip in Red Team's ready room. It was a huge informal room, mostly neutral in color. Mission briefs, real-world intel, and other briefings were done in a special room. Pictures of Red Team exploits decorated one wall. An ornate totem pole and an authentic Indian headdress stood as Team symbols. In the largest part of the room were four big tables with eight to ten chairs that could sit a boat crew at each table. Carpeting covered the floor. The FNGs were responsible for cleanliness and keeping the two refrigerators stocked with various brands of beer. The Team chief and Team leader shared one office adjoining the Team room. Also adjoining the Team room was a computer room for general use. Just outside the Team room were the individual cages where we kept our gear.

Casanova and I sat at a table. Little Big Man arrived with an envelope from the Randall knife company. He had offered to send his knife, tell his story, and sponsor their company—*SEAL Team Six sniper saved by Randall knife.*

"How much they going to pay you?" Casanova asked.

Little Big Man opened the letter and read, "Thank you for sharing your story with us. We'll give you ten percent off if you want to buy another knife."

"Dumb-asses," Little Big Man said.

Casanova laughed loudly and boisterously. I laughed so hard, I almost swallowed my chewing tobacco.

I recovered rapidly and returned to the Team. My first contact with Lieutenant Commander Buttwipe was when he took over command of Red Team as senior officer, Red Team leader. Buttwipe lived for appearances more than getting the job done, which ruffled a lot of operators' feathers. A number of people left Red Team to go to Blue and Gold Teams because of him. He had a fake chuckle, especially in the presence of senior officers. When he laughed with us, it felt like he was really thinking about something else. Because he was part Japanese, we made jokes behind his back about losing

World War II. Short in stature, he cut his hair short, too, in a flattop style.

He must've loved the smell of my gluteus maximus, because he rode it constantly. Maybe Buttwipe felt self-conscious that he lacked talent. Although he ran and swam well, he brought up the rear during CQB shooting drills, and he lacked good timely tactical decisions. Maybe he resented never seeing combat, or not earning a Silver Star. Regardless of his reason, somehow Buttwipe found out that Delta wanted me. The Delta operators at the hospital in Germany encouraged me to join them. A Delta colonel told me at the Andrews Air Force Base hospital how I could laterally transfer out of the SEALs and into Delta. In retrospect, Delta probably would've understood and respected me more—I know of no stronger bond than the bond with people I'd been in combat with. My relationship with Casanova, Little Big Man, the Delta operators, the CCTs, and the PJs was stronger than my relationship with other Teammates.

"I'll support you if you stay here," Buttwipe said, "but if you try to leave, I'll be your worst nightmare."

Buttwipe's actions gave me more motivation to transfer to Delta. Yet his words said he didn't want me to leave. He made no sense. I remained because I trained to be a SEAL, was still a SEAL, and wanted to continue being a SEAL. It's what I did best.

In the sum of things, Buttwipe didn't support me. He even gave me a hard time about showing up at the Delta memorial unshaven in civilian clothes. I really couldn't understand his argument—I'd almost died of staph infection while making the trip to the ceremony. Surviving day to day took nearly all the energy I had. Shaving was a luxury I couldn't afford. I despised his incompetence as much as I despised the incompetence of Clinton. Buttwipe should've been a politician instead of an operator. Just remembering him now makes me want to kick him in the face.

Laura and I divorced. The baby she was pregnant with wasn't mine—wasn't even the same race. It happened while I was gone. That's all I'm going to say about that. I'd been unfaithful, too. Rachel and Blake went to live with their mom because I wouldn't be able to take care of them when I had to be away for work. I hadn't spent enough time with Rachel, and now I'd be spending even less time with her. Her mother let her do most of the things she wanted, but I didn't. When Rachel became old enough to choose, she chose to live with her mom. Later, when Rachel was a senior in high school, her mother let her move in with her boyfriend— something I would never allow. My relationship with Rachel would deteriorate. Even though I was stricter with Blake than with Rachel, he chose to live with me when he turned thirteen. Although I should've known that family ties are stronger than job ties, I'd sacrificed my family for the Teams.

In spite of my sacrifices for the Teams, I could never return to being 100 percent of the sniper I used to be. My thinking became darker. One day, I held my SIG SAUER P-226 pistol in my hand. *How bad would it be if I took this P-226 and ended everything with one 9mm bullet? There are worse things than death.* I convinced myself that everyone would be better off. They could collect on my life insurance.

Blake was visiting me. "Dad."

That one word snapped me out of it. Ending my life would've been selfish. *If I don't have anything else to live for, at least I have my children.* I never had those dark thoughts again.

Although it had looked initially like I'd lose my leg, I didn't. I walked on crutches before I was supposed to, used a cane before I was supposed to, walked unassisted before I was supposed to, and started swimming before I was supposed to. Although people thought I would never walk without a limp, I did. Even though many thought I'd never run again, I did. After returning to the Team, I hit the gym every morning and did PT with them. I couldn't always keep up, but I consistently worked hard at it.

15.
AMBASSADOR DEATH THREATS

Although still experiencing daily pain and sleepless nights from my injuries, I recovered to the point that I could receive an assignment to protect Ambassador to the Philippines John Negroponte, who had received some death threats. A Yale graduate, he dropped out of Harvard Law School to become a diplomat. Of Greek descent, he spoke English, French, Greek, Spanish, and Vietnamese.

With me from Team Six came Johnny. He had been stationed in the Philippines before, possibly on a deployment with SEAL Team One, and had a lot of friends—many of them female. He had volunteered for the assignment to have some fun.

Johnny always had a lighthearted attitude. We were living in a condo on the tenth floor of a building in Makati, an upscale neighborhood in Manila. One evening, an earthquake hit. It woke us up, along with our maid, Lucy. Johnny and I both came out of our rooms, he in his boxer shorts and I in my birthday suit. Outside the window, buildings swayed side to side. I could feel our building sway, too. "What do you want to do?" I asked.

Johnny had that big smile on his face. "Nothing we can do. Just sort it out when we hit the ground."

We laughed it off and went back to bed.

Our job included training Philippine nationals, some from the Philippine National Police force, to protect the ambassador. We showed the Filipinos how to do diplomatic advances, run a three-vehicle motorcade, walk a detail diamond (one agent walking point, one on each side of the principal, and one bringing up the rear), and more. We took them out to shoot with their Uzis. Uzis are poor weapons for accuracy, and the Philippine nationals were poor marksmen with any weapon. The ambassador was fortunate they didn't have to shoot anyone to protect his life. Our recommendation to the assistant regional security officer was to let Filipinos carry shotguns instead of Uzis, so they had a better chance of hitting something. The change wasn't made.

Sitting down with the commandant and assistant regional security officer, and drawing on my experiences running a CIA safe house in Somalia, we came up with an improved defense and E&E plan for the embassy. Also, we took the Marine embassy guards out to the range for shooting practice. "Hey, we're marines. We know how to shoot." After spending a few days on the range with Johnny and me, the marines' eyes opened up. "Good stuff!"

Ambassador Negroponte never seemed to stop, always meeting with people, and he played tennis well. He treated us like we were part of the family. I felt close to his children, whom we also protected. His British wife was polite and sweet. They invited Johnny and me to Thanksgiving dinner at the American Residence in

Baguio, a mansion complete with chandeliers and oil paintings.

One day, Johnny and I did an advance for the ambassador's visit to a chiropractor. I wore my Oakley sunglasses. We walked up to the front desk and introduced ourselves. The receptionist invited us in. As we searched rooms for bad guys, we interrupted the chiropractor during her lunch. We apologized and continued on.

Later, we received a call from the ambassador, asking us to see him. We left our condo in Makati and met with him. He politely told us, "Next time you go to the chiropractor's office, don't go all roughshod. That chiropractor also happens to be a friend." This was before 9/11, so security was less of a priority, but we had done our advance the way we were trained. He explained, "I have a shoulder injury from tennis, and if she doesn't realign my spine, I'm in pain."

I was skeptical about chiropractors and didn't think they would be effective in easing the constant pain I had in my leg and neck, but I filed our conversation in the back of my mind anyway.

At the embassy, Johnny and I met a middle-aged American doctor who feared for his life. "I'm doing charity work as a doctor. Just trying to help people. And the mob is trying to rob and kill me."

"How do you know?"

"They're following me. People call my hotel, checking if I'm there. They're at the hotel waiting for me."

Johnny and I told the assistant regional security officer (ARSO), working for the State Department. "We think the mob is really going to kill this guy."

Johnny and I wore civilian clothes. Not wanting to stick out like Secret Service agents or diplomatic security, we didn't carry radios. I liked to wear khaki Royal Robbins pants because they're easy to run in, have a lot of pockets, and look nice. Over a navy blue T-shirt, I wore a photographer's vest with a pair of binoculars and a blowout kit in the pockets. In a pancake holster on my hip was my SIG SAUER, which held one fifteen-round magazine. In the mag holder on my belt, I carried two more magazines. Over the vest I wore an unbuttoned button-down shirt, concealing my pistol and spare magazines.

Leaving the doctor at the embassy, the two of us ran a mini countersurveillance of the doctor's hotel. It wasn't a high-class place like the Intercontinental, but it wasn't a dive, either. Three blocks away from his hotel, Johnny and I stood on one of the top floors of a building. I called the hotel's front desk and introduced myself as working for diplomatic security. Explaining the situation, I asked the desk clerk to open the curtains in the doctor's room. Also, I told him what I looked like and what time I'd arrive.

When the curtains opened, we could see inside with the binoculars we'd brought from the Team—pocket-sized waterproof Bausch & Lombs (now licensed with Bushnell) with antiglare coating, enhanced light transmission, and high color contrast. No one seemed to be waiting in the room. I felt relieved that we wouldn't have to do a forced entry and get into a gun battle. The desk clerk verified that no one was inside. So far, so good. Then again, he could be setting us up.

We moved in a wide square around the hotel area, looking for anyone running surveillance. Then we moved in closer toward the hotel, making concentric squares.

A junky old vehicle sat in front of the hotel with two guys in it. My spider senses tingled. *These are the two guys I need to look out for.* They weren't dressed like businessmen and didn't seem to be there to pick anyone up. No one else in the area seemed to be a threat.

Johnny parked our Jeep Cherokee near the corner of the building where he could see the doctor's room above and the thugs in front of him. I transferred my SIG SAUER from my holster to my vest pocket, keeping my hand on it with my finger near the trigger. Then I stepped out of our vehicle and walked to the hotel.

Inside the lobby, my eyes scanned for anyone or anything out of place. At that point in my career, I could take a glance at people, note their posture and body language, and know if they were a threat. Part of my awareness seemed to be a heightened sixth sense—like when you think somebody is watching you and you turn around to find out somebody really is watching you.

The desk clerk, probably a relative of the hotel owner, escorted me to the stairway. An elevator can be a death trap. It can be stopped between floors. There could be somebody on top of the elevator—it doesn't just happen in movies. Or a big surprise could be waiting when the elevator opens. If this was a setup, the desk clerk would become more nervous as we neared the doctor's room. He would know he stood a good chance of getting killed during an ambush. If the ambush didn't kill him, I would.

We entered the stairway. I drew my pistol and bladed the stairs as we walked up—scanning the overhead for a muzzle or someone about to drop a brick on our heads, then scanning the stairs in front of me.

As we reached the fourth floor, I was going to ask the clerk to walk out in front of me, but he already had. He led me through the hallway and unlocked the doctor's door. Inside the room, I locked the door behind us, including the bar latch. I didn't want any surprise visitors from behind. The clerk went to the center of the room and began packing up the doctor's belongings—perfect; if anyone was going to attack us, they'd go after the clerk first. Also, his relaxed state gave me further evidence that he wasn't setting me up. I searched the room for bogeymen: shower, closets, under the bed—everywhere. When everything was clear, I closed one curtain halfway over the window, signaling Johnny we were in and all was clear. Maybe I could've waved at him from the window, but I didn't take the chance of eating a sniper's bullet. If I hadn't given the signal within five minutes after leaving Johnny, he'd've been coming to back me up.

The clerk packed a rolling suitcase, a garment bag, and a briefcase full of U.S. currency. I wondered how the doctor had acquired the stacks of money—thousands of dollars from what I could see. Maybe he brought the cash from the States to survive on. Maybe he'd been involved in something he shouldn't have been.

After the clerk finished packing everything, he

carried the luggage down the stairs. Feeling more comfortable, I still had my weapon out but wasn't aiming at every potential hazard. Reaching the bottom of the stairs, I put the pistol back in my pocket. I quickly looked around the lobby. Everything seemed OK.

I thanked the clerk and took the luggage. After hooking the garment bag to the suitcase, I pulled it with my left hand while carrying the briefcase in my right.

When I exited the hotel, the two thugs saw me. They seemed to know what I was there for, and they seemed to know that I knew what they were there for. *Is it worth it for you to try taking me down?* If they made a move, I'd have to drop the briefcase in my right hand and draw my pistol from my pocket. I could move while shooting, and they would be confined to their vehicle. If they tried it, I'd make them have a bad day. Even so, my anus puckered.

Johnny brought up the Jeep Cherokee and stopped at an angle behind them. If they wanted to get out and shoot at the Jeep, they'd have to get out and turn—without their door as a shield between them and us. Johnny stepped out with his weapon drawn and held down at his side. The door shielded his lower body from the direction of the two thugs. Johnny's presence gave me peace of mind.

I walked past the thugs, threw the luggage in the back, and sat down in the passenger seat. The thugs had cranked their heads around to look at us, becoming highly animated, speaking rapidly back and forth. Johnny drove us out and circled the block, and when we returned, the two thugs were gone.

We picked up the doctor at the embassy, gave him

his luggage, and took him to a U.S. commissary in Manila where they had shopping and a restaurant. We kept him there until his flight was ready to leave. He thanked us over and over again.

As we drove the doctor to the airport, we had another of our vehicles drive out front to make sure the route was clear.

"You two saved my life." He continued to thank us. We loaded the doctor onto a plane.

Later, he wrote the embassy thanking them for our help, which resulted in big kudos for us. We found out later that the doctor had been dating a mob boss's daughter. She lost her virginity to him, and he promised to marry her—even though he had plans to leave the country. When the mob boss discovered this, he put a contract out on the doctor. Maybe he deserved it.

I'd come a long way in recovering from my wounded leg. I still had daily pain and sleepless nights, though, and the diplomatic security assignment was an easy job as far as SEAL Team Six assignments went—a cakewalk. I knew I wouldn't be able to work the tough assignments again.

After completing the diplomatic security assignment, I returned to the Team. We did our routine workups: running, kill house, shooting range. I realized, *This isn't going to work out*.

I spoke to Six's command master chief. "I'm going to pack my stuff and head to Georgia. I'm in constant pain. My leg throbs all day. A lot of hip pain. Neck pain. I can't sleep too well." At the time, I didn't know what was wrong with me. Having adjusted for my gunshot wound by changing my gait, I was carrying myself wrong—my externally rotated foot was affecting my hip. My neck compensated by going the other way. Sort of like a house: If the basement tilts to the right and sinks a little, the roof follows—except the neck pulls the opposite way.

"I understand exactly where you're coming from. If you want, I'll transfer you to any Team you want, send you to BUD/S to be an instructor . . . You can pick a division here: air ops, boat ops, demo . . . Whatever you want to do. Just tell me and it's yours."

I'd never be able to do what my Teammates were doing. I remembered going up the stairs in the kill house—holding up the last three guys in the train. That had never happened to me before. I knew when I was at the top of my game. Now I was not. It was a harsh reality to face. *I'm not as good, not as fast, and my senses are not as keen as they used to be. Definitely not physically doing what I used to do.* "Thank you, Master Chief. But if I'm not going to be one of the Team guys doing the job, I'd rather just get on with the next phase of my life. Do something different. See what's out there."

Most of my adult life, I had been in the military. It would be a new adventure: *What can I do in the civilian world?*

16.
FISH OUT OF WATER

Outside of the military, my situation would be feast or famine. While processing out of the navy on a medical retirement, I received an offer to train the 1996 Summer Olympics security teams in Atlanta. Fifteen hundred dollars a week seemed like huge money to me then—especially compared to military pay. I left the navy and took the job. Also, I trained the Federal Bureau of Prisons Special Operations and Response Teams and others. It involved a lot of travel. Charging five hundred dollars a day, I thought I'd get rich.

In the tactical game, I was paid well for each assignment, but the assignments came and went. Between assignments, I struggled financially.

Hoping for more stability, I became a police officer just north of Miami Beach in Hallandale Beach, Florida, a place known for its greyhound racetrack and Canadian tourists. After more than half a year of training, I became a police officer, just like the ones who treated me well as a kid.

While patrolling, I wore Revo sunglasses, made with NASA technology by the same Italian eyewear company,

Luxottica, that owns Ray-Ban and Oakley. The Revos had the clearest lenses and the best polarized protection, and they stayed on comfortably. Because I was a rookie, a recruit training officer (RTO) rode in the patrol car with me. One day, I spotted a stolen Cadillac driving in front of us. I called it in. Another patrol car joined me, and we turned on our flashing lights. The stolen Cadillac pulled over. Just as it stopped, the passenger, a black kid in his late teens, bailed out and took off running. We stopped behind the stolen vehicle. My RTO jumped out of the passenger seat of our patrol car, ran to the stolen Cadillac, and apprehended the driver, an obese kid. After I opened my door on the driver's side, my feet hit the ground running.

I chased the runner for what seemed like forever. Over shrubs and fences. Underneath bushes. My ASP telescoping tactical baton fell out somewhere during the chase. The radio mike clipped to my lapel fell off and dragged behind me. I didn't lose my sunglasses, though. We ran through people's yards and ended up all the way in the next town, South Hollywood. Suddenly, I lost visual and audible contact with the runner. A man watering the grass in his front yard pointed to the back of his house. I snuck up behind the house, but the runner spotted me and took off again. Finally, as he ran across the middle of the street, I tackled him on the asphalt. A motorcycle police officer stopped and helped me. It felt good to catch the guy.

"That's the longest foot chase I've ever heard of," the policeman said.

If the runner hadn't been holding his pants up the whole time he was running, he could've outrun me.

When I stood him up with the handcuffs on, his pants fell down. I took out a flexicuff, pulled his pants up, and zip-tied his belt loop to his handcuffs to keep his pants on.

My RTO arrived with our patrol car.

The kid turned and looked at my name tag. "You ain't going to beat me, Officer Wasdin?"

"Of course not. Why do you ask that?"

"I just thought that's what you cops did. Beat us. That's why I was running."

"Man, you got the wrong idea of cops."

When I started to put him in the car, another officer actually pushed the kid into the vehicle.

"Hey, take your hands off my prisoner," I said. "And don't touch him again."

Later, I'd catch flak from some of the guys who'd been around a while. "You should've been rougher on the kid. Show him you don't run from cops. There's a way to put cuffs on somebody, then there's *a way to put cuffs on somebody*."

I understood their point, but I didn't adhere to it. That wasn't my type of police work. It turned out that the fat kid had stolen the car. The runner was a mule, paid probably twenty or thirty dollars a day, to deliver crack, then carry the buyer's money back to the dealer. He had three or four pieces of the off-white colored rock on him. The dealers used kids under the age of eighteen, so they couldn't be prosecuted as adults.

I put the fat driver in the back of my vehicle with the runner and drove away.

"Why didn't you get your fat ass out and start running?" the runner said.

"Nigger, please. You got caught by a white man," the fat kid argued. "What you talking 'bout?"

"This wasn't no ordinary white man. Every time I turned around, he was still coming."

I smiled.

At the Hallandale Beach Police Department, I processed the two suspects. Then I took them to the Broward County Sheriff's Department to drop them off at the jail. I noticed the runner's hands and knees were sliced up from my tackling him on the asphalt. He was going to need a couple of stitches. Since it's the arresting officer's job to take him to the hospital, that's what I did.

After checking him in at the hospital, we had a forty-five-minute wait. Having missed lunch, I cuffed the kid to a railing and went to the McDonald's in the hospital. I returned and ate my Quarter Pounder Value Meal.

The kid looked at my food.

"Are you hungry?" I asked.

"Uh, not too bad."

"When's the last time you ate something?"

"I had some soup last night."

Oh, crap. I went back to McDonald's and bought him a Quarter Pounder. When I returned, I asked, "If I'm nice enough to buy you a hamburger, am I going to have to chase your tail down if I take that handcuff off and let you eat like a human being?"

"No, sir, Officer Wasdin. I promise you. I ain't running again. I promise."

"Just so you know, I'm tired of running. So if you run again, I may just shoot you."

We chuckled.

I took off the handcuffs, and he thanked me. He gulped down his Quarter Pounder. Then I went back and got him some more food.

Finished eating, we sat in the emergency room. "You ain't like most *po*-lice, is you?" he said.

"More police are like me than you think."

"I would've never thought a police officer would buy me something to eat."

"You know what? If you went up to most police officers and asked them for food, they'd probably give it to you. They probably wouldn't give you money, but they'd at least give you a pack of crackers or something."

"Thank you."

He was very polite. Wouldn't stop thanking me. He seemed like a good kid. Just in with the wrong crowd. I felt good to be able to help him in that way, but I felt bad at how destitute his situation was.

Later, when I saw him on the street, whatever he was doing, he made it a point to stop and wave at me. Occasionally, he came over and talked.

For a couple of weeks after the big foot chase, my body paid for it. My neck and lower back were killing me. A police officer from North Miami Beach had been recommending over and over that I visit a chiropractor, but I blew her off. Now I was desperate. I remembered Ambassador Negroponte's chiropractor.

Finally I went. The chiropractor evaluated me. "Compensatory to your gunshot wound, you've got an external foot rotation affecting your right hip. From your pelvis it worked its way up to your neck. This is why you aren't sleeping well and experience constant pain."

After three adjustments, I slept all the way through the night for the first time in years, nearly pain free. Just by visiting the chiropractor twice a month. *Wow!* After all the neurologists, orthopedic surgeons, and other doctors, a chiropractor gave me back my quality of life.

At that point, I thought chiropractors were like massage therapists or something like that. I had no idea that they studied to become doctors. *There really is something to this chiropractor thing.*

As a police officer, I didn't find a kid with the marks of beatings like the ones I'd received on a weekly basis as a child. If I had, there would've been no questions asked. That child would've been turned over to the authorities, and the father would go straight to jail.

Financially, as a single father, I realized I couldn't make it as a police officer. Forty-two thousand dollars a year went far in Jesup, Georgia, but not in Hallandale Beach, Florida.

The world's leading manufacturer of body armor for military and law enforcement, Point Blank Body Armor, part of Point Blank Body Armor–PACA (Protective Apparel Corporation of America), offered me a job in Tennessee. Seventy-five thousand dollars a year would go far—especially in Tennessee. So I left law enforcement and took the job. Living in a small town, I felt rich. Blake fit in well at his new school, and life went smoothly.

As part of promoting the body armor, Point Blank assigned me to teach SWAT to Kane Kosugi, a Japanese American martial arts actor, for a popular Japanese TV series called *Muscle Ranking* (*Kinniku Banzuke*). Kane wore a Special Mission and Response Team (SMART) vest that I had designed. He was a hard worker who learned fast.

With Point Blank I had to travel internationally all the time: Abu Dhabi, Dubai, Paris, and wherever there was a huge military or police contract. Blake stayed with friends while I was gone. When Point Blank Body Armor–PACA changed hands, I didn't like the new management.

I moved back to Jesup so Blake and I could be closer to my daughter, Rachel. I had worked out a plan to train the United Arab Emirates police SWAT teams via a Switzerland contact. My friend Tom McMillan had secured a range for me in Folkston, Georgia, to facilitate the training. It was going to be great. I had never earned five thousand dollars a week before. I was looking forward to finally having my years of military training pay off big-time. On September 11, 2001, we were putting the final stages of the plan into effect when the twin towers of the World Trade Center were hit by terrorists. That changed everything, putting the training on hold. Looking for a temporary solution until the matter could be resolved, Brother Ron recommended a job to me. "You'd be good at it. GMC car salesman."

I had to do something, so I took it in order to put food on the table. To my surprise, I made more money selling cars than I had made doing anything else up to that point. The customers loved me. Blake settled into high school.

I even dated. One date turned out to be a stalker. It

wasn't funny. She would call me and say, "It usually takes you twenty minutes to get from work to home. Today it took you thirty-five minutes. What happened?"

"Are you serious?"

My cousin Sandy joked with me one night. "She's outside standing in your azaleas, looking in your window."

I laughed it off.

Sandy laughed, too.

After I hung up, I thought, *Maybe I'd better go check*. The stalker wasn't in my azaleas, but she sat in her car a block away watching my house. I just couldn't pick the right woman. It was frustrating.

On one occasion, I went on a date with an attractive woman. Feeling the vibes, I was ready for sex—it had been a while. While eating dinner at a restaurant, I asked, "What do you like to do? Have you read any good books lately?"

"I haven't read anything since high school when I had to read."

"What do you do for a hobby?"

"I listen to my police scanner and watch rasslin'."

I kept a straight face. "Really."

"Yeah. Listening to the scanner keeps me tied into the community. So I know who's getting in trouble and where all the excitement is. If there's going to be a big arrest or fire, I go and watch."

Holy crap. "And your other hobby is what?"

"Rasslin'. I like Stone Cold Steve Austin."

If she could've kept her mouth shut, she would've been great. After dinner, I took her home. Didn't even kiss her good night.

She was upset.

I am not going out on any more dates. There are no girls in Wayne County I really want to date.

On a Saturday afternoon, January 19, 2002, I was headed home in my truck with two chicken boxes from Sybil's Family Restaurant. People drive from a hundred miles to eat Sybil's chicken. Blake and I had plans to eat chicken and watch *O Brother, Where Art Thou?*, which I had already rented. My cousin Edward called me up: "Deidre and I are going out tonight. She's got a friend, and we want you to come out with us." Classical ambush.

"No."

Two minutes later, Deidre called. "Howard, please. I've never asked you for anything. Debbie just got out of a really bad marriage, and she's going out with us, but she doesn't want to feel like the third wheel. Just show up for company. You're a fun-loving guy. I'll never ever ask you to do anything else again. I promise. Just do this for me."

Total guilt trip. I was irritated, but I dropped off the chicken boxes. "Blake, I'm going on a date."

"Really? I thought you weren't going to date."

"Yeah, me, too."

Edward and Deidre took me to Debbie's apartment. Deidre told Debbie, "This is the guy I was telling you about who needs a date."

Deidre had set up Debbie and me.

All four of us rode in one vehicle. I acted like, *Hey, I am Howard Wasdin. You need to humble yourself before me. Show proper respect.*

She threw my attitude back at me. *Hey, I don't care who you are.*

Wow. That's different—and she actually speaks in complete sentences using words with more than two syllables. Where the hell did she come from?

The two of us ended up having a great dinner, laughing a lot and enjoying our conversation and company. We even showed our appreciation to Edward by using words he could understand.

I remember the first time my hand touched hers. We were watching a *Sports Illustrated* bloopers video with Deidre and Edward. The spark of energy from that touch rushed through both of us. We continued our visit for a few minutes, and then I drove Debbie back to her apartment.

When we arrived at her home, we continued our conversation inside. Our talking led to laughter, the laughter led to a connection, that connection led to kissing, and the kissing rocked my world. The chemistry was unlike any I had ever felt. I lost track of time, but I knew that if I was going to be a gentleman, I'd better leave. We were both blindsided. Neither of us was looking for a relationship. Neither of us wanted a relationship, but our guardian angels had put the two of us in the right place at the right time.

We walked to the door to say good night. Leaving took all of my self-control. "I had a great time tonight," I said.

"Me, too."

"Why don't you give me a call tomorrow?" I asked. Now, I had been raised in Screven, Georgia, by strict parents who would accept nothing less than gentlemanly behavior from me. It wasn't that I was no longer a gentleman. It's just that I was Howard Wasdin. I didn't have to pick up a phone and call a woman. They called me. This girl had been raised to be a *lady*, though.

"I don't know how you were raised, but my mama raised me not to call boys. If you want to talk to me, you are going to have to call me." She closed the door.

Wow. It hit me. *Girls who call boys today just don't get it—they're missing being chased and the thrill of it.*

On the drive home reality set in. The speed limit was 55 miles per hour, but I doubt I exceeded 45. I was embarrassed and disappointed in myself. Even though I was raised to be a gentleman, I had become arrogant. She was absolutely right. *What is wrong with me?* I knew better than to say, "Hey, I'm Howard Wasdin, give me a call." I respected her even more.

Sunday, I waited all day. I started to call her several times, but I didn't call. *Yeah, she'll call me.*

She never did.

Monday morning, I called her. We went to lunch. When the weekend came, we dated. Every weekend after that, we dated. Until we got married. Although I'd sworn I'd never tie the knot again, Brother Ron married Debbie and me on January 17, 2003. Even today, when we see him in public, he notices how happy we are together and makes the comment, "When I married you two, I used good glue."

Car sales wasn't fulfilling—even though the good people of Wayne County bought from me, showing their love and appreciation. They knew me from growing up in their community and were thankful for my military service. I had thought about becoming a chiropractor. I tried working at a chemical plant. My old CIA friend Condor told me about a job at a security firm in Brazil. I probably would've ended up in the security field forever. Like other Team guys who leave the navy. *Do security work until I'm too old or too dead.*

In October 2004, Debbie and I talked with my Veterans Affairs representative. They would pay for my college expenses to become a chiropractor. Debbie and I visited the university, but on the way back, I came up with all kinds of reasons I shouldn't do it. "I won't be able to work full-time and go to school full-time. We'll have to tighten our budget. It's going to take a long time. I'll have to live near school until I graduate. A lot of driving back and forth . . ."

Debbie threw the BS flag. "You can go the rest of your life being miserable—never feeling fulfilled, never finding a job you really like again—or you can just do this. The sooner you get started, the sooner you'll be done, and you'll be happy with your occupation again. If you don't, you'll look back after four years and say, 'If I'd gone to school, I'd be finished by now.'" I married the right woman.

In January 2005, at Life University in Marietta, Georgia, I started school to become a chiropractor. Although I enjoyed my studies, a small percentage of my classmates were hippie crackpots who opposed medical doctors, needles, and medication. Even one of my professors told us, "I will not give CPR or mouth-to-mouth to someone who is dying." He would try to give the dying person a chiropractic adjustment and that was it. A husband and wife who were both chiropractors had met and married while in school. Three years after they graduated, the wife died from an ear infection because they refused to receive medical treatment for her—simple antibiotics would've saved her life. Their attitude was that chiropractors had the only pure discipline to cure people. Their mantra was *Innate will provide*. They reminded me of the witch doctor who unsuccessfully tried to cure the boy I helped in Somalia. Most of my other classmates and professors didn't think this way, nor do chiropractors as a whole. It's the small percentage of crackpots who give all chiropractors a bad name.

During my last year at school, my father had an abdominal aortic aneurysm. His abdominal aorta was blowing up like a balloon.

17.
HEALING

I drove 268 miles to see my father at the hospital in Savannah—but appearances would be deceiving. He was awake, joking with my sisters. The surgical doctor said, "Your father is going to be OK. He's in recovery." So that night I left him to prepare to take final exams at Life University.

Several hours later, after I'd returned home, my youngest sister, Sue Anne, called to tell me that our father had had a heart attack. An hour later, around midnight, my cousin Greg told me Dad had passed away. Nobody saw it coming.

I tried to take my exams anyway. During the first final exam, Dr. Marni Capes told me, "Howard, you need to get up and walk out of here right now."

"No, no. I can do it. I can do it."

I found out I wasn't as tough as I thought I was. My head was not in it. After I had become a SEAL, I didn't worry about Dad kicking the crap out of me anymore. Our relationship had improved. After Somalia, I told him I loved him for the first time—then I told him every time I saw him after that. We hugged. The passage

of time had mellowed him, too. During a family re-
union shortly before his death, he told me how he approved of my new wife, Debbie. "She's a keeper. Don't
mess up." He loved her. Regarding my new profession,
he said, "When you open up your clinic, I'll be one of
your first patients." Coming from a man who wouldn't
go to a doctor unless he was dying, which was part of
his undoing, his confidence in my future skills as a chiropractor meant a lot to me. I had received the acceptance, respect, and approval from my father that I'd
always longed for.

My mother told me that later in life Dad was disappointed that he and I didn't have a better relationship. I
didn't have the heart to tell her that when I was home,
he had always been a dictator. He didn't have conversations with me—didn't build a relationship. I didn't cry
as much about his death as I had about Uncle Carroll's.
As a kid, I could ask Uncle Carroll questions like, "Is it
normal for me to wake up every morning with a hard
pee-pee? Is there something wrong with me?" My uncle
laughed. "No, that's normal, son." Still, my dad raised
me the only way he knew how, and I was sad when he
died.

One day, about nine months later, Blake asked out of
the blue, "Would you like to meet him?"

"Meet who?" I asked.

"Your real dad."

My biological father could have walked past me in
the grocery store, and I wouldn't have known who he
was. "Yeah, Blake. You know, I think I would."

We did a people search and found him. Then I
made the phone call. At Christmas, I went to see Ben

Wilbanks, my biological father. Ben said that my mother had taken us kids and run off to Georgia with Leon. In my mind, Ben's story kind of explains the quick move from Florida to Georgia and the quick adoption. I'm inclined to believe him, due to conflicting stories I got from my mother and sisters. Ben said he had spent years looking for me and could never find me. He turned out to be one of the nicest and most loving men I'd ever met. When he hugged me, I knew that I was really being hugged. Seeing Ben Wilbanks seemed to explain where I got my affectionate side—my capability for compassion and emotion. Ben had served in the army as a military policeman and worked most of his career as a truck driver, which is what he still does.

Blake and I continue to maintain a relationship with my biological father, Blake's grandfather. Whatever happened between my mother and Ben, she still hasn't forgiven him. Nor forgotten. For my part, I refuse to hold decisions made in their youth against either of them, because I wouldn't want to be held in contempt for all the decisions made by me in my youth.

When I was getting ready to graduate from clinic, I received a message from Captain Bailey. He'd seen a magazine article about me in his chiropractor's office and sent an e-mail congratulating me, asking if I remembered him from BUD/S. It was a no-brainer remembering my commanding officer at BUD/S. I could be on my deathbed and still remember him securing us from Hell Week.

I graduated with honors as a doctor of chiropractic on September 24, 2009. I have always been a "show me" person and resisted going to a chiropractor for a long time, but chemicals couldn't fix my structural problem. The chemicals only hid my pain. A general practitioner can't do everything for a patient, and a chiropractor can't do everything. Working as a team, as I learned my whole life, we become more effective. Local doctors refer patients to me, and I refer patients to them. The patients benefit the most.

When I first started seeing patients was when I knew I'd made the right decision. They trust me, I figure out what's wrong with them, I help them feel better, and they love me for it.

I am now focused on my new career. Construction of my new clinic, Absolute Precision Chiropractic, was completed in April 2010. From the day I opened the doors, I have been blessed with busy days treating members of the local and surrounding communities. One of my patients, a thirteen-year-old boy, had been suffering from chronic headaches for four years. It turned out he experienced a bad car accident when he was little and lost the curve in his neck. He went from nearly twelve headaches a month on frequent medication to one or two headaches in the first ten weeks I saw him. Success stories like this let me know I made the right decision. I truly feel that this is the path God intended for me when he spared my life in Somalia.

Another affirmation for me occurred when I treated a young lady who had brachial palsy. Her arm hadn't formed correctly, and she had a lot of nerve damage—she was barely able to move her right arm. I had been helping her with electrical stimulation, adjusting her, and administering other chiropractic techniques. She laterally moved her arm 42 degrees for the first time in her life. Then she flexed her arm forward toward me 45 degrees for the first time. My assistant cried. The fifteen-year-old girl cried from her exertion and success. Her father cried. I stepped out of the room—and cried. I had to walk around a little until I could hold back the tears. I grabbed a tissue and wiped my eyes. Then I returned to my patient as if everything were OK and said, "All right, here's your exercise for next week." Seeing her move that arm after hard work on both our parts fulfilled me. Helping patients like her helps lessen the guilt that still makes me wonder why I'm still alive when better men than me like Dan Busch are not. I understand better why God spared me—he really did have a purpose for me after my life as a SEAL.

Even though Blake is in his twenties now, whenever he visits, I give him a good-night hug. I give the same affection to my stepdaughter, Eryn, whom I consider my own daughter. I give my wife, Debbie, a hug or a kiss every time I leave or return to the house. Debbie and I are so affectionate that friends tell us, "Get a room." Years ago I had questioned why my life had been spared. Today I am thankful that God spared my life and equally thankful for the path that was laid before me. I once again have a positive mind, body, and spirit. Professionally and personally, life is good again.

EPILOGUE

Four Somali pirates boarded an American cargo ship, the MV *Maersk Alabama,* 280 miles off the Somali coast—the first ship registered under an American flag to be hijacked since the 1800s. The pirates took Captain Richard Phillips hostage in a 25-foot lifeboat.

The USS *Bainbridge* (DDG-96) arrived and asked the pirates to release Captain Phillips. A P-3 Orion flew overhead, monitoring the situation. The pirates refused to release the captain until they received a million-dollar ransom.

Under the cover of darkness, a SEAL team parachuted into the ocean and linked up with the *Bainbridge.*

The lifeboat ran out of fuel, and the wind churned up the ocean. Becoming anxious about the rough seas, the pirates allowed the *Bainbridge* to tow it into calmer waters.

Sunday night, April 12, 2009, nearly 30 yards apart, both the *Bainbridge* and the lifeboat pitched and rolled in the dark. Inside the *Bainbridge,* one of the pirates negotiated a million-dollar ransom. On the fantail, three snipers and their spotters, dressed in black, observed the lifeboat, relaying information on all activity to the SEAL commander. Even with KN-250 night-vision scopes, the best, everything is flat—two-dimensional.

"Tango aiming AK at Hotel's back," a spotter reported. The terrorist was aiming his rifle at the hostage.

Two other pirates poked their heads above deck to see what was going on.

Each sniper had a square of Velcro on each side of his Win Mag. Attached to the Velcro was a signaling device. When a sniper had a pirate in his sights, he pressed the device, sending a signal back to the SEAL commander that shone as a green light. One light for each sniper.

Over their radio earpieces, the snipers heard their commander give the execute order: "Stand by, stand by. Three, two, one, execute, execute." From the *Bainbridge*'s fantail, the three snipers each simultaneously fired one head shot. The three pirates fell. An assault team motored to the lifeboat and freed Captain Phillips. Other SEALs apprehended the pirate negotiating on board the *Bainbridge*.

Once again, the SEAL Team Six sniper standards have been tested—and the standards remain high. Most of the snipers' missions remain classified to the general public, their own families, and even fellow SEALs. It is difficult for people to comprehend or appreciate the incredible amounts of training and risks those men undergo. For the most part, their commitment, sacrifice, and patriotism will continue to remain hidden.

SPECIAL OPERATIONS WARRIOR FOUNDATION

The Special Operations Warrior Foundation was founded in 1980 as the Colonel Arthur D. "Bull" Simons Scholarship Fund to provide college educations for the seventeen children surviving the nine special operations men killed or incapacitated in April of that year at Desert One in Iran during the failed attempt to rescue American hostages from the U.S. Embassy in Tehran. It was named in honor of the legendary Army Green Beret, Bull Simons, who repeatedly risked his life on rescue missions.

Following creation of the U.S. Special Operations Command, and as casualties mounted from actions such as Operations Urgent Fury (Grenada), Just Cause (Panama), Desert Storm (Kuwait and Iraq), and Restore Hope (Somalia), the Bull Simons Fund gradually expanded its outreach program to encompass all special operations forces. Thus in 1995 the Family Liaison Action Group (established to support the families of the Iranian hostages) and the Spectre (air force gunship) Association Scholarship Fund merged to form the Special Operations Warrior Foundation. In 1998 the

Warrior Foundation extended its scholarship and financial aid counseling to cover training fatalities as well as operational fatalities since the inception of the foundation in 1980. This action immediately made 205 more children eligible for college funding.

The Warrior Foundation's mission is to provide a college education to every child who has lost a parent serving in the U.S. Special Operations Command and its units in any branch of the armed forces during an operational or training mission. These personnel are stationed in units throughout the United States and at overseas bases. Some of the largest concentrations of special operations forces are at military bases at Camp Lejeune and Fort Bragg, North Carolina; Hurlburt Field, Florida; Coronado Naval Station, California; Dam Neck, Virginia; MacDill Air Force Base, Florida; Fort Lewis, Washington; Fort Stewart, Georgia; Fort Campbell, Kentucky; Little Creek, Virginia; Fort Carson, Colorado; Cannon Air Force Base, New Mexico; Royal Air Force Mildenhall, United Kingdom; and Kadena Air Base, Japan.

The Warrior Foundation also provides immediate financial assistance to special operations personnel severely wounded in the war against terrorism.

Today, the Warrior Foundation is committed to providing scholarship grants, *not loans,* to more than seven hundred children. These children survive more than six hundred special operations personnel who gave their lives in patriotic service to their country, including those who died fighting our nation's war against terrorism as part of Operation Enduring Freedom in Afghanistan and the Philippines, as well as Operation Iraqi Freedom.

To date, 121 children of fallen special operations

warriors have graduated from college. Children from all military services have received or been offered Warrior Foundation scholarships.

Contact information:
Special Operations Warrior Foundation
P.O. Box 13483
Tampa, FL 33690
www.specialops.org
E-mail: warrior@specialops.org
Toll-free phone: 1-877-337-7693

ACKNOWLEDGMENTS

Howard's Acknowledgments

I'd like to thank my Lord and Savior Jesus Christ for all my blessings. Thanks for the guardian angels that kept me alive while in harm's way.

I'm very thankful for the people of Wayne County, Georgia, who have always stood behind me and been a source of strength, motivation, and inspiration.

Special thanks to my patients, who have allowed me to be their chiropractor. I love you all.

Thanks to my coauthor, Steve Templin, who resurrected a dead project in this book and worked tirelessly to perfect it.

I'm truly blessed to have been given two careers that were/are exceptional and that I truly loved. I'm happy every day to come to work and help people, which, as corny as it sounds, was the reason I became a SEAL in the first place.

God bless America and our fighting men and women.

Steve's Acknowledgments

I've been blessed. During Basic Underwater Demolition/ SEAL training with Class 143, I first met Howard Wasdin. We'd finished another brutal day of training, and Howard asked, "Who wants to go with me for a jog on the beach?" I thought he was nuts. *Hadn't we had enough for the day?!* Even nuttier were the guys who followed him. Howard and I became friends. We hung out with the guys in Tijuana on Saturday, and he dragged me to church on Sunday. Our paths split when I injured myself and rolled back to Class 144, but I never forgot him.

Years later, waiting for a flight at Los Angeles International Airport, I slipped into the bookstore to kill some time and soon found myself in the middle of a war zone—I had picked Mark Bowden's excellent book *Black Hawk Down*. I looked in the index to see if any SEALs were involved. To my surprise, I ran across Howard's name. *No way.* I thought for sure somebody would write the rest of his story, and I'd be one of the first to buy it. Years went by, though, and no book. Thanks to Facebook, I hooked up with Howard again. I'm fortunate he waited to tell his story. Coauthoring his biography has been the ride of a lifetime—thanks, Howard!

I'm also blessed that my wife, Reiko, and children, Kent and Maria, have given me a taste of heaven. Of course, I couldn't have come into this world without my mother, Gwen, who has always been there to support me and let me do my own thing; some of my fondest early memories are exploring the Arizona desert alone before I was old enough to attend school. I'm thankful to my father, Art, for the times he was there for me. My grandfather Robert taught me how to negotiate 10 percent off a can of paint at the hardware store. Grandpa loved me like a son, and I loved him like a father. I'm sure he's looking down on this book with a smile—writing has been my dream since early elementary school. Carol Scarr gave Howard and me excellent writing advice on earlier drafts and has been a great friend.

It would be difficult to write and research without the support of Meio University, where I am an associate professor. Scott Miller of Trident Media Group showed Howard and me all the professionalism an agent can show and more. He read our manuscript during his Easter vacation; when he returned to work, he found us our first publisher within twenty-four hours. Marc Resnick at St. Martin's Press outshined the others to seal the deal and has maintained his enthusiasm, making this process a joy.

I'm deeply honored that General Henry Hugh Shelton (Retired) took time from his busy schedule to give support. Also, the Delta Force major who wrote *Kill Bin Laden,* Dalton Fury, offered his help early on, for which I'm grateful. Kudos to Marine sniper Jack Coughlin, author of *Shooter,* for his encouragement. Thanks to Randy "Kemo" Clendening (former SEAL Team Two operator) for assistance, too.

I'd like to thank Debbie Wasdin for her friendship and help. Eryn Wasdin chauffeured me and made me smile.

While I worked with Howard to finish up the book, Tammie Willis, a licensed medical massage therapist at Absolute Precision, gave me the best massage I've ever had—you're awesome, Tammie. The rest of the Absolute Precision staff was wonderful, too: Miki, Kelly, and everyone.

Thank you to the people of Wayne County, Georgia, who made me feel at home during my stay.

REFERENCES

Boesch, R., with K. Dockery. "Master Chief Boatswain's Mate Rudy Boesch, USN (Ret.)." In *Hunters and Shooters*, ed. B. Fawcett, 1–32. New York: Avon, 1995.

Bosiljevac, T. L. *SEALs: UDT/SEAL Operations in Vietnam.* Boulder, Colo.: Paladin Press, 1990.

Bowden, M. *Black Hawk Down.* New York: Signet, 2001.

Carney, J. T., and B. F. Schemmer. *No Room for Error: The Covert Operations of America's Special Tactics Units from Iran to Afghanistan.* New York: Ballantine Books, 2002.

Chalker, D., and K. Dockery. *One Perfect Op: An Insider's Account of the Navy SEAL Special Warfare Teams.* New York: HarperCollins, 2002.

Couch, D. *The Warrior Elite: The Forging of SEAL Class 228.* New York: Three Rivers Press, 2001.

Coulson, D. O., and E. Shannon. *No Heroes: Inside the FBI's Secret Counter-Terror Force.* New York: Pocket Books, 1999.

Eversmann, M., and D. Schilling, eds. *The Battle of Mogadishu: Firsthand Accounts from the Men of Task Force Ranger.* New York: Presidio Press, 2006.

Gormly, R. A. *Combat Swimmer: Memoirs of a Navy SEAL*. New York: Dutton, 1998.

Lechner, J. O. *Combat Operations in Mogadishu, Somalia, Conducted by Task Force Ranger*. Fort Benning, Ga.: United States Army Infantry School, 1994.

Loeb, V. "After-Action Report . . . In Somalia with the CIA." *Washington Post,* February 27, 2000.

———. "Confessions of a Hero." *Washington Post,* April 29, 2001.

Marcinko, R., and R. Weisman. *Rogue Warrior*. New York: Pocket Books, 1992.

Maren, M. "Somaliarchive: The Mysterious Death of Ilaria Alpi." http://www.netnomad.com/ilaria.html (accessed September 20, 2010).

Murphy K. M., II. *Multi-National Combined Arms Breaching (MOUT) in Somalia*. Fort Benning, Ga.: United States Army Infantry School, 1994.

Norris, T. *Medal of Honor Series: Thomas Norris*. Pritzker Military Library. January 29, 2009. http://www.pritzkermilitarylibrary.org/events/2009/01-29-thomas-norris.jsp (accessed September 20, 2010).

Norris, T., and M. Thornton. *Medal of Honor Series: Thomas Norris and Michael Thornton*. Pritzker Military Library. November 9, 2006. http://www.pritzkermilitarylibrary.org/events/2006/11-09-thornton-norris.jsp (accessed September 20, 2010).

Pfarrer, C. *Warrior Soul: The Memoir of a Navy SEAL*. New York: Random House, 2004.

Rysewyk, L. A. *Experiences of Executive Officer from Bravo Company, 3rd Battalion, 75th Ranger Regiment and Task Force Ranger during the Battle of the Black Sea on 3–4 October, 1993 in Mogadishu,*

Somalia. Fort Benning, Ga.: United States Army Infantry School, May, 1994.

Stubblefield, G. with H. Halberstadt. *Inside the U.S. Navy SEALs*. Osceola, Wisc.: MBI Publishing, 1995.

Walsh, M. J., with G. Walker. *SEAL!* New York: Pocket Books, 1994.

INDEX